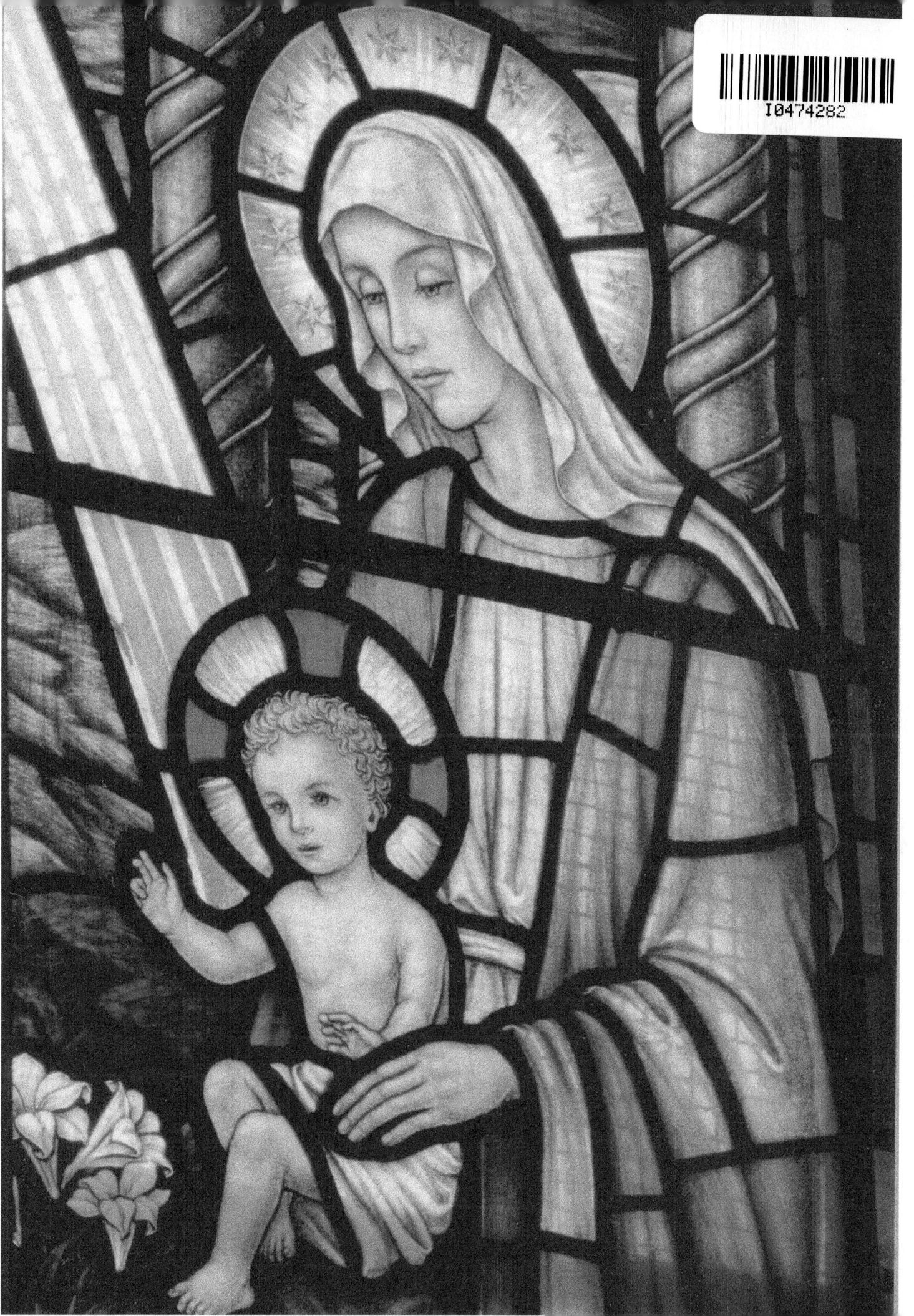

Claire's Traditional Carolbook

Claire & Eros Mungal

ISBN 978-0-244-64760-5

Traditional Carols

In Two Easy Keys

NOW INCLUDES AULD LANG SYNE!

AND A NEW CAROL FOR KIDS-LITTLE ANGELS!

Claire's

CAROLBOOK

Words and Piano Fingering

Easy Arrangements

Songsheets with full verses

Piano, Keyboard, Guitar, Violin, Flute

Appendix:

Auld Lang Syne, Little Angels   Carol, Guitar chords,
Practice pieces, fingering for   recorder, Note charts.

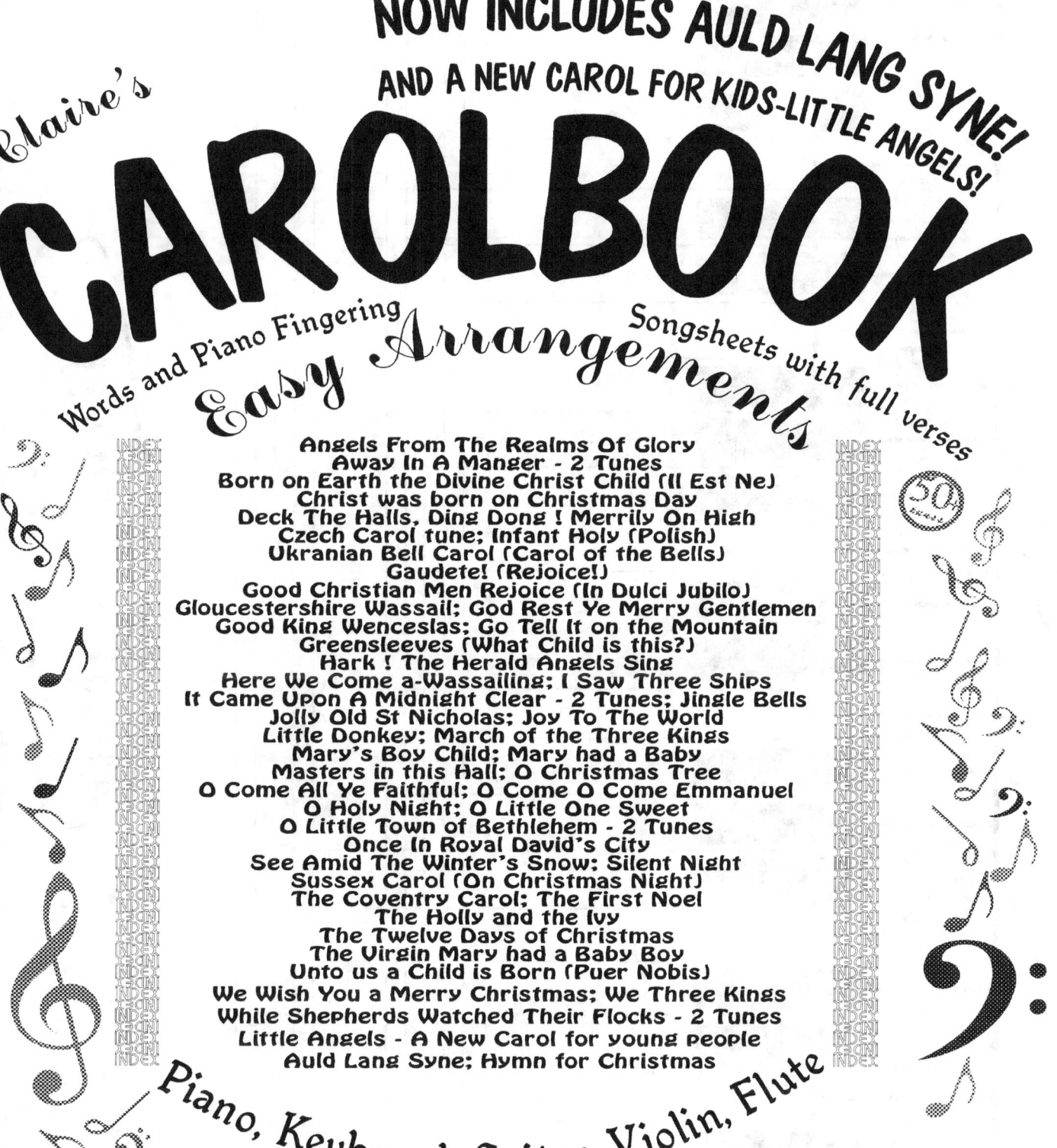

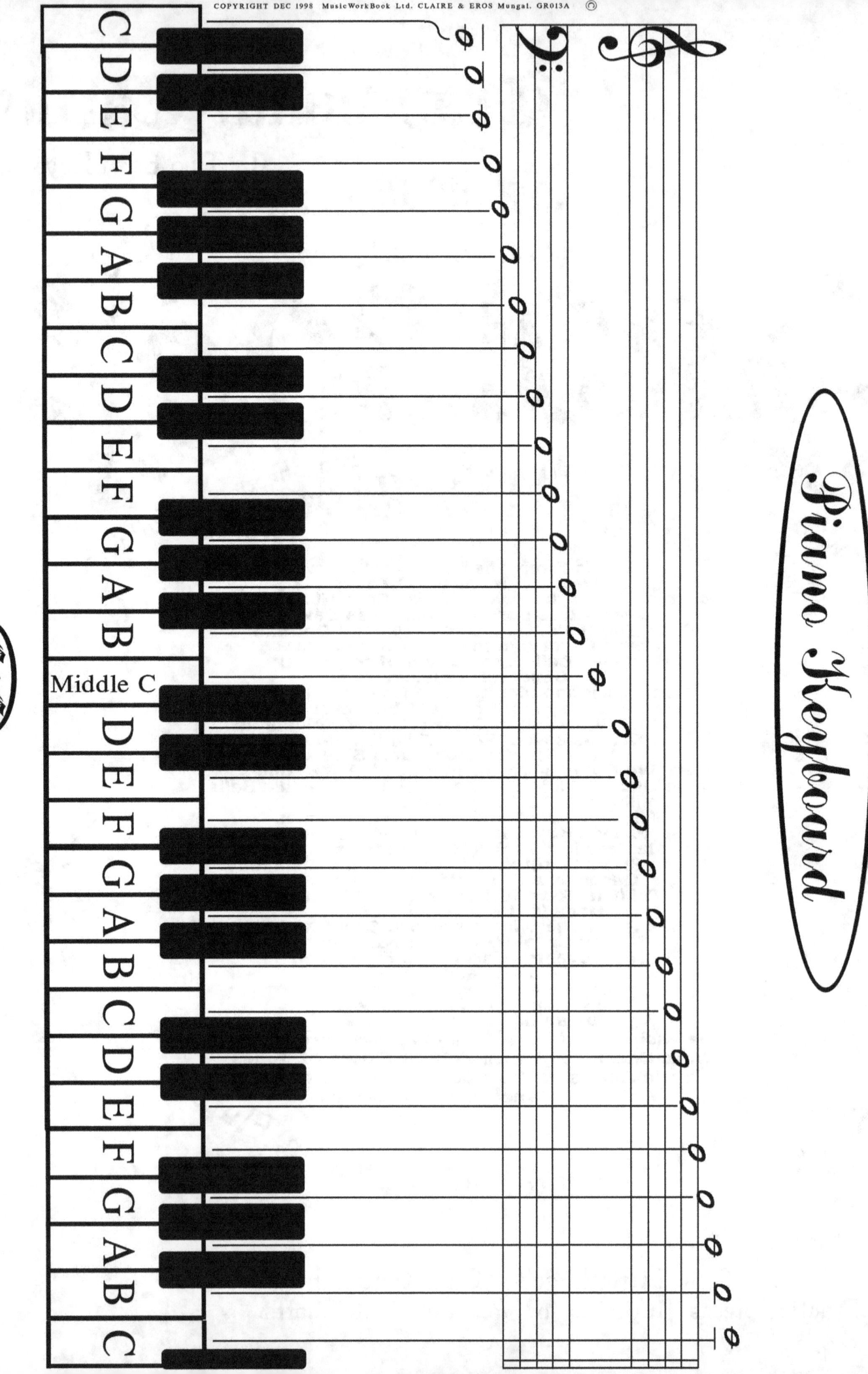

Preface

These Carols are arranged in two easy keys C and G major. No key signatures have been used, and for arrangements in the key of G, the F notes are individually sharpened. Importance has been given to practical accompaniments with easy left-hand positions. The "1 plus 2" note arrangements lead to easy sight reading and playability by students, especially young pianists.

The "two note" left hand chords are designed to give maximum harmony with the right hand generally with only three notes. The accompaniments are also designed to maintain a steady rhythm while maintaining harmonic interest with the minimum of complexity. In pieces where there are suggestions of diminished chords or passing notes, D sharp or C sharp, the sharps may be ignored without destroying the harmony as long as the pianist remembers the F sharps !

It is advised that the student pianist practise the exercises in the appendix, the "left hand pairs" are designed to introduce the left hand style. In pieces where there are 4 crotchet pairs to the bar, for example "Angels from the realms of glory", the second and fourth pairs can be omitted without interrupting the rhythmic flow of the music.

For electronic keyboards, simple 4 crotchet beat rhythms can be used, example 8 beat types at a tempo of 105, for example in "Little Angels". For pieces in three crotchet beat time, for example "We wish you a Merry Christmas" or "We Three Kings", a simple waltz time at a starting tempo of 100 will be effective. More complex rhythms will tend to confuse and not help students.

For Guitar players the carols that are written in the key of C major can be accompanied by the major chords of C,F,G. Also any carols written in the key of G major can be accompanied by the major chords of G,C,D. Those in the key of G with have at least one F sharp. For guitar chords see the appendix where there are also other useful chords.

From the same publishers:
"Claire's Music Workbook", Music Theory and Exercises.
US and Canada edition: ISBN 1-555395-678-8.
United Kingdom: 0-9544406-0-9. Caribbean: 0-9544406-4-1.
MusicWorkbook Ltd., Bryant Avenue, Slough, SL2 1LF. Tel. +44(0)701 7000 559.

First published 1999 in the United Kingdom.
Written by Claire and Eros Mungal.
Revised 2011 by Christopher, Darren and Eros Mungal.
Claire's Traditional Carolbook: ISBN 0-9544406-1-7
Published by MusicWorkBook Ltd., 5 Bryant Avenue,
Slough, SL2 1LF, England, United Kingdom.
Tel. +44 (0)701 7000 559
E-MAIL musicworkbook@aol.com

Teacher guidelines, hints and tips for playing pieces and updates will be included on the internet. See webpages for updates.

www.musicworkbook.com
www.theorybook.co.uk
ISMN 979-0-900-2079
Library Catalogue (UK) 782.528

Also by the same authors:
Claire's Music Workbook Caribbean Edition: ISBN 0-9544406-4-1
Claire's MusicWorkBook ISBN (US) 1-55395-678-8
ISBN (UK) 0-9544406-0-9.

Image of stained glass window from St. Mary's Church, Slough, Berks. by kind permission of the vicar the Rev. Andrew Allen.
Thanks also to the resident organist Malcolm Stowell for editorial suggestions.

Dedicated to the memory of Claire Louise Mungal,
who was suddenly taken away from us on the 1st July 2002.

Daughter

Co-author

Music teacher

University student

Friend

May God rest her Soul

Traditional Carols

Angels From The Realms Of Glory

Arr. Claire

Allegro

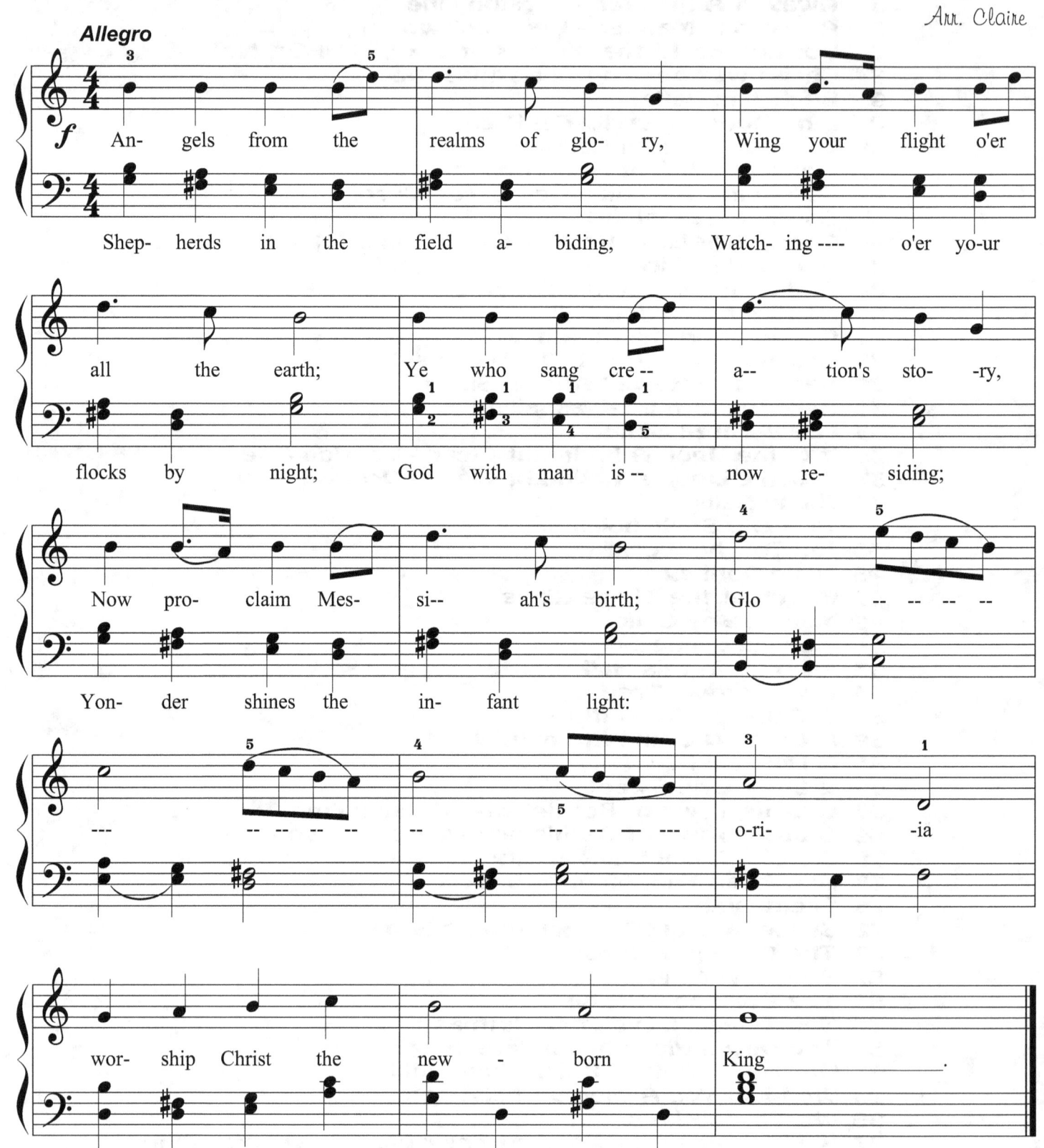

Angels from the realms of glory

Angels from the realms of glory,
Wing your flight o'er all the earth;
Ye who sang creation's story,
 Now proclaim Messiah's birth:

Chorus: Come....... and worship,
        Worship Christ the new-born King.

Shepherds in fields abiding,
Watching o'er your flocks by night,
God with man is now residing;
Yonder shines the infant light.

Chorus: Come....... and worship,
        Worship Christ the new-born King.

Sages, leave your contemplations;
Brighter visions beam afar;
Seek the great Desire of Nations;
Ye have seen His natal star.

Chorus: Come....... and worship,
        Worship Christ the new-born King.

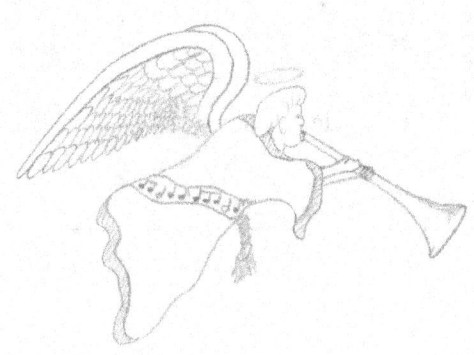

Away In A Manger

Version 1

Arr. Claire

Adagio

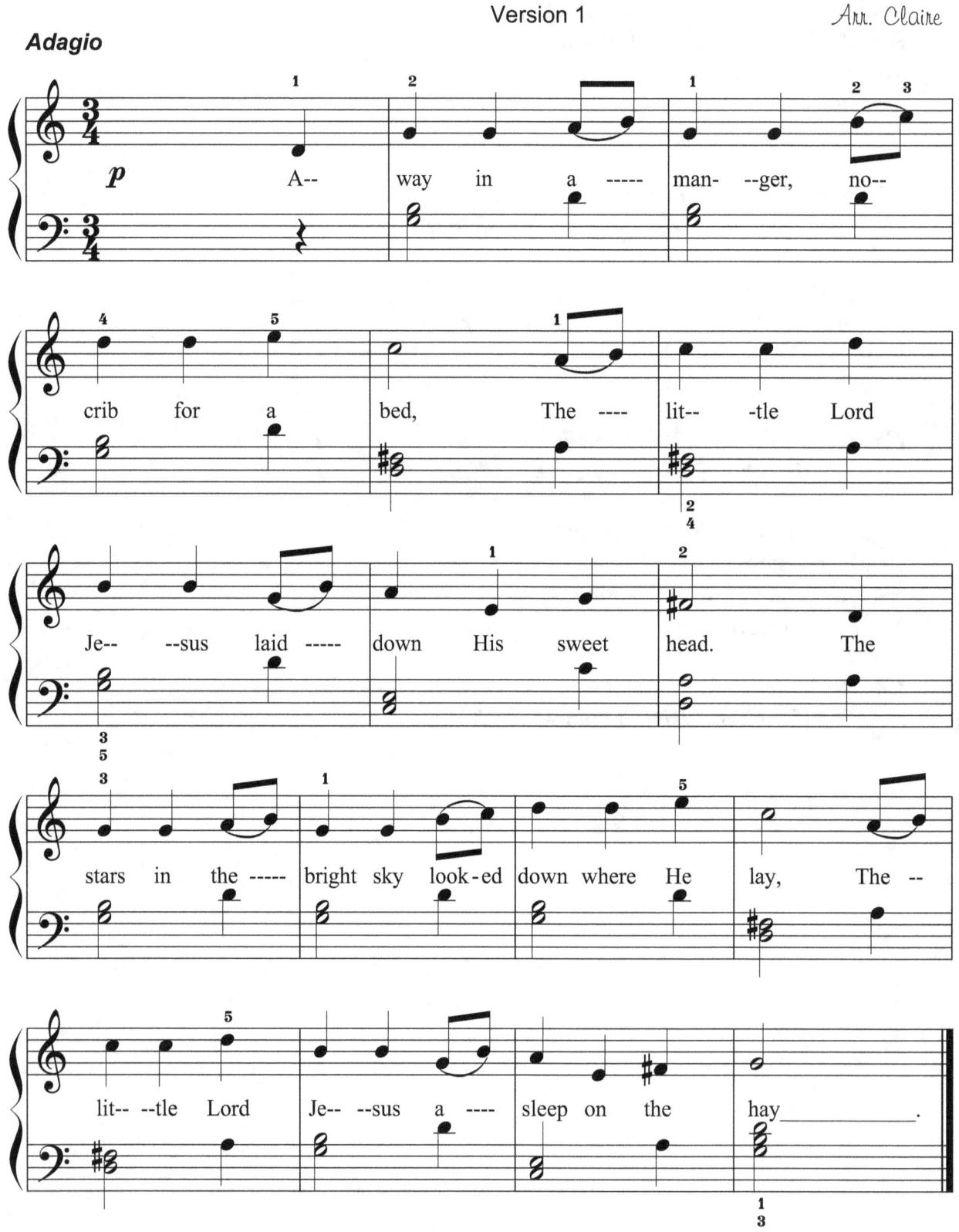

Away In A Manger

Away in a manger, no crib for a bed,
The little Lord Jesus laid down his sweet head.
The stars in the bright sky looked down where he lay,
The little Lord Jesus asleep on the hay.

The cattle are lowing, the Baby awakes,
But little Lord Jesus no crying he makes.
I love thee, Lord Jesus! Look down from the sky,
And stay by my side until morning is nigh.

Be near me, Lord Jesus; I ask Thee to stay,
Close by me for ever, and love me, I pray.
Bless all the dear children in thy tender care,
And fit us for heaven, to live with Thee there.

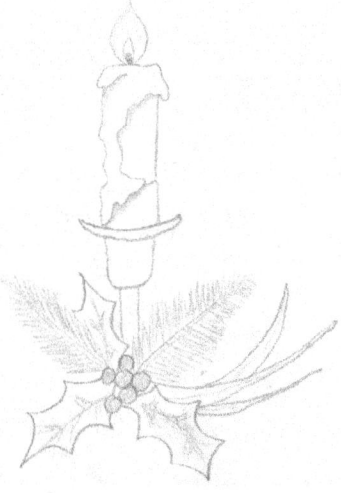

Away In A Manger

Version 2

Traditional American

Arr. Claire

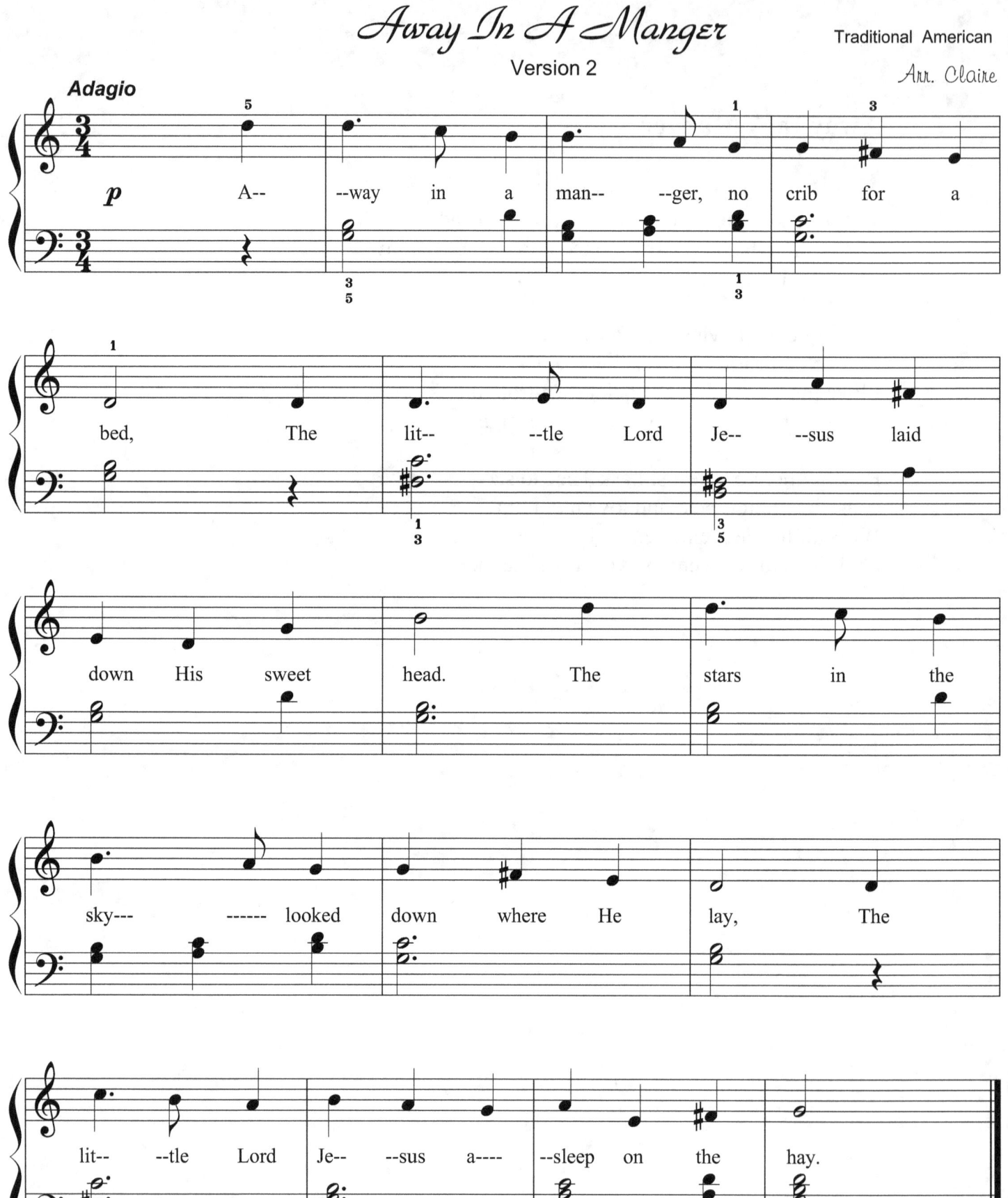

Away In A Manger

Away in a manger, no crib for a bed,
The little Lord Jesus laid down his sweet head.
The stars in the bright sky looked down where he lay,
The little Lord Jesus asleep on the hay.

The cattle are lowing, the Baby awakes,
But little Lord Jesus no crying he makes.
I love thee, Lord Jesus! Look down from the sky,
And stay by my side until morning is nigh.

Be near me, Lord Jesus; I ask Thee to stay,
Close by me for ever, and love me, I pray.
Bless all the dear children in thy tender care,
And fit us for heaven, to live with Thee there.

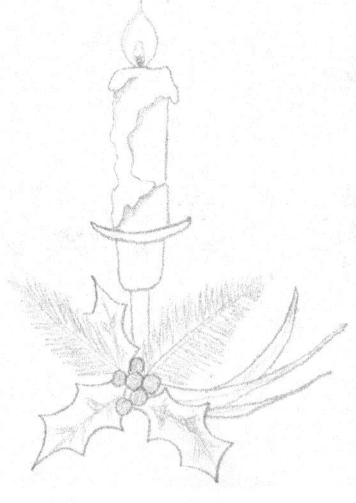

Born on Earth the Divine Christ Child

IL EST NE LE DIVIN ENFANT

Arr. Eros

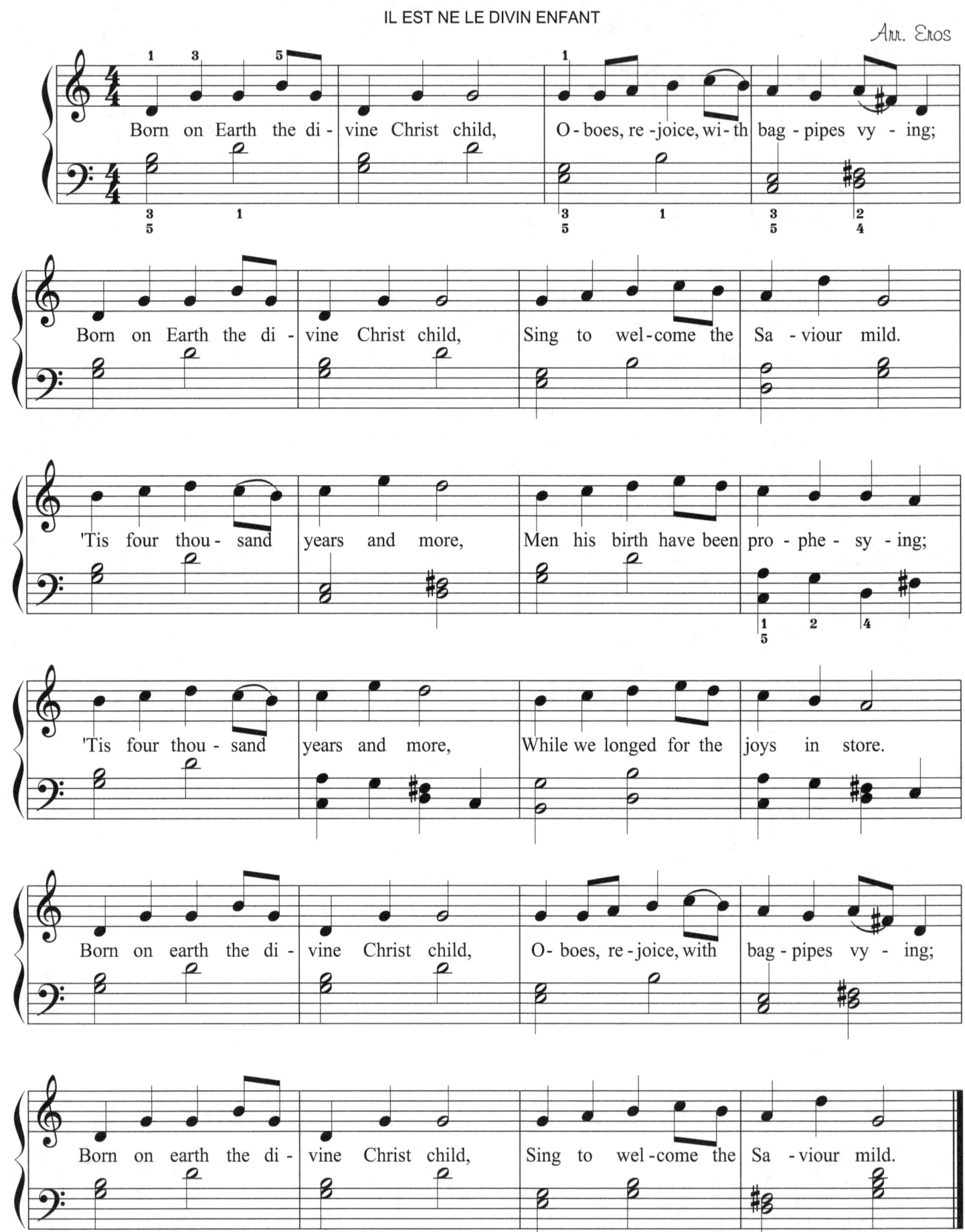

Christ was born on Christmas day

14 Century German

Arr. Eros

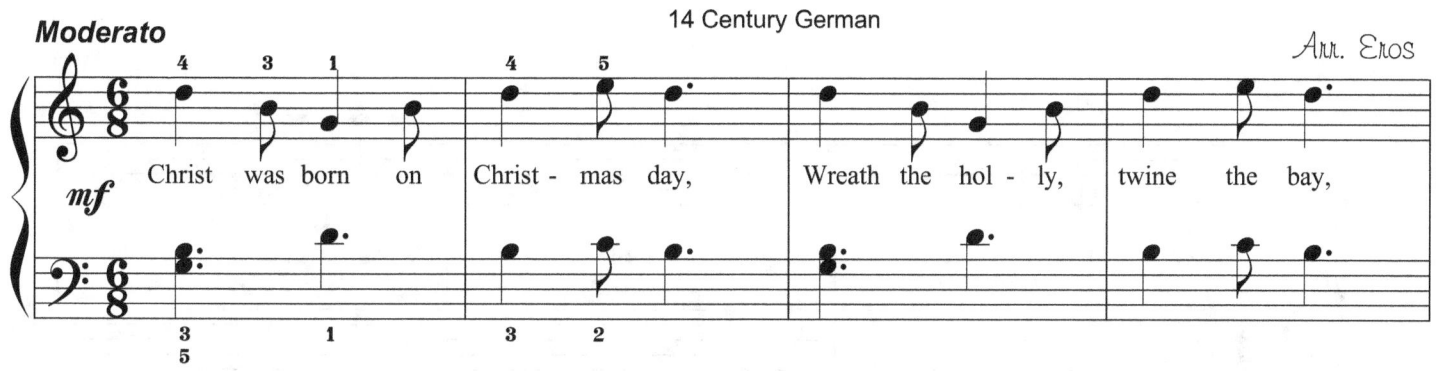

Christ was born on Christ - mas day, Wreath the hol - ly, twine the bay,

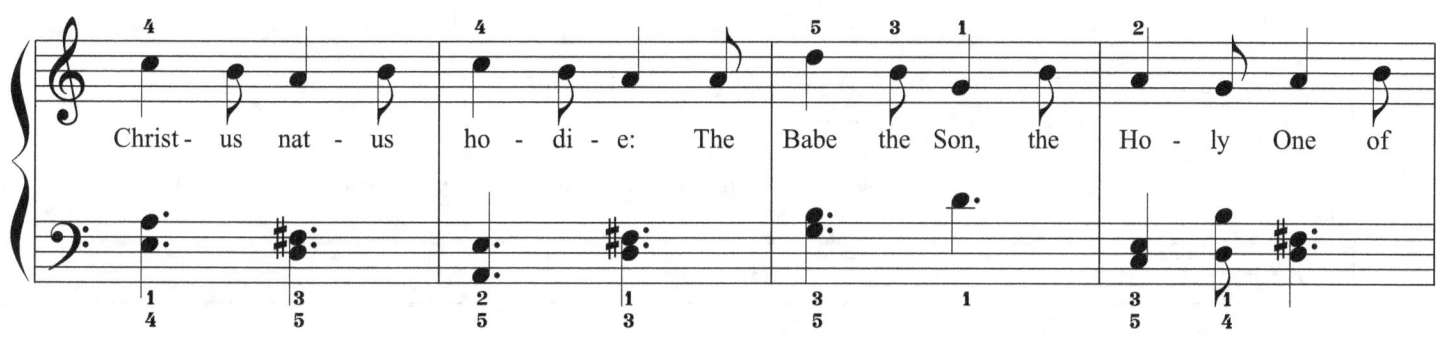

Christ - us nat - us ho - di - e: The Babe the Son, the Ho - ly One of

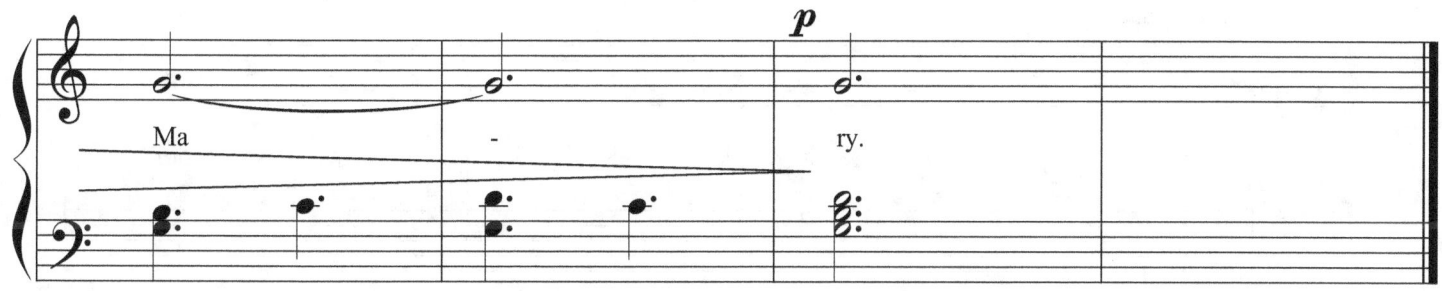

Ma - ry.

1 Christ was born on Christmas day,
   Wreath the holly, twine the bay,
   Christus natus ho-di-e:
   The Babe, the Son, the Holy One of Mary.

2. He is born to set us free,
   He is born our Lord to be,
   Ex Maria Virgine:
   The God, the Lord, by all adored forever.

3. Let the bright red berries glow
   Ev'rywhere in goodly show,
   Christus natus ho-di-e:
   The Babe, the Son, the Holy One of Mary.

4. Christian men, rejoice and sing;
   'Tis the birthday of a King,
   Ex Maria Virgine:
   The God, the Lord, by all adored forever.

Deck The Halls

Arr. Claire

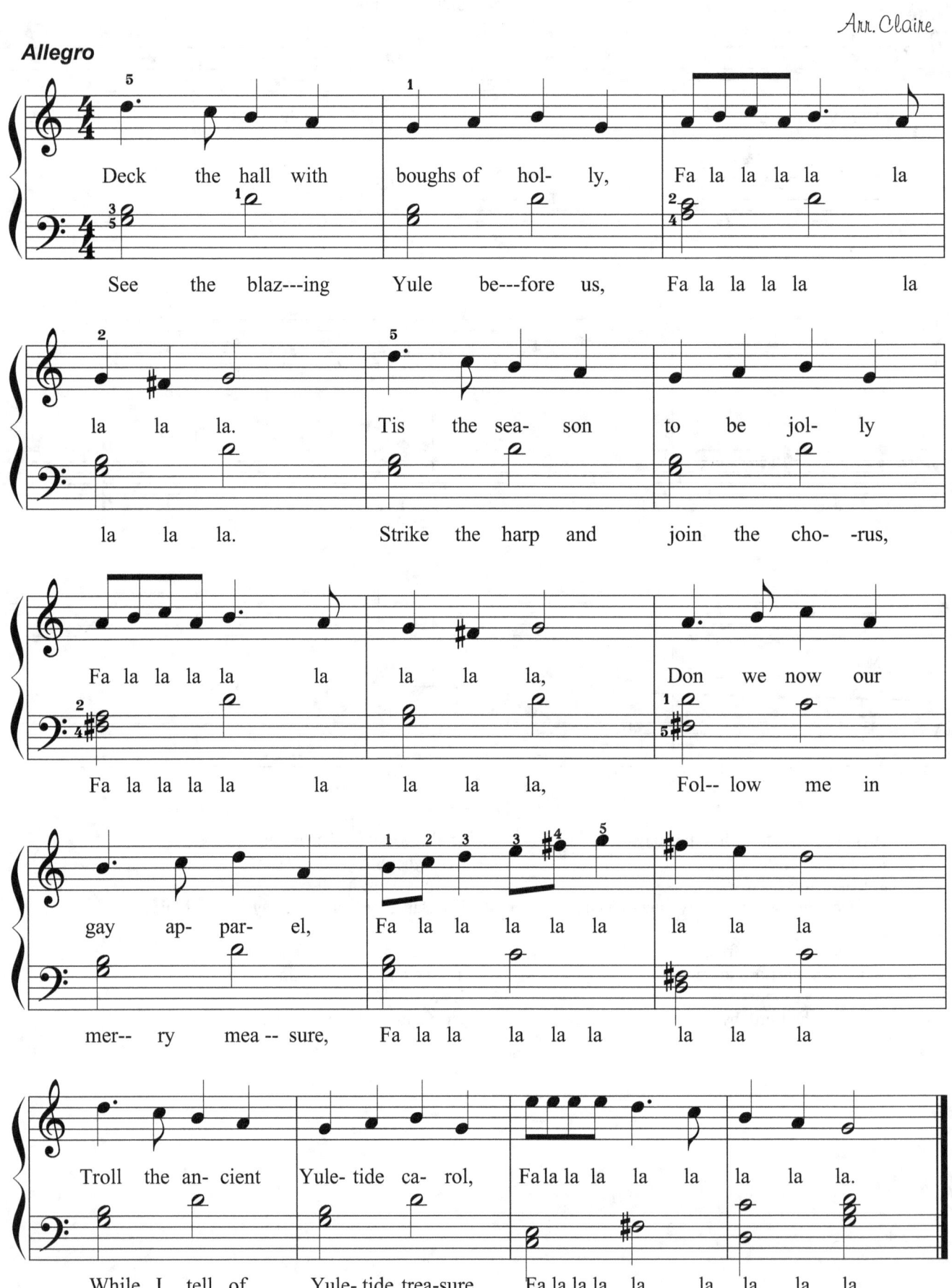

Deck the halls

Deck the halls with boughs of holly,
Fa, la, la, la, la, la, la, la, la.
Tis the season to be jolly,
Fa, la, la, la, la, la, la, la, la
Don we now our gay apparel,
Fa, la, la, la, la, la, la, la, la,
Troll the ancient Yule-tide carol,
Fa, la, la, la, la, la, la, la, la.

See the blazing Yule before us,
Fa, la, la, la, la, la, la, la, la
Strike the harp and join the chorus,
Fa, la, la, la, la, la, la, la, la
Follow me in merry measure,
Fa, la, la, la, la, la, la, la, la
While I tell of Yule-tide treasure,
Fa, la, la, la, la, la, la, la, la

Fast away the old year passes,
Fa, la, la, la, la, la, la, la, la
Hail the new, ye lads and lasses,
Fa, la, la, la, la, la, la, la, la
Sing we joyous all together,
Fa, la, la, la, la, la, la, la, la
Heedless of the wing and weather,
Fa, la, la, la, la, la, la, la, la.

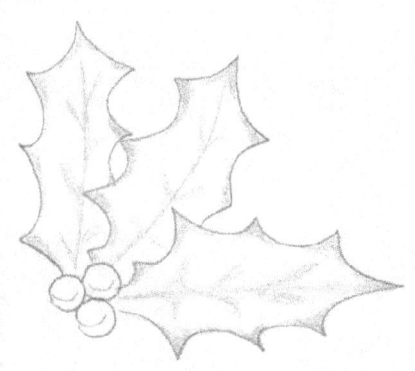

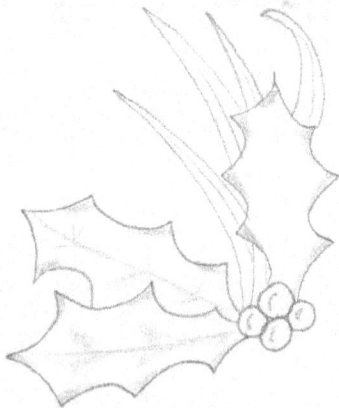

Ding Dong Merrily On High

Traditional French
Arr. Claire

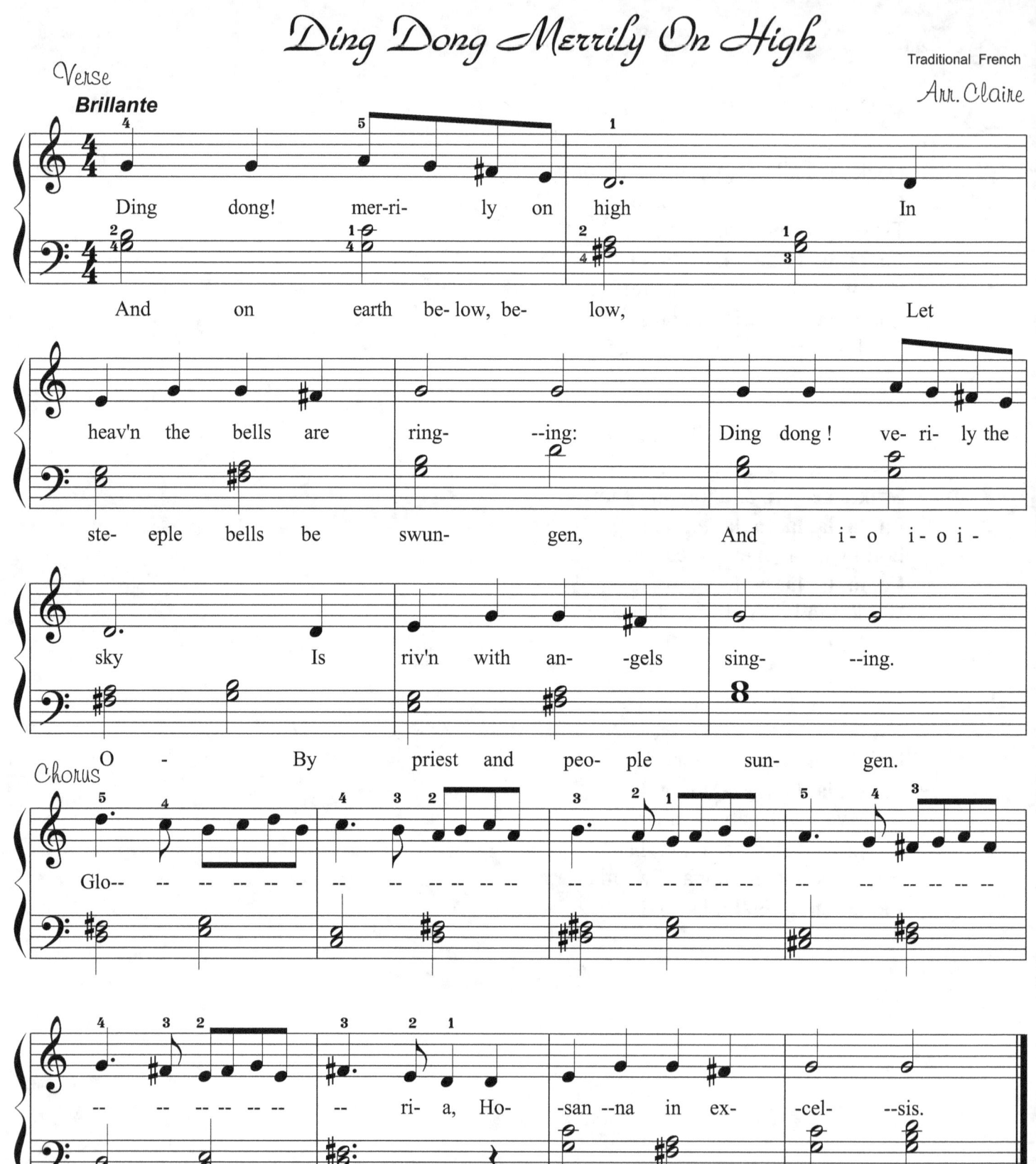

Verse
Brillante

Ding dong! mer-ri- ly on high In

And on earth be- low, be- low, Let

heav'n the bells are ring- --ing: Ding dong! ve- ri- ly the

ste- eple bells be swun- gen, And i- o i- o i-

sky Is riv'n with an- gels sing- --ing.

O - By priest and peo- ple sun- gen.

Chorus

Glo-- -- -- -- -- -- -- -- -- -- -- -- -- -- -- -- -- --

-- -- -- -- -- -- ri- a, Ho- -san --na in ex- -cel- --sis.

Ding, Dong, Merrily on High

Ding, Dong, merrily on high,
In heaven the bells are ringing,
Ding, Dong, verily the sky,
Is riv'n with angel-singing:

Gloria.....Hosanna in excelsis.

E'en so here below, below,
Let steeple bells be swungen,
And i-o, i-o, i-o,
By priest and people sungen:

Gloria.....Hosanna in excelsis.

Pray you, dutifully prime,
Your matin chime, ye ringers;
May you beautifully rhyme,
Your evetime song, ye singers:

Gloria.....Hosanna in excelsis.

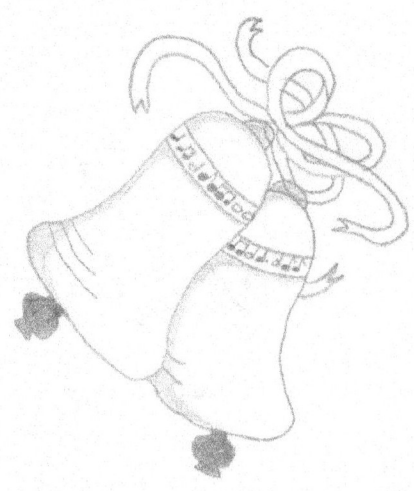

Czech Carol

The Sleigh Bell Carol

Arr. Claire

Cantabile

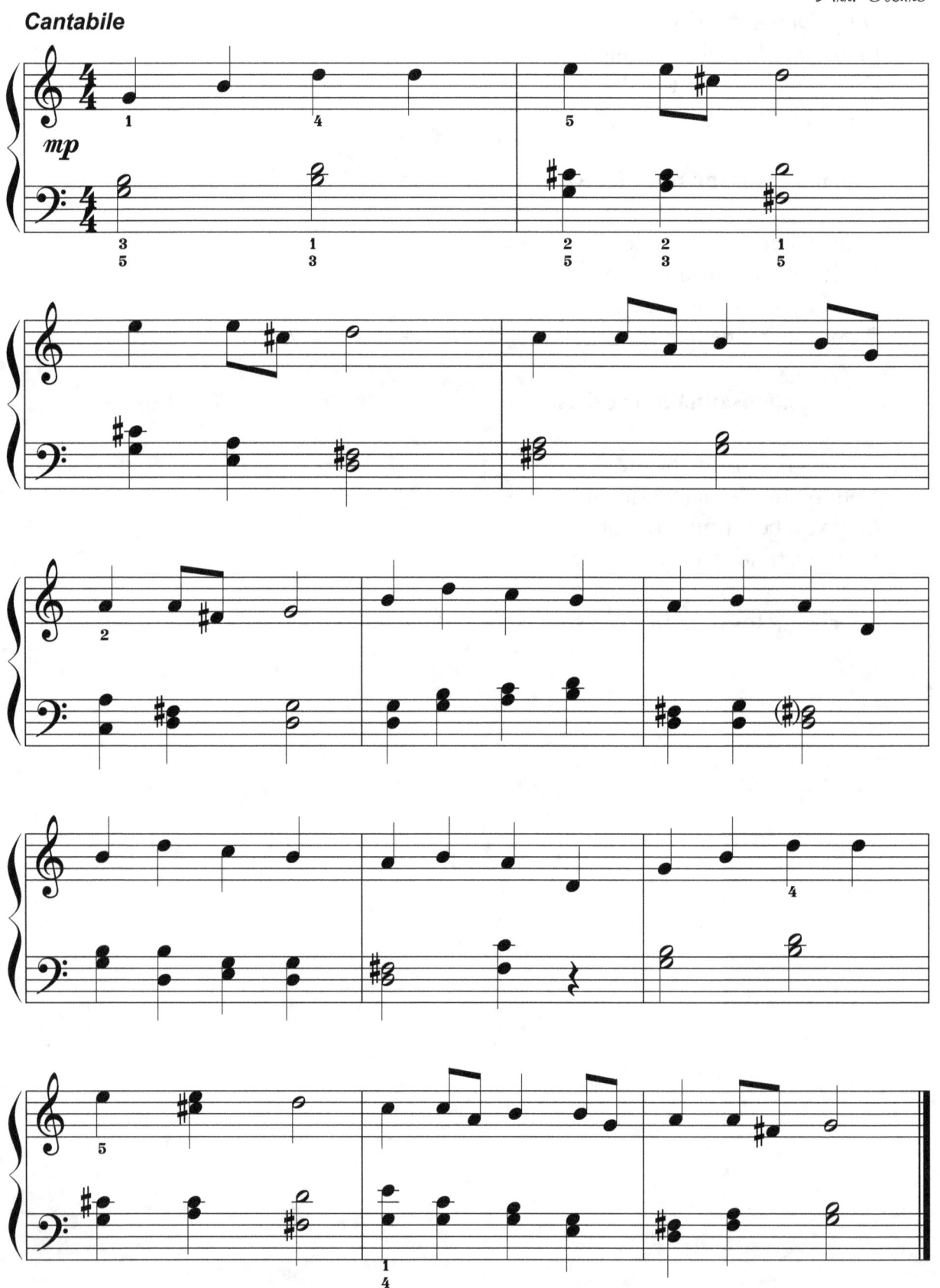

This is also known as the Sleigh Bell Carol ("Over the Snow") and is played at a much faster pace.

Search for the words or lyrics on the internet: "Sleigh Bell Carol"; also search "Czech Carol, Rocking".

Infant Holy, Infant Lowly

Traditional Polish

Arr. Eros

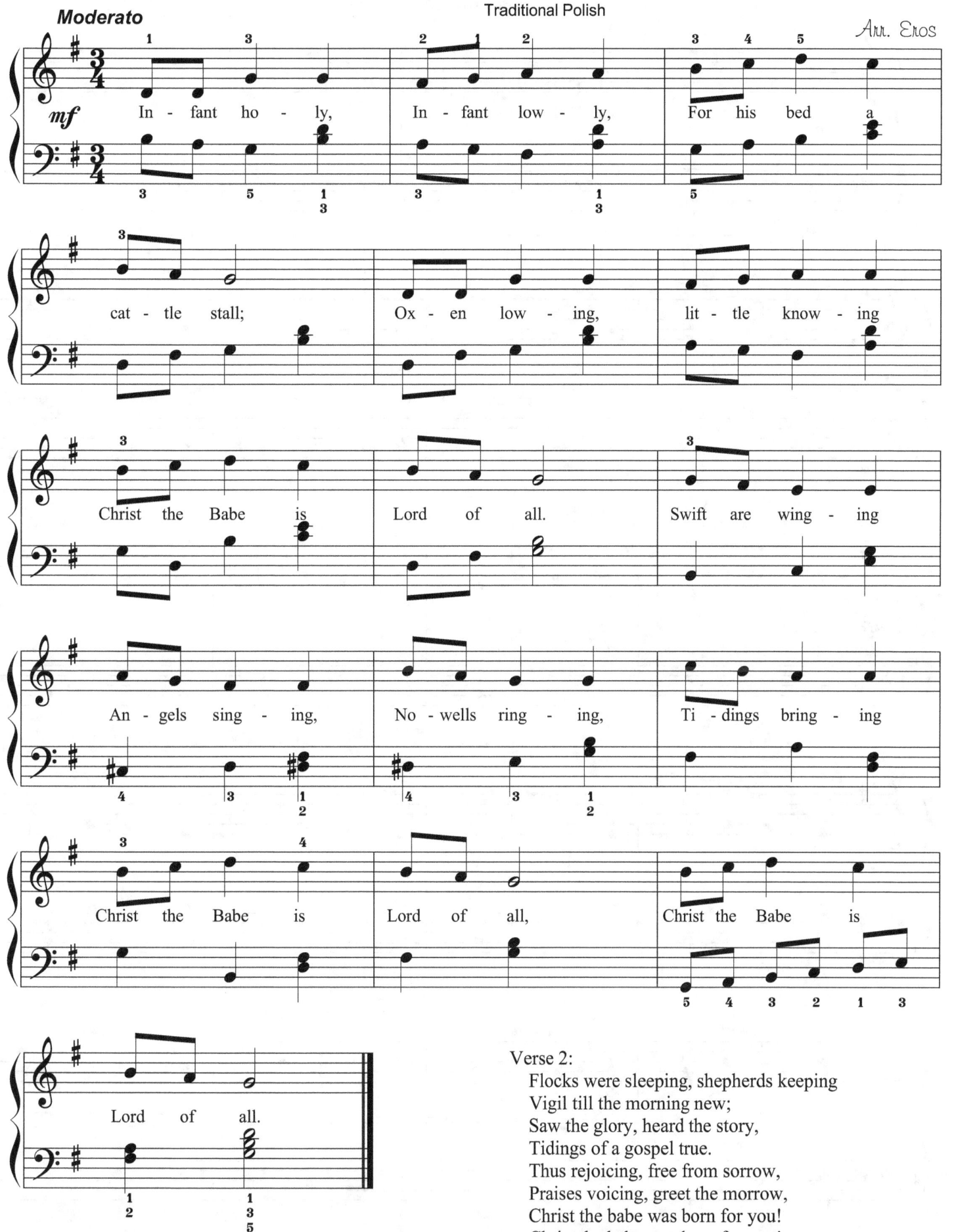

Verse 2:
Flocks were sleeping, shepherds keeping
Vigil till the morning new;
Saw the glory, heard the story,
Tidings of a gospel true.
Thus rejoicing, free from sorrow,
Praises voicing, greet the morrow,
Christ the babe was born for you!
Christ the babe was born for you!

Translation Edith M. Reed

Carol of the Bells

Ukranian Carol - Leontovich. *For keyboards, select a bell sound.*

Arr. Eros

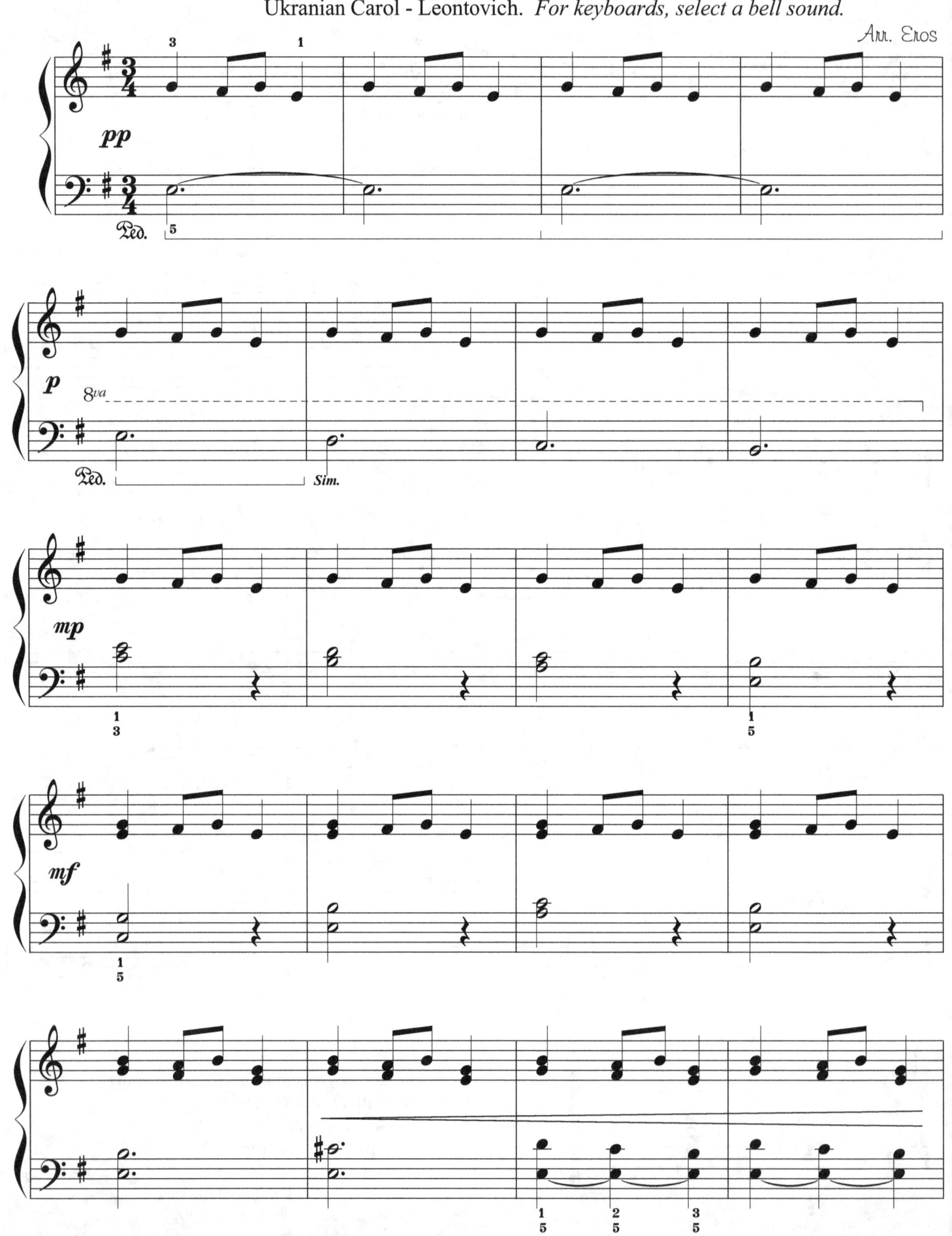

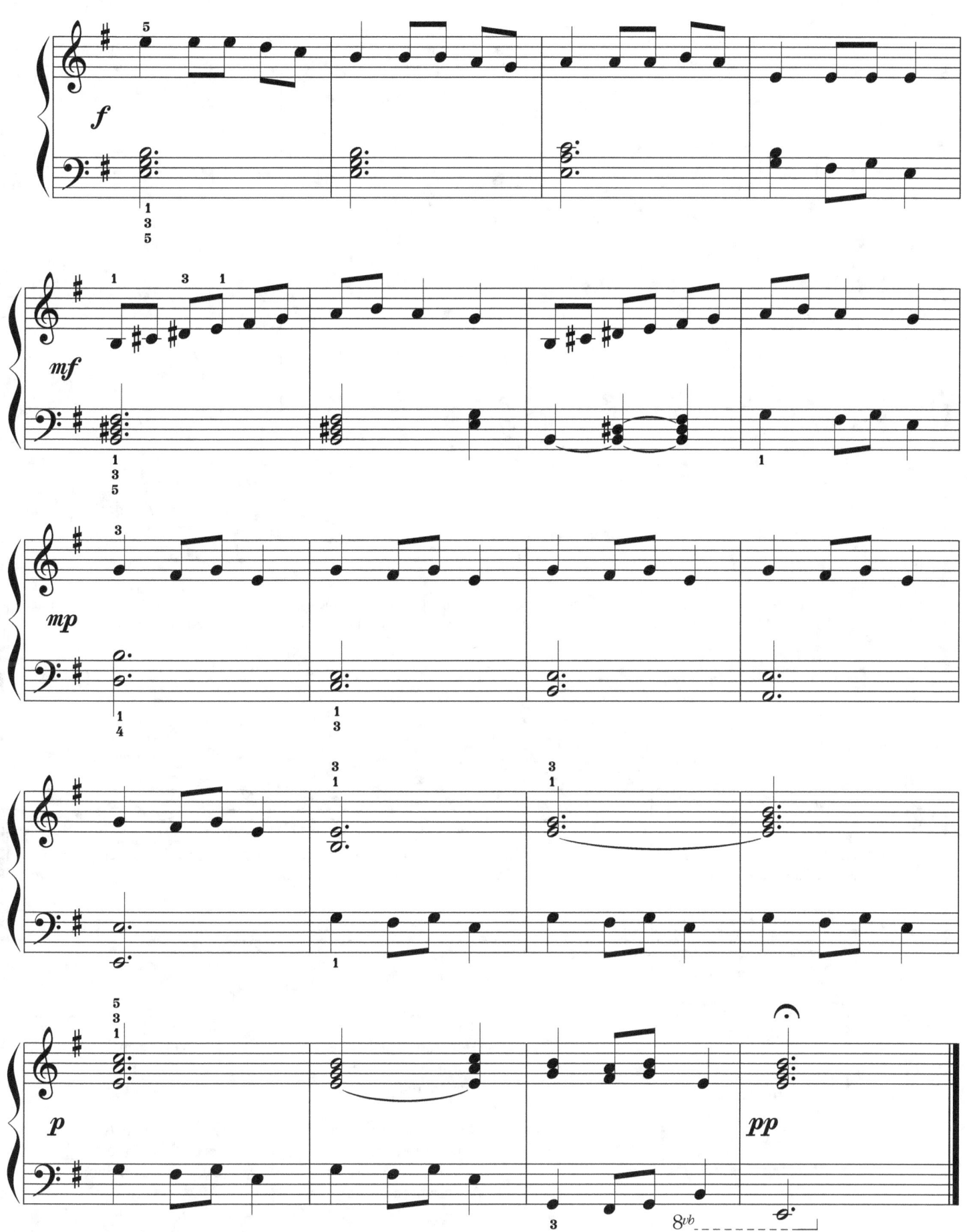

Gaudete (Rejoice)

Piae Cantiones 158.

Arr. Eros M.

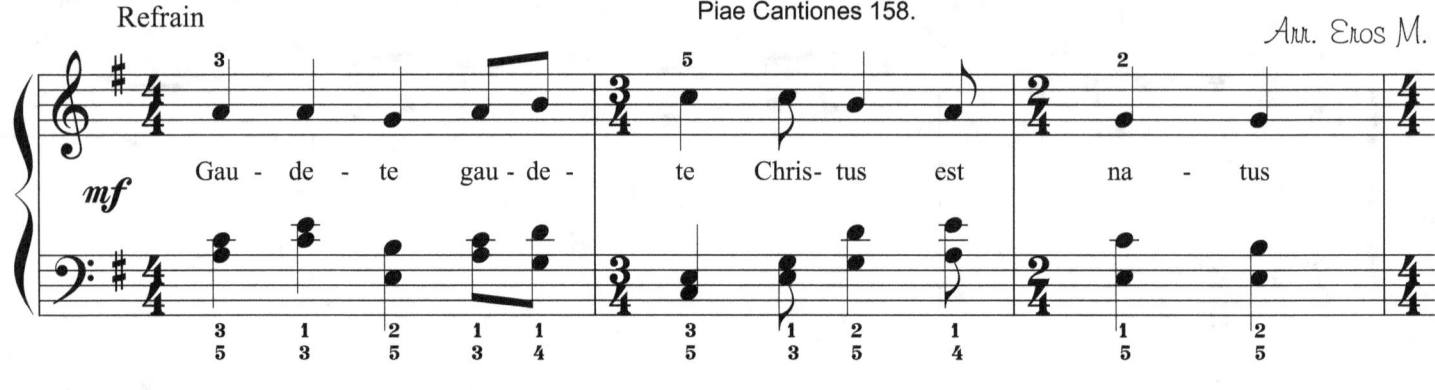

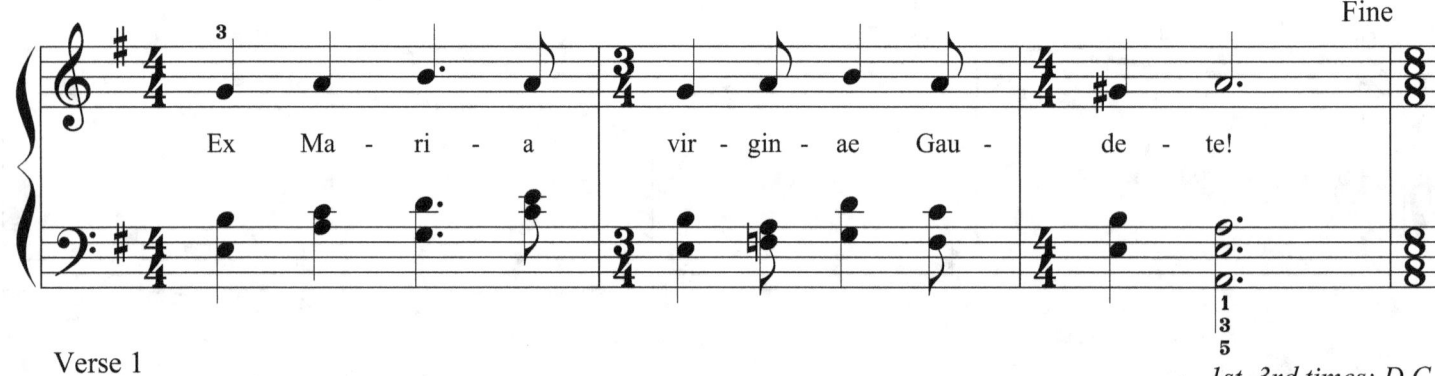

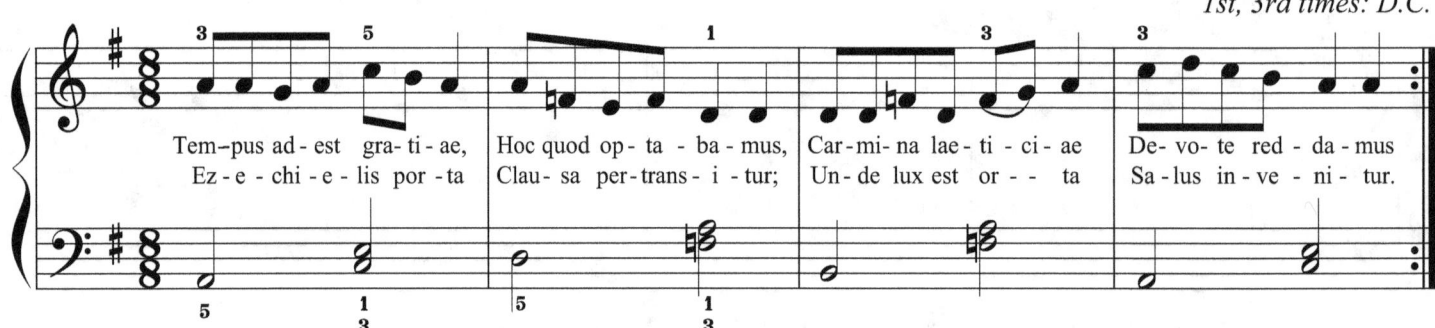

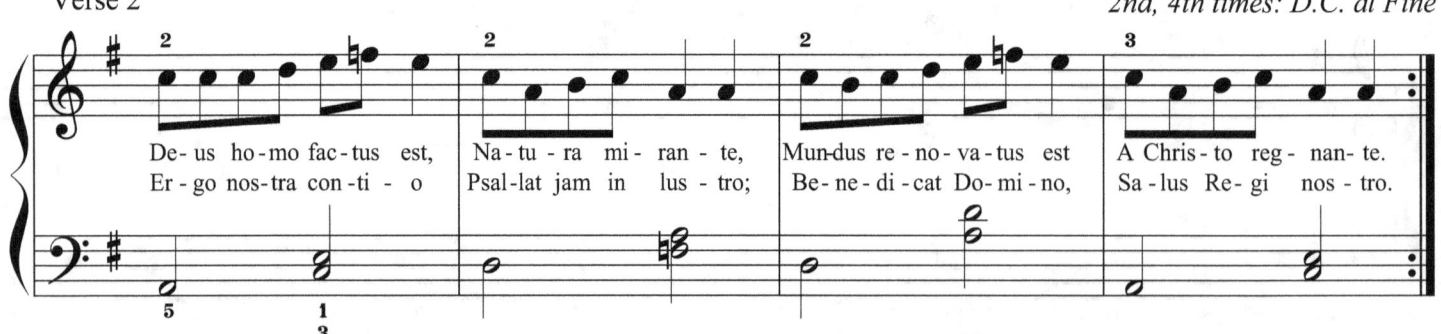

Refrain:

Gaudete, Gaudete,
Christus est natus,
Ex Maria virginae,
Gaudete.

Verses:

1. Tempus adest gratiae,
   Hoc quod optabamus;
   Carmina laeticiae,
   Devote reddamus.

2. Deus homo factus est,
   Natura mirante;
   Mundus renovatus est
   A Christo regnante.

3. Ezechielis porta
   Clausa pertransitur,
   Unde lux est orta,
   Salus invenitur.

4. Ergo nostra contio
   Psallat jam in lustro,
   Benedicat Domino,
   Salus Regi nostro.

Good Christian Men Rejoice

In Dulci Jubilo

Arr. Eros

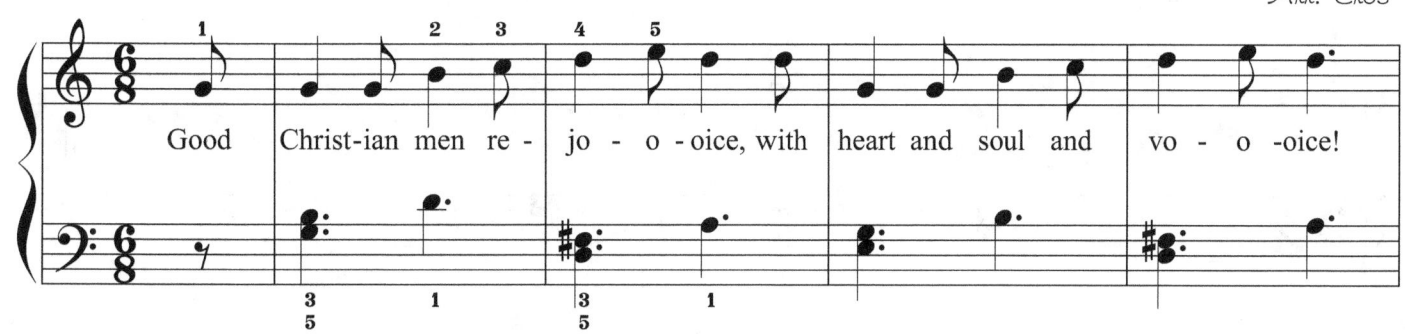

Good Christ-ian men re - jo - o -oice, with heart and soul and vo - o -oice!

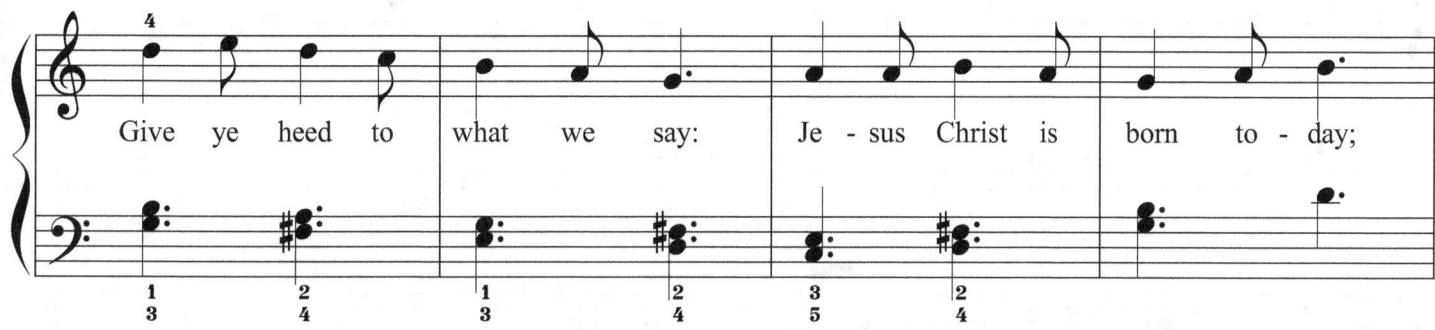

Give ye heed to what we say: Je -sus Christ is born to - day;

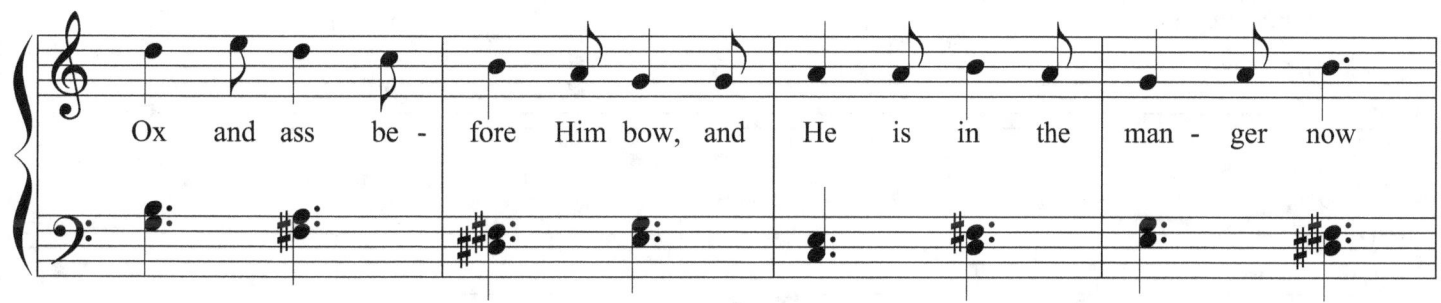

Ox and ass be - fore Him bow, and He is in the man - ger now

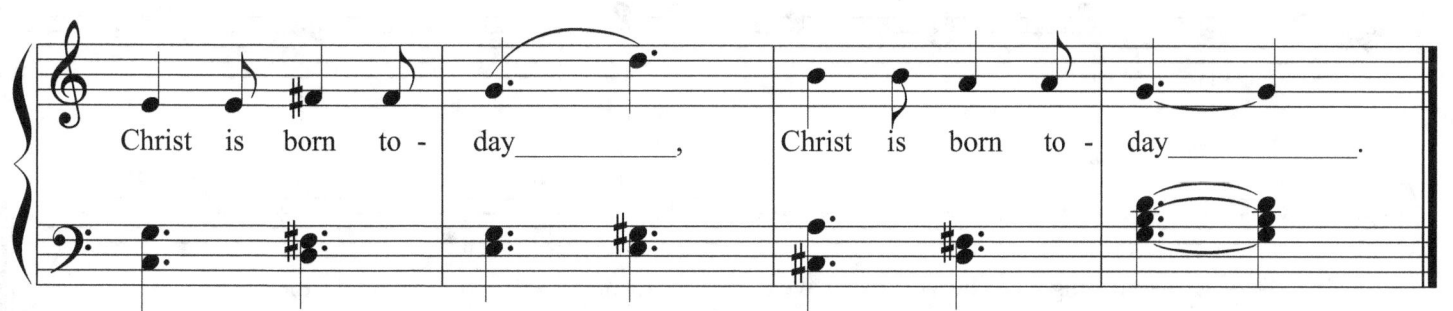

Christ is born to - day_____, Christ is born to - day_____.

2. Good Christian men, rejoice
   With heart and soul and voice!
   Now ye hear of endless bliss:
   Jesus Christ was born for this,
   He hath ope'd the heav'ly door,
   And man is blest for evermore,
   Christ was born for this.

3. Good Christians all, rejoice
   With heart and soul and voice!
   Now ye need not fear the grave
   Jesus Christ was born to save;
   Calls you one, and calls you all
   To gain His everlasting hall,
   Christ was born to save.

Gloucestershire Wassail

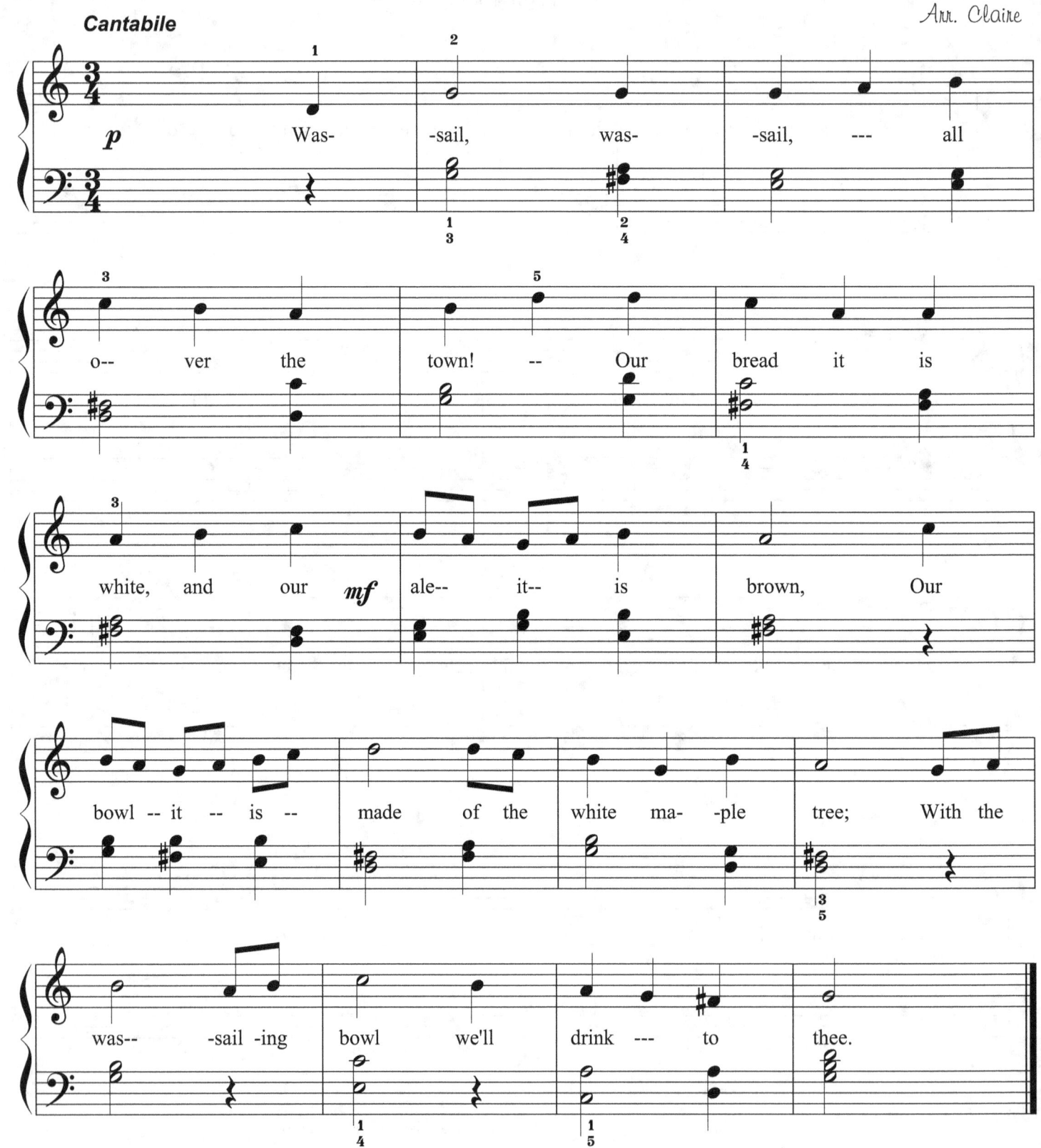

Gloucestershire Wassail

Wassail, wassail, all over the town !
Our bread it is white, and our ale it is brown,
Our bowl it is made of the white maple tree,
With the was sailing bowl we'll drink to thee.

And here is to horse and to his right eye,
Pray God send our master a good Christmas pie,
And a good Christmas pie that we may all see,
With our wassailing bowl we'll drink to thee.

And here is to cow and to her left ear,
Pray God send our master a happy New Year,
And a happy New Year as e'er he did see,
With our wassailing bowl we'll drink to thee.

Come, butler, come fill us a bowl of your best,
Then we hope your soul in Heaven may rest,
But if you do bring us a bowl of the small,
Then down shall go butler, bowl and all.

Then here's to the maid in the lily white smock,
Who tripped to the door and slipped back the lock,
Who tripped to the door and pulled back the pin,
For to let us jolly wassailers in.

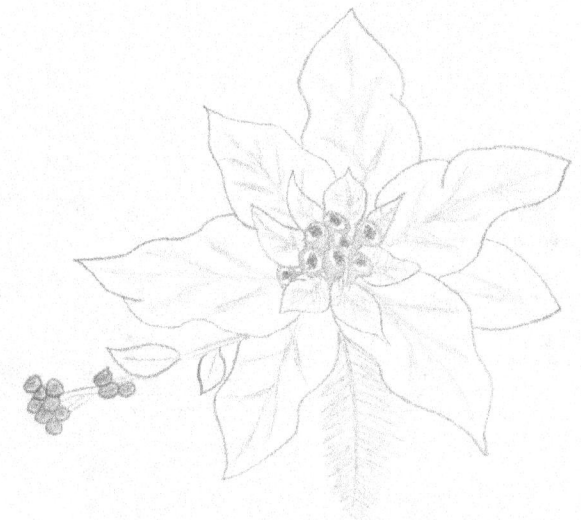

God Rest Ye Merry Gentlemen

Arr. Claire

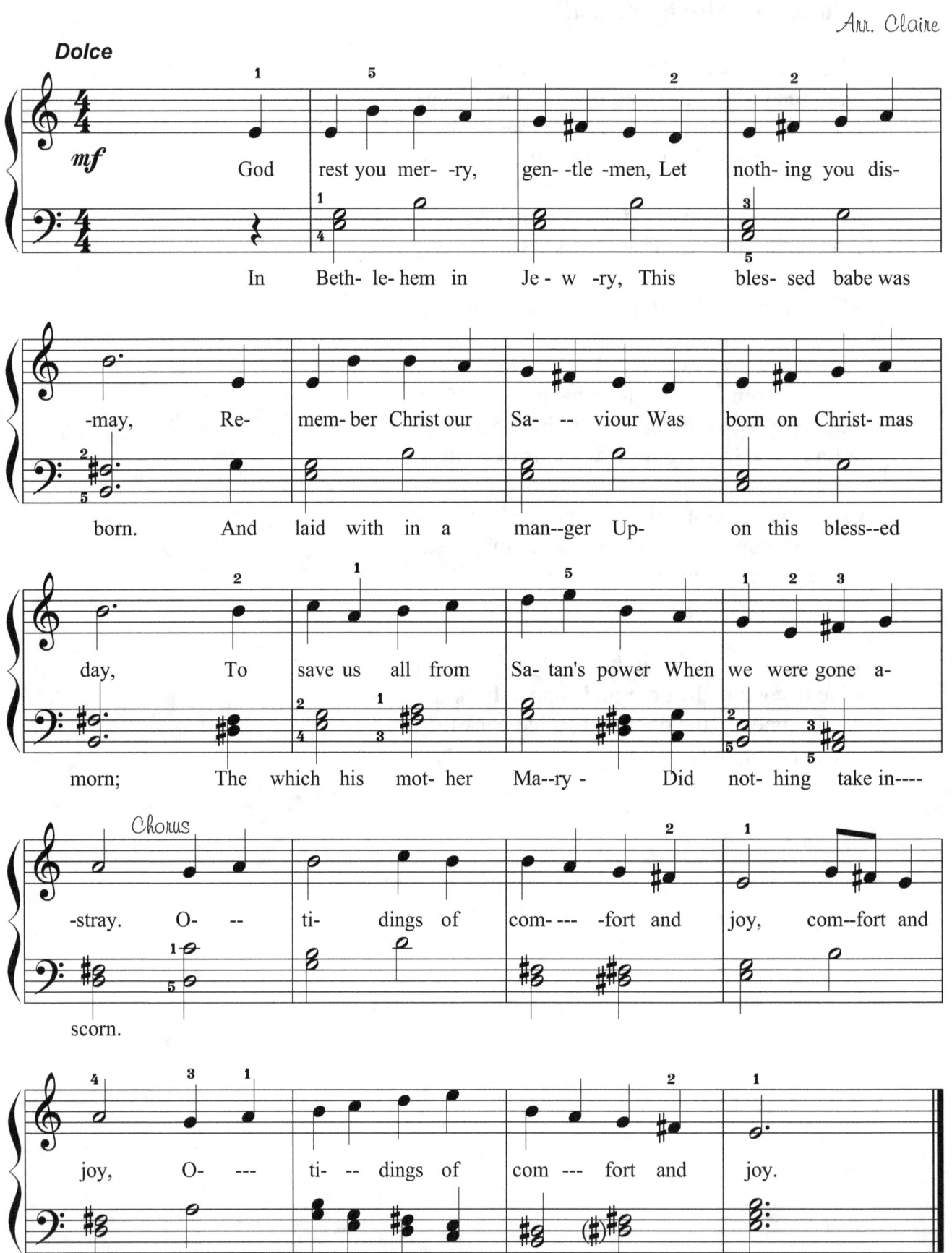

Dolce

God rest you mer- -ry, gen- -tle -men, Let noth- ing you dis-

In Beth- le- hem in Je- w -ry, This bles- sed babe was

-may, Re- mem- ber Christ our Sa- --- viour Was born on Christ- mas

born. And laid with in a man--ger Up- on this bless--ed

day, To save us all from Sa- tan's power When we were gone a-

morn; The which his mot- her Ma--ry - Did not- hing take in----

Chorus

-stray. O- --- ti- dings of com- ----fort and joy, com--fort and

scorn.

joy, O- ---- ti- -- dings of com --- fort and joy.

God Rest You Merry, Gentlemen

God rest you merry, gentlemen, let nothing you dismay,
For Jesus Christ, our Saviour, was born on Christmas day,
To save us all from Satan's power when we had gone astray,

O tidings of comfort and joy ! Comfort and Joy,
O tidings of comfort and of joy.

From God, our heavenly Father, a blessed angel came,
And unto certain shepherds brought tidings of the same,
How that in Bethlehem was born the Son of God by name.

O tidings of comfort and joy ! Comfort and Joy,
O tidings of comfort and of joy.

"Fear not, then,"said the angel, "let nothing you affright;
This day is born a Saviour, of virtue, power and might,
So frequently to vanquish all the friends of Satan quite."

O tidings of comfort and joy ! Comfort and Joy,
O tidings of comfort and of joy.

The shepherds at those tidings rejoiced much in mind,
And left their flocks a-feeding in tempest, storm and wind,
And went to Bethlehem straightway, the Blessed Babe to find.

O tidings of comfort and joy ! Comfort and Joy,
O tidings of comfort and of joy.

But when to Bethlehem they came, whereat this infant lay,
They found Him in a manger, where oxen feed on hay;
His mother, Mary, kneeling, unto the Lord did pray.

O tidings of comfort and joy ! Comfort and Joy,
O tidings of comfort and of joy.

Now to the Lord sing praises, all you within this place,
And with true love and brotherhood each other now embrace;
This holy tide of Christmas all other doth deface.

O tidings of comfort and joy ! Comfort and Joy,
O tidings of comfort and of joy.

Good King Wenceslas

Arr. Claire

Maestoso

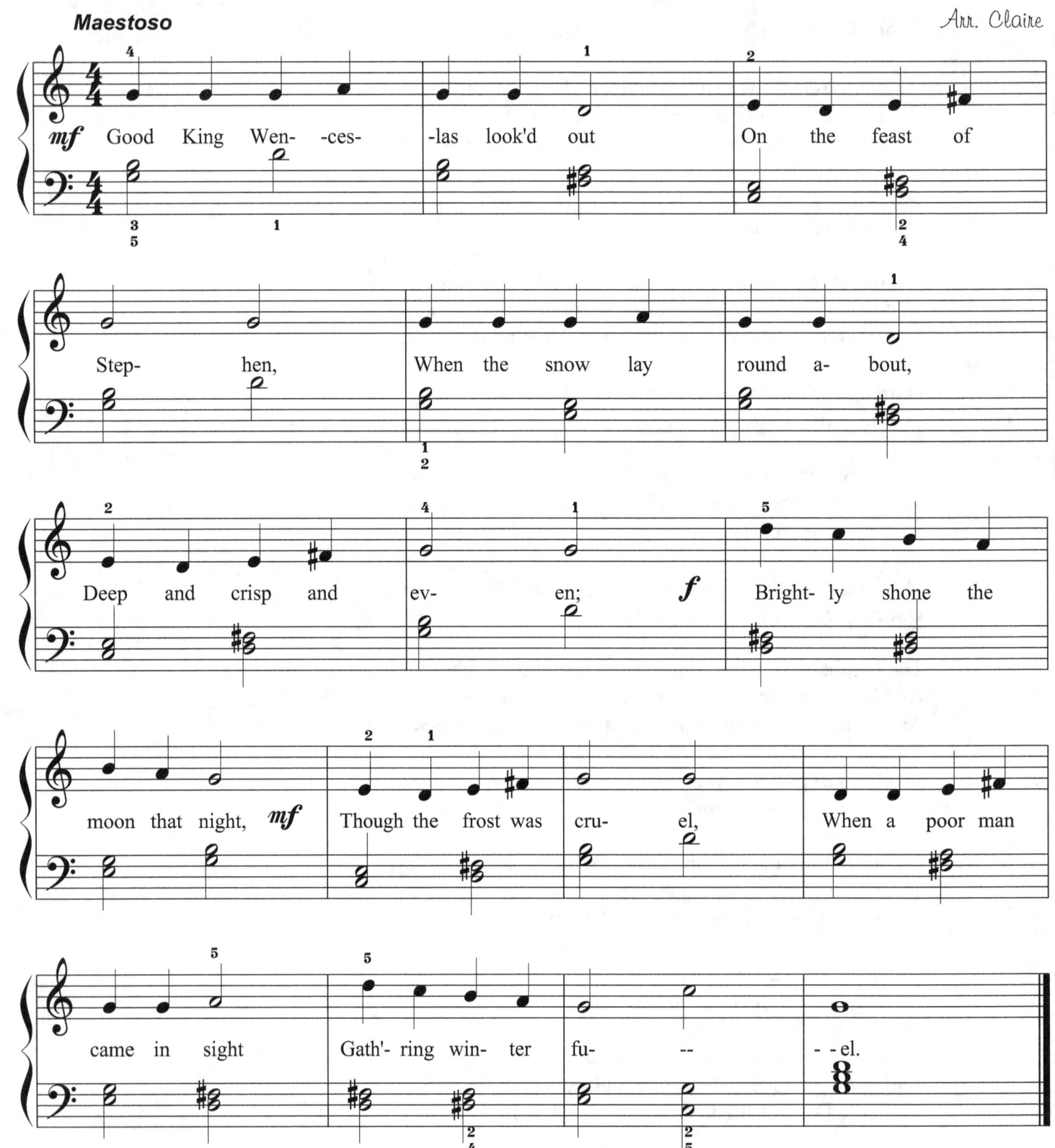

Good King Wenceslas

Good King Wenceslas look'd out
On the feast of Stephen,
When the snow lay round about,
Deep and crisp and even;
Brightly shone the moon that night,
Though the frost was cruel,
When a poor man came in sight,
Gath'ring winter fuel.

"Hither, page, come, stand by me
If thou know'st it telling,
Yonder peasant, who is he ?
Where and what his dwelling ?
"Sire, he lives a good league hence,
Down beneath the mountain:
Close against the forest fence,
By Saint Agnes' fountain!"

Bring me flesh, and bring me wine,
bring me pine logs hither:
Thou and I, we'll see him dine,
when we bear them thither."
"Page and monarch, on they went,
On they went together:
Through the rude wind's wild lament,
Through the bitter weather.

"Sire the night is darker now,
And the storm grows stronger,
Fails my heart, I know not how,
I can go no longer."
Mark my steps, be brave, my page:
Tread thou in them boldly;
Then thou'lt find the winter's rage
Freeze thy blood less coldly."

In his master's steps he trod
Where the snow lay dinted:
Heat was in the very sod
Which his foot had printed.
Therefore Christian men, be sure,
Wealth or rank possessing,
Ye who now do bless the poor,
Shall yourselves find blessing.

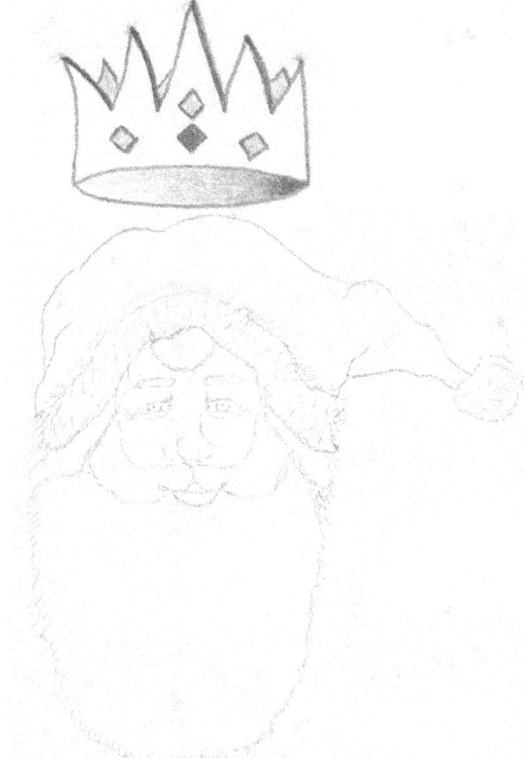

Go Tell It On The Mountain

Traditional American
Arr. Claire

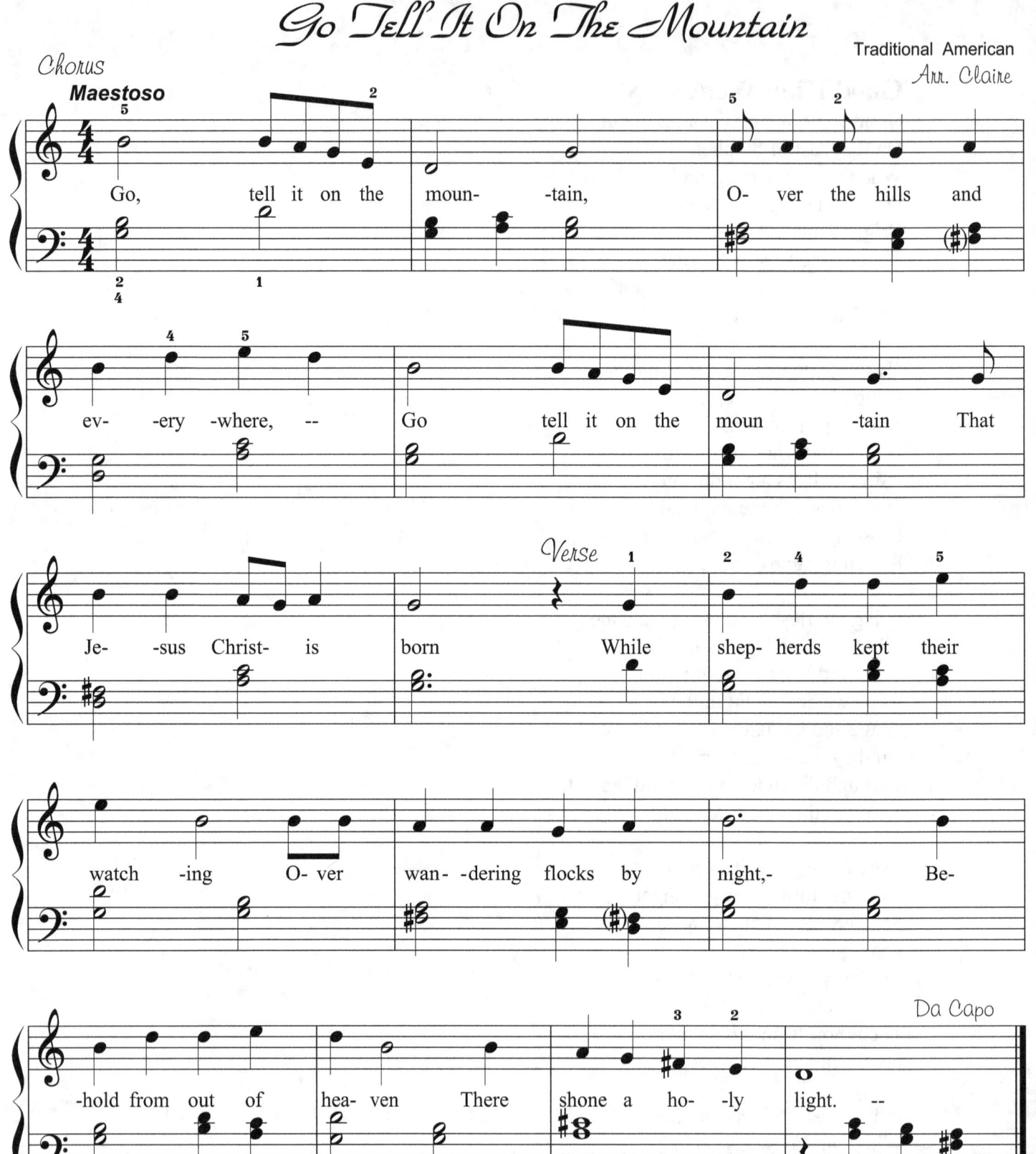

Go Tell It On The Mountain

CHORUS:

Go, tell it on the mountain,
Over the hills and everywhere,
Go tell it on the mountain,
That Jesus Christ is born.

While shepherds kept their watching,
Over wandering flocks by night,
Behold from out of heaven,
There shone a holy light.

Chorus

And lo, when they had seen it,
They all bowed down and prayed,
They travelled on together,
To where the babe was laid.

Chorus

When I was a seeker,
I sought both night and day;
I asked my Lord to help me,
And he showed me the way.

Chorus

He made me a watchman,
Upon the city wall,
And if I am a Christian,
I am the least of all.

Chorus

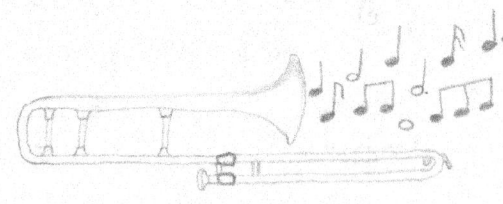

Greensleeves
What Child Is This?

Arr. Claire

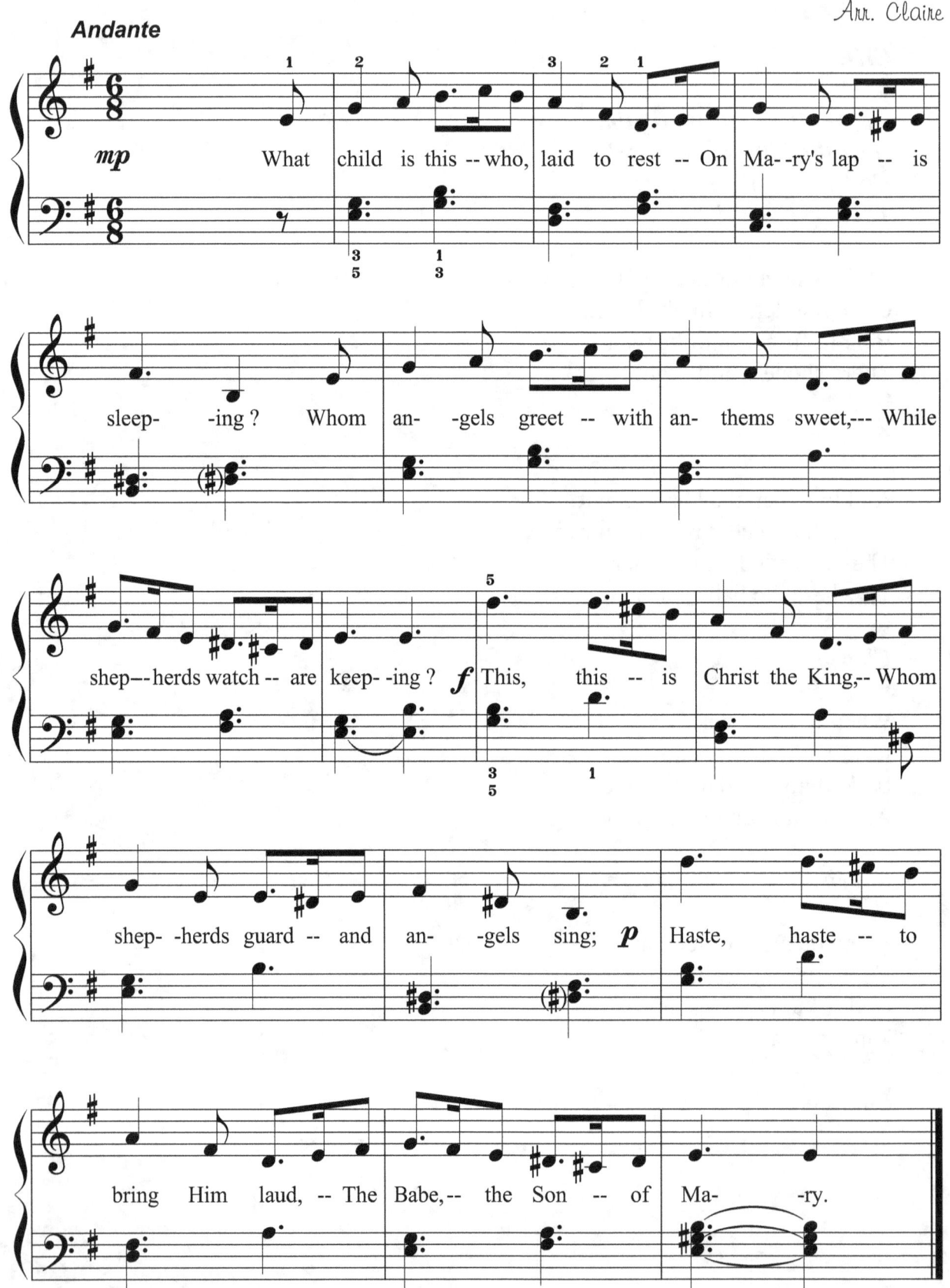

Andante

mp   What child is this -- who, laid to rest -- On Ma--ry's lap -- is

sleep- -ing?   Whom an- -gels greet -- with an- thems sweet,--- While

shep--herds watch -- are keep- -ing? *f* This,   this -- is   Christ the King,-- Whom

shep- -herds guard -- and an- -gels sing; *p* Haste,   haste -- to

bring Him laud, -- The Babe,-- the Son -- of Ma- -ry.

What Child is This ?

What Child is this who,
Laid to rest on Mary's lap is sleeping ?
Whom angels greet with anthems sweet,
While shepherds are keeping ?
This, this is Christ the King,
Whom shepherds guard and Angels sing,
Haste, haste to bring Him laud,
The Babe, the Son of Mary !

Why lies He in such mean estate,
Where ox and ass are feeding ?
Good Christian, fear for sinners here,
The silent Word is pleading,
Nails, spear, shall pierce Him through,
The Cross be borne for me, for you,
Hail, hail the Word made flesh,
The Babe, the Son of Mary !

So bring Him incense, gold and myrrh,
Come peasant, king to own Him,
The King of kings salvation brings,
Let loving hearts enthrone him.
Raise, raise the song on high,
The Virgin sings her lullaby
Joy, joy for Christ is born,
The Babe, the Son of Mary

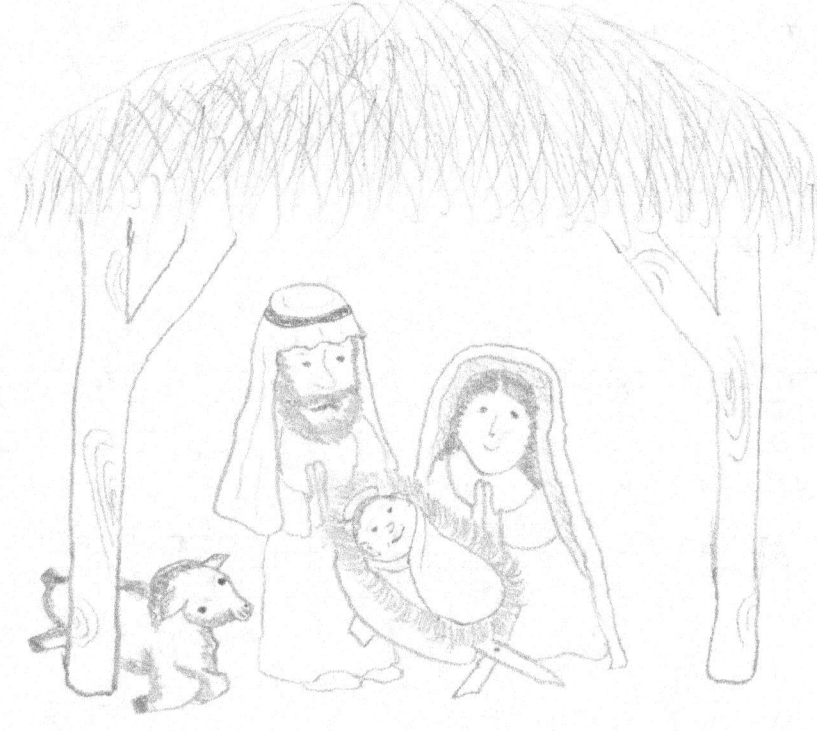

Hark! The Herald Angels Sing.

Arr. Claire

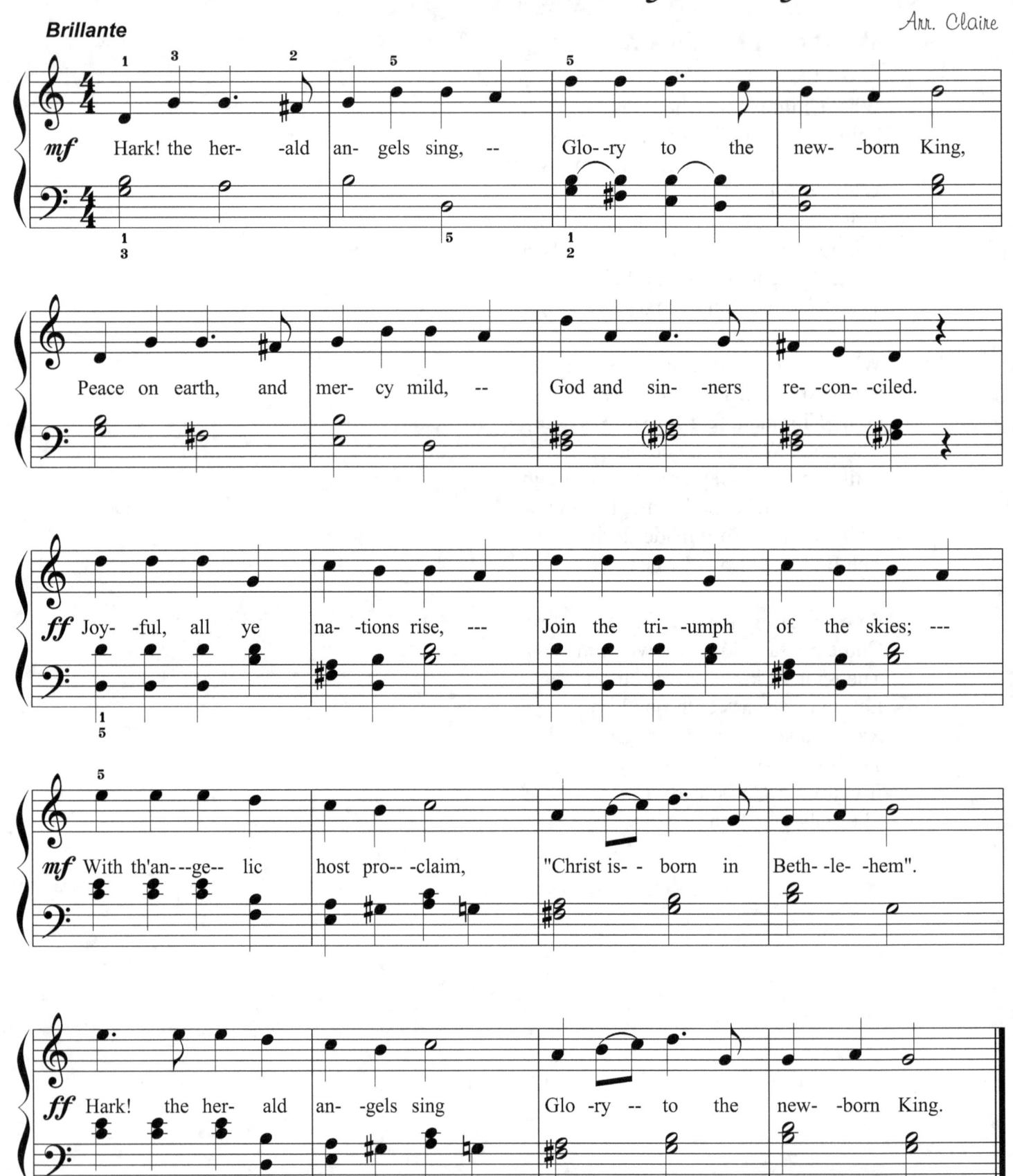

Hark! The Herald-Angels Sing

Hark! The Herald-Angels Sing,
"Glory to the new-born King.
Peace on earth and mercy mild:
God and sinners reconciled."
Joyful, all ye nations, rise,
Join the triumph of the skies:
With th'Angelic host proclaim,
"Christ is born in Bethlehem."

Hark! The herald-angels sing
Glory to the new-born King.

Christ, by highest heav'n adored,
Christ the everlasting Lord;
Late in time behold Him come,
Offspring of a Virgin's womb.
Veil'd in flesh, the Godhead see:
Hail, the Incarnate Deity:
Pleased as man with man to dwell,
Jesus our Emmanuel!

Hark! The herald-angels sing
Glory to the new-born King.

Hail, the heaven-born Prince of Peace!
Hail, the Son of Righteousness:
Light and life to all He brings,
Risen with healing in His wings.
Mild He lays His glory by,
Born that man no more may die,
Born to raise the sons of earth,
Born to give them second birth.

Hark! The herald-angels sing
Glory to the new-born King.

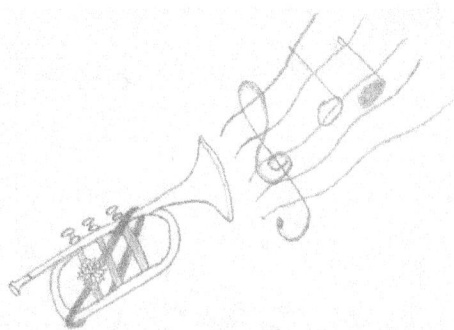

Here We Come a-Wassailing

Arr. by Eros

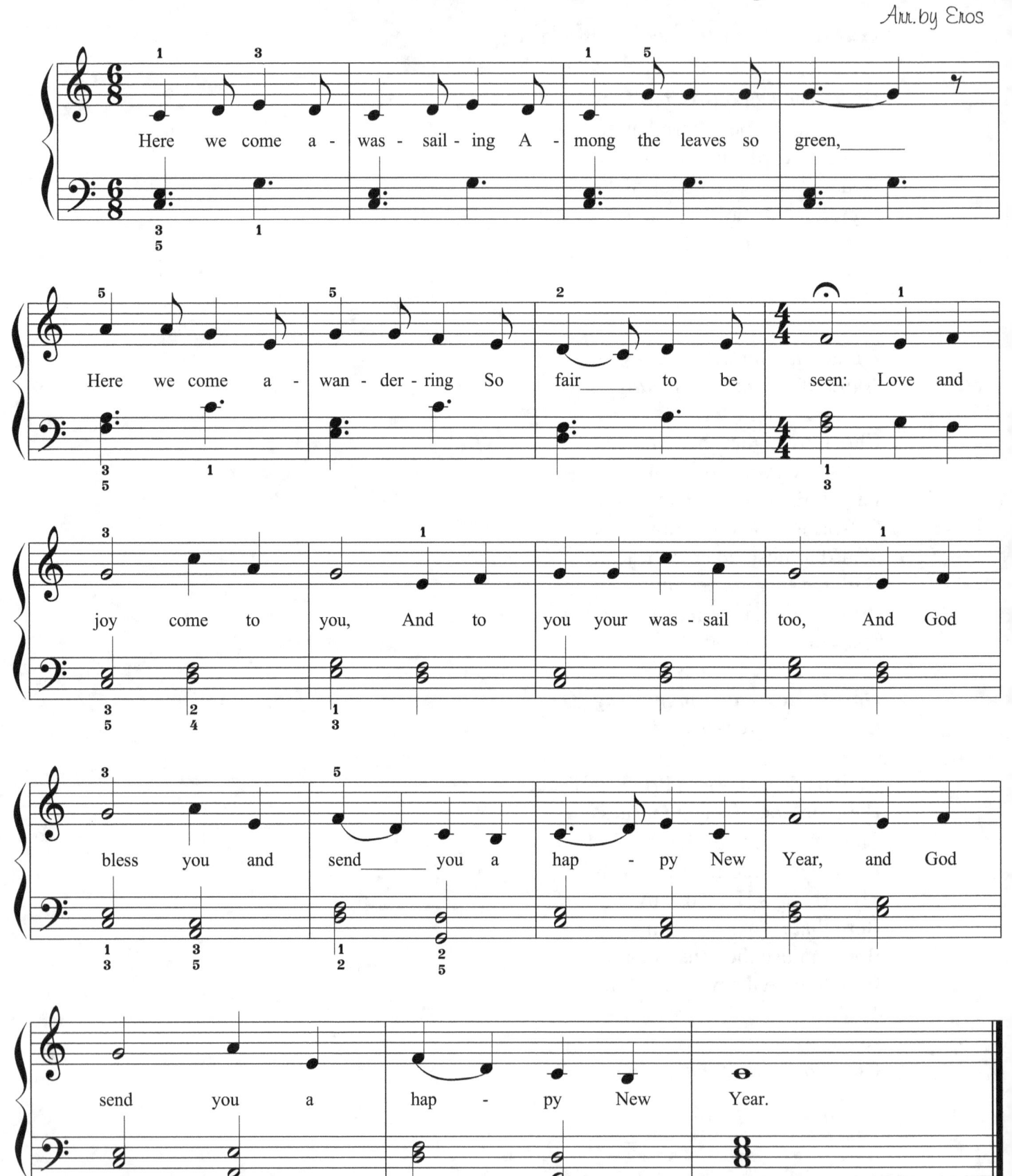

Here We Come a-Wassailing

Here we come a-wassailing
Among the leaves so green,
Here we come a-wandering
So fair to be seen.

Love and joy come to you,
And to you your wassail too,
And God bless you send you a
happy New Year,
And God send you a happy New Year.

Our wassail cup is made
Of the rosemary tree,
And so is your beer
Of the best barley.

We are not daily beggars
That beg from door to doors,
But we are neighbours' children
Whom you have seen before.

Good Master and good Mistress,
As you sit by the fire,
Pray for us poor children
Who're wand'ring in the mire.

We have got a little purse
Of stretching leather skin;
Give some of your small change
To line it well within.

Call the butler of this house,
Put on him golden ring;
Let him bring us pots of beer:
The better we shall sing.

Bring us out a table
And spread it with a cloth
Bring us out a mouldy cheese,
And some of your Christmas loaf.

God bless the Master of this house,
Likewise the Mistress too;
And all the little children
That round the table go.

And all your kin and kinsfolk
That dwell both far and near;
I wish you Merry Christmas,
And happy New Year.

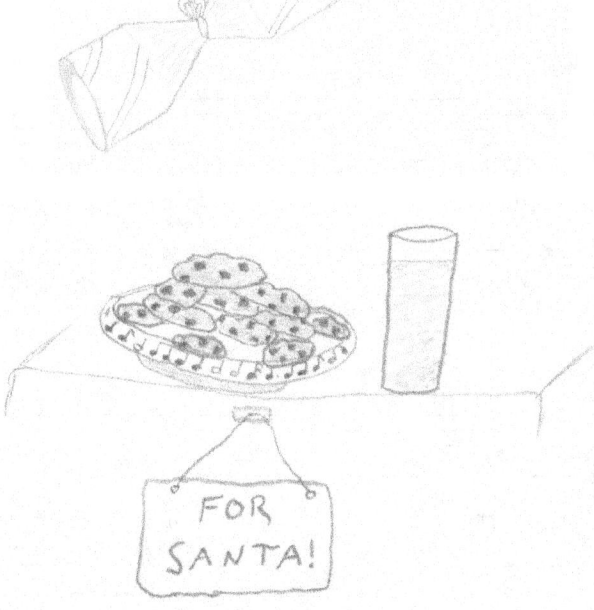

I Saw Three Ships

Arr. Claire

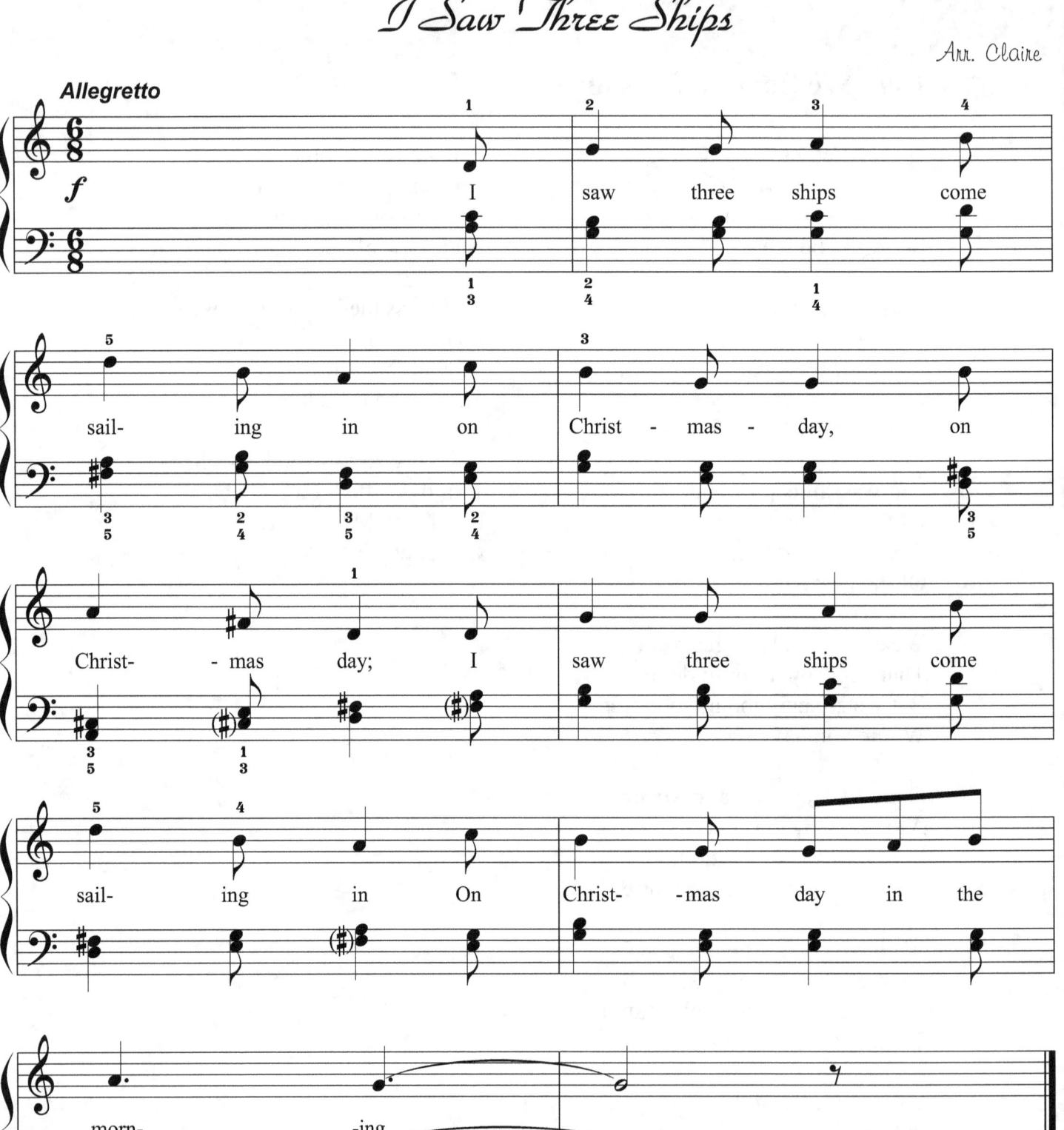

Allegretto

f

I saw three ships come sail- ing in on Christ - mas - day, on Christ- -mas day; I saw three ships come sail- ing in On Christ- -mas day in the morn- -ing

I saw Three Ships

I saw three ships come sailing in,
On Christmas Day, on Christmas Day,
I saw three ships come sailing in,
On Christmas Day in the morning.

And what was in those ships all three ?
On Christmas Day, on Christmas Day,
And what was in those ships all three ?
On Christmas Day in the morning.

Our Saviour Christ and his lady,
On Christmas Day, on Christmas Day,
Our Saviour Christ and his lady,
On Christmas Day in the morning.

Pray, whither sailed those ships all three ?
On Christmas Day, on Christmas Day,
Pray, whither sailed those ships all three ?
On Christmas Day in the morning.

O, they sailed in to Bethlehem,
On Christmas Day, on Christmas Day,
O, they sailed in to Bethlehem,
On Christmas Day in the morning.

And all the bells on earth shall ring,
On Christmas Day, on Christmas Day,
And and all the bells on earth shall ring,
On Christmas Day in the morning.

And all the angels in Heaven shall sing,
On Christmas Day, on Christmas Day,
And all the angels in Heaven shall sing,
On Christmas Day in the morning.

And all the souls on earth shall sing,
On Christmas Day, on Christmas Day,
And all the souls on earth shall sing,
On Christmas Day in the morning.

Then let us all rejoice again,
On Christmas Day, on Christmas Day,
Then let us all rejoice again,
On Christmas Day in the morning.

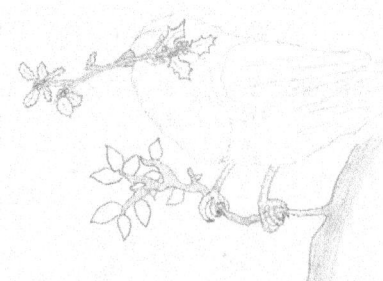

It Came Upon The Midnight Clear

Version one

Traditional American

Arr. Claire

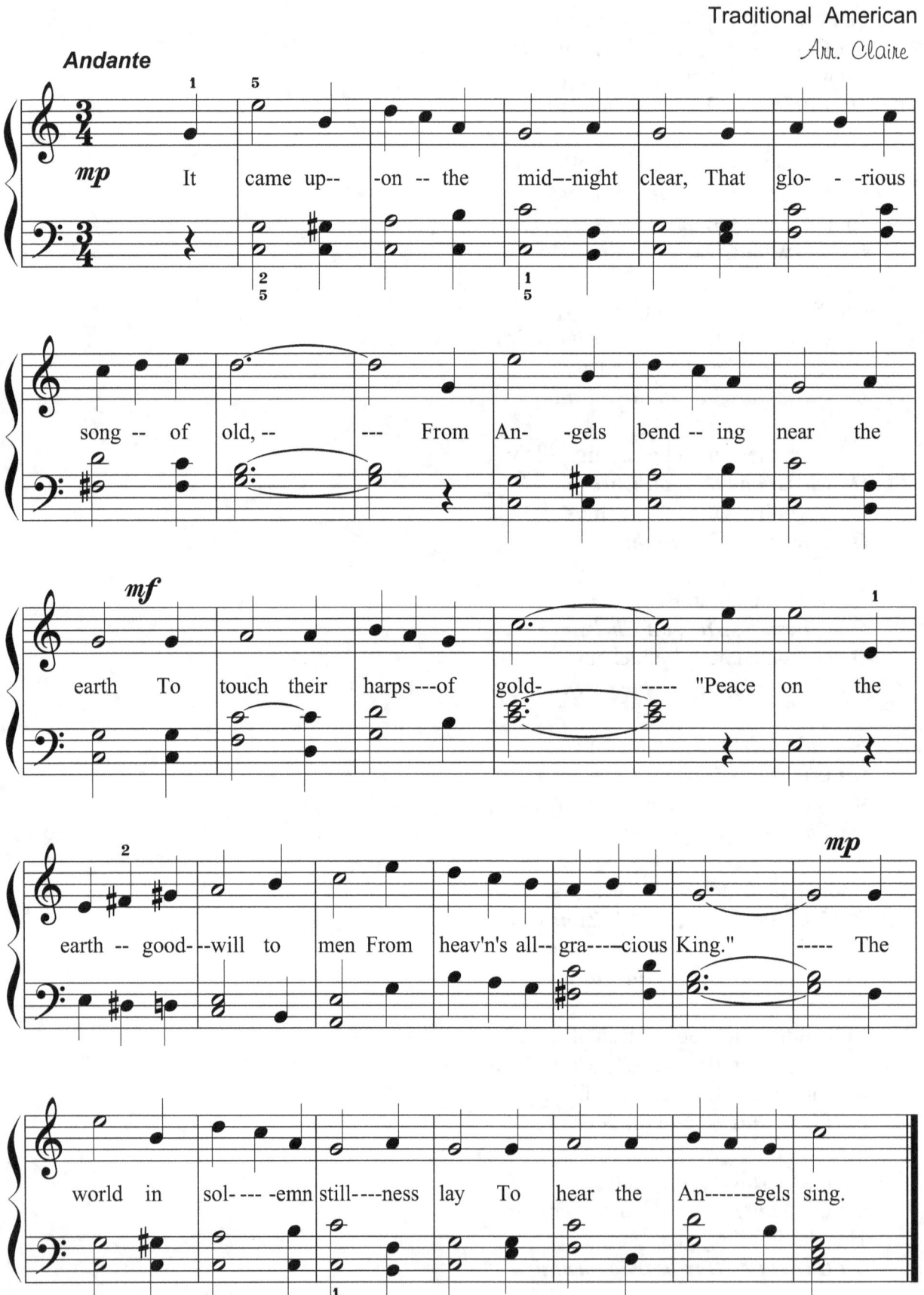

Andante

mp It came up-- -on -- the mid--night clear, That glo- -rious

song -- of old, -- ---- From An- -gels bend -- ing near the

mf earth To touch their harps ---of gold---- ----- "Peace on the

earth -- good---will to men From heav'n's all-- gra----cious King." ----- The

world in sol---- -emn still----ness lay To hear the An------gels sing.

35

It Came Upon The Midnight Clear

It came upon the midnight clear,
That glorious song of old,
From angels bending near the earth,
To touch their harps of gold:
"Peace on earth, good will to men"
From heaven's all gracious King;
The world in solemn stillness lay
To hear the angels sing.

Still through the cloven skies they come,
With peaceful wings unfurled,
And still their heavenly music floats
O'er all the weary world;
Above its sad and lowly plains
They bend on heavenly wing,
And ever oe'r its Babel-sounds
The blessed angels sing.

Yet with the woes of sin and strife
The world has suffered long;
Beneath the angel-strain have rolled
Two thousand years of wrong;
And man, at war with man, hears not
The love-song which they bring:
O hush the noise, ye men of strife,
And hear the angels sing!

For lo! The days are hastening on,
By prophet-bards foretold,
When with the ever-circling years
Comes round the age of gold:
When peace shall over all the earth
Its ancient splendours fling,
And the whole world send back the song
Which now the angels sing.

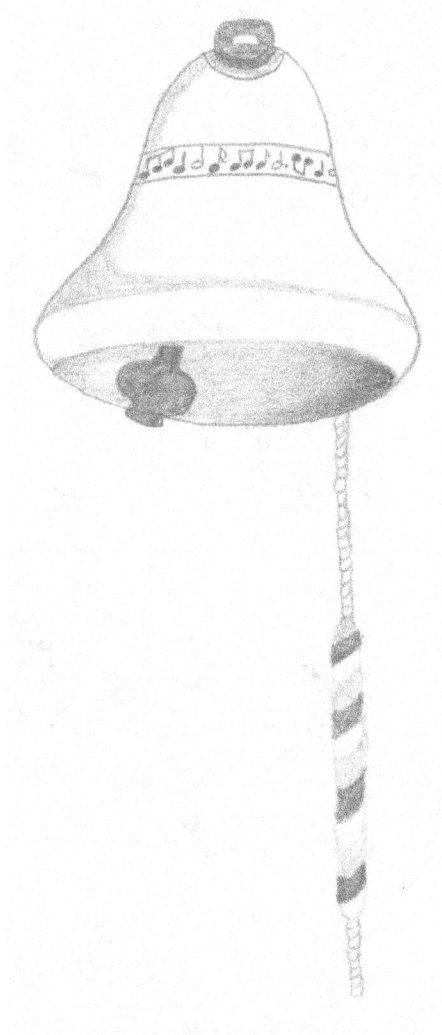

It Came Upon The Midnight Clear

Version Two

Traditional English
Arr. Claire

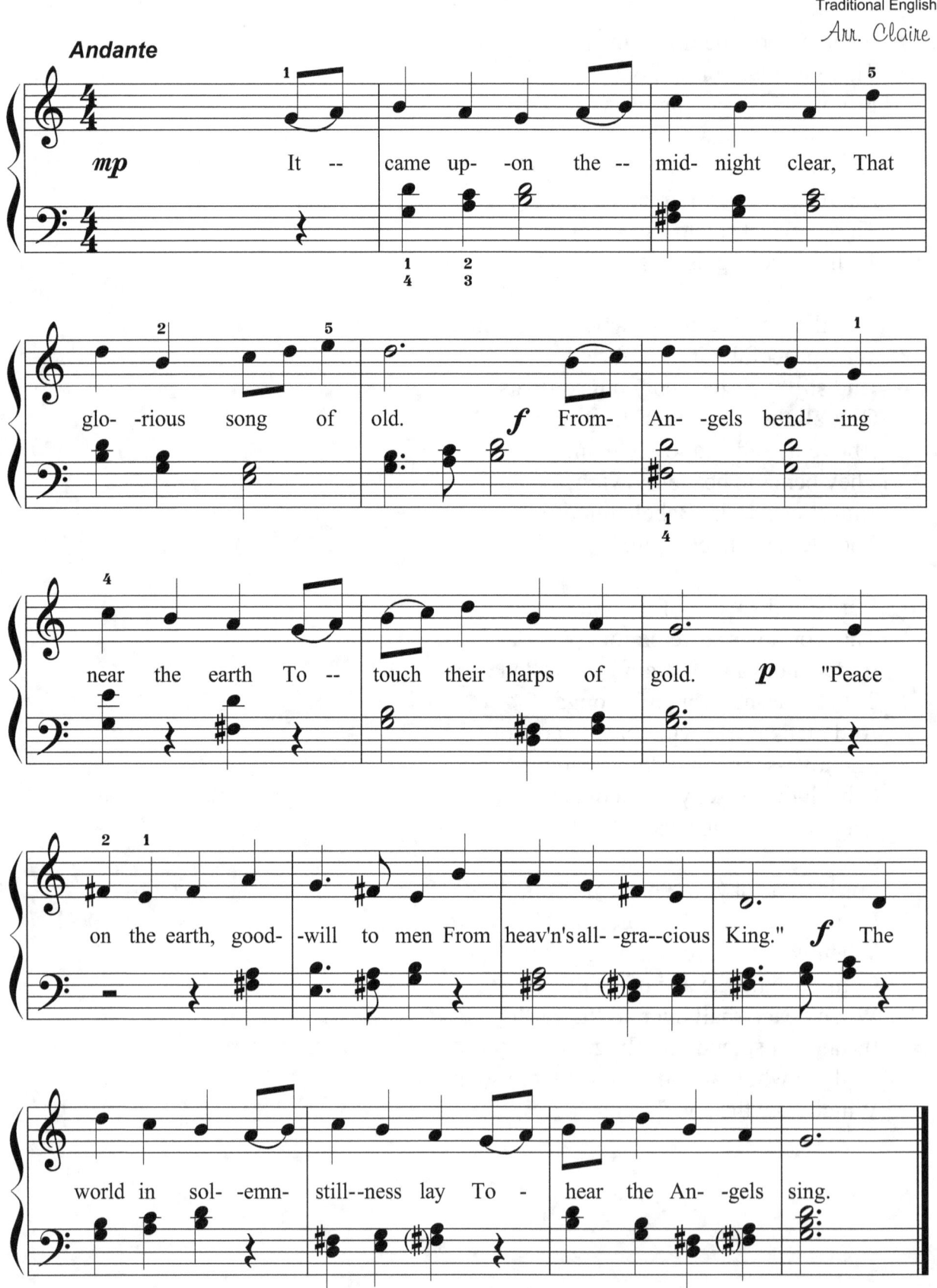

Andante

It -- came up- -on the -- mid- night clear, That glo- -rious song of old. *f* From- An- -gels bend- -ing near the earth To -- touch their harps of gold. *p* "Peace on the earth, good- -will to men From heav'n's all- -gra--cious King." *f* The world in sol- -emn- still--ness lay To - hear the An- -gels sing.

37

It Came Upon The Midnight Clear

It came upon the midnight clear,
That glorious song of old,
From angels bending near the earth,
To touch their harps of gold:
"Peace on earth, good will to men"
From heaven's all gracious King;
The world in solemn stillness lay
To hear the angels sing.

Still through the cloven skies they come,
With peaceful wings unfurled,
And still their heavenly music floats
O'er all the weary world;
Above its sad and lowly plains
They bend on heavenly wing,
And ever oe'r its Babel-sounds
The blessed angels sing.

Yet with the woes of sin and strife
The world has suffered long;
Beneath the angel-strain have rolled
Two thousand years of wrong;
And man, at war with man, hears not
The love-song which they bring:
O hush the noise, ye men of strife,
And hear the angels sing!

For lo! The days are hastening on,
By prophet-bards foretold,
When with the ever-circling years
Comes round the age of gold:
When peace shall over all the earth
Its ancient splendours fling,
And the whole world send back the song
Which now the angels sing.

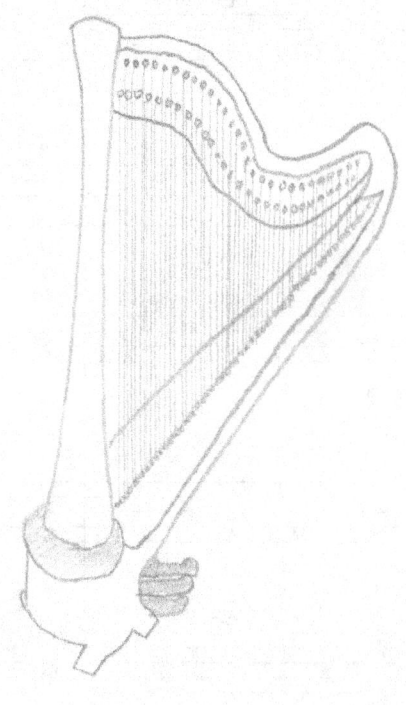

Jingle Bells

Arr. Claire

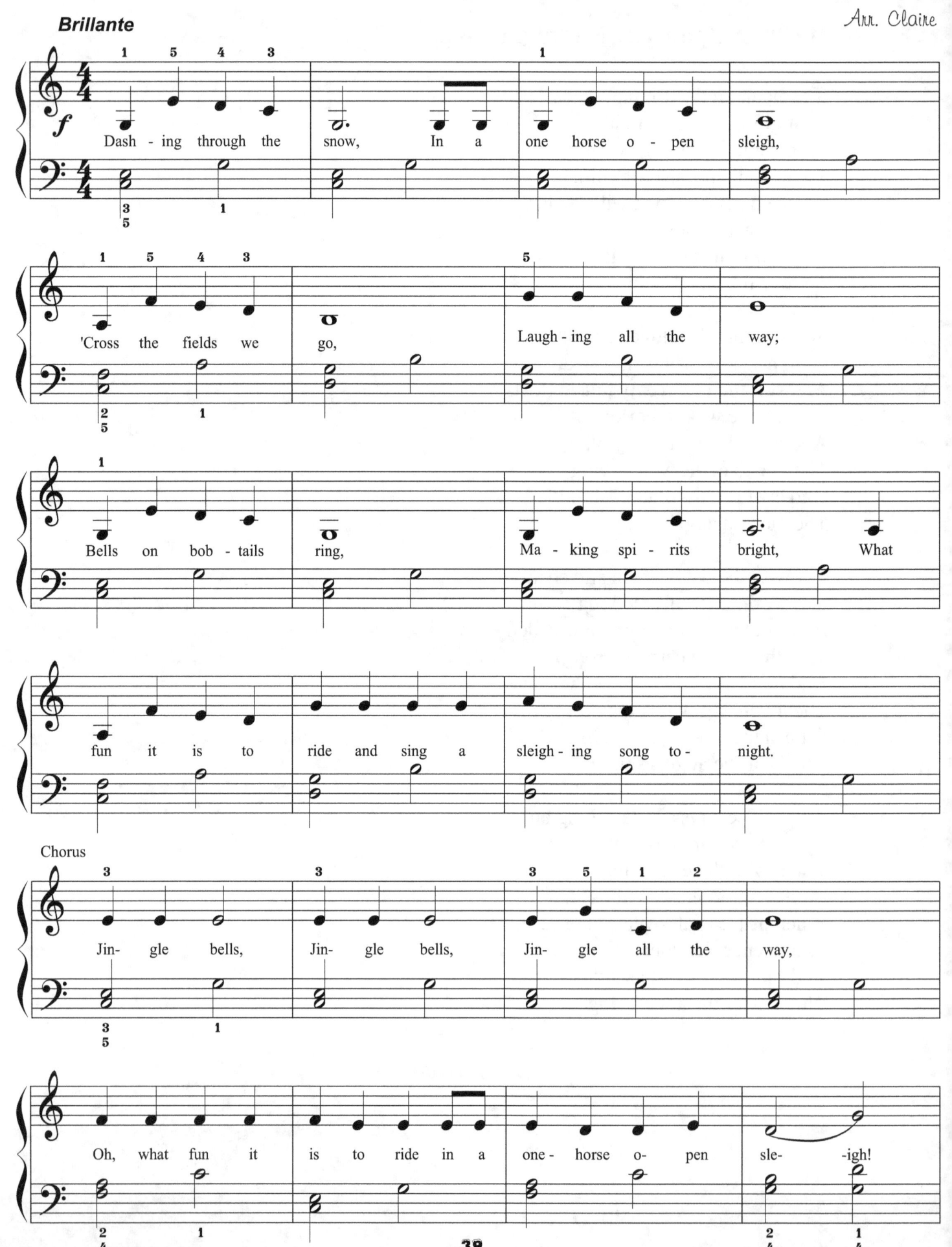

39

Jingle Bells

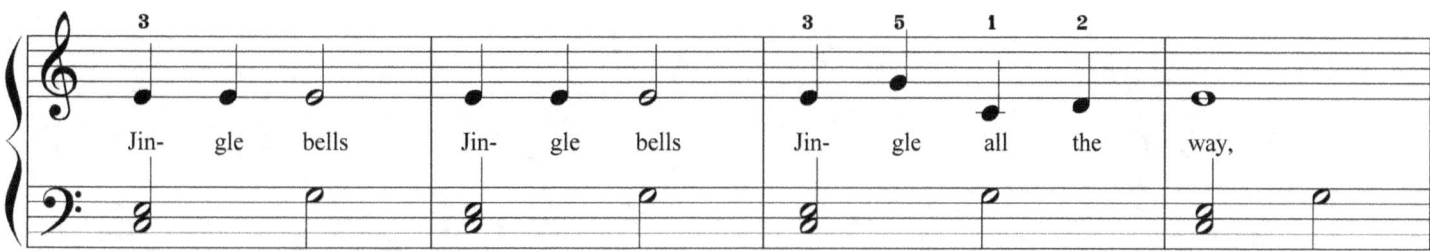

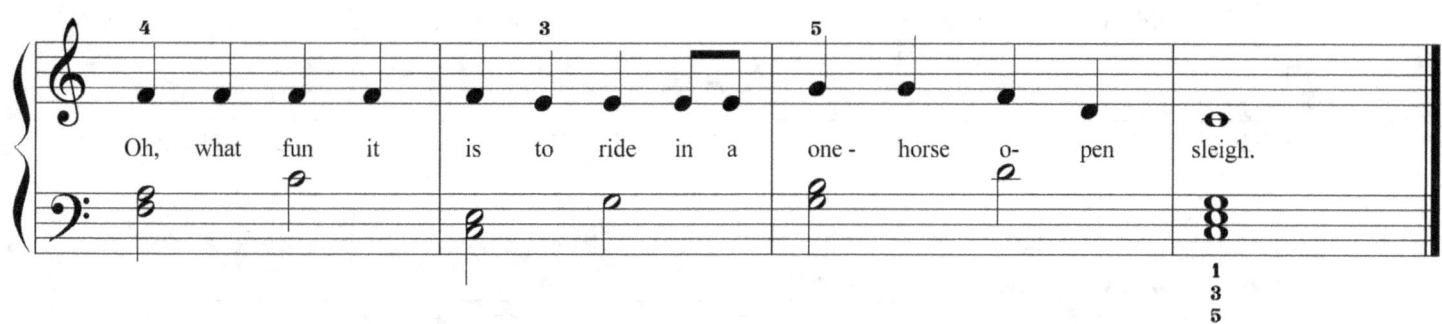

1 We're dashing through the snow,
   In a one-horse open sleigh,
   'Cross the fields we go,
   Laughing all the way;
   The bells on bobtails ring,
   They're making spirits bright,
   What fun it is to ride and sing
   A sleighing song tonight.
   Chorus

3 Now the ground is white,
   Go it while you're young!
   Take the girls tonight,
   And sing this sleighing song.
   Just get a bobtail'd bay,
   Two-forty for his speed,
   Then hitch him to an open sleigh
   And crack! You'll take the lead.
   Chorus

2 Day or two ago,
   I thought I'd take a ride,
   Soon Miss Fanny Bright
   Was seated at my side.
   The horse was lean and lank,
   Misfortune seemed his lot,
   He got into a drifted bank,
   And we, we got upsot!
   Chorus

Chorus:
Jingle bells, Jingle bells,
Jingle all the way,
Oh, what fun it is to ride
In a one-horse open sleigh;
Jingle bells, Jingle bells,
Jingle all the way,
Oh what fun it is to ride
In a one-horse open sleigh.

Jolly Old Saint Nicholas

Traditional American

Arr. Claire

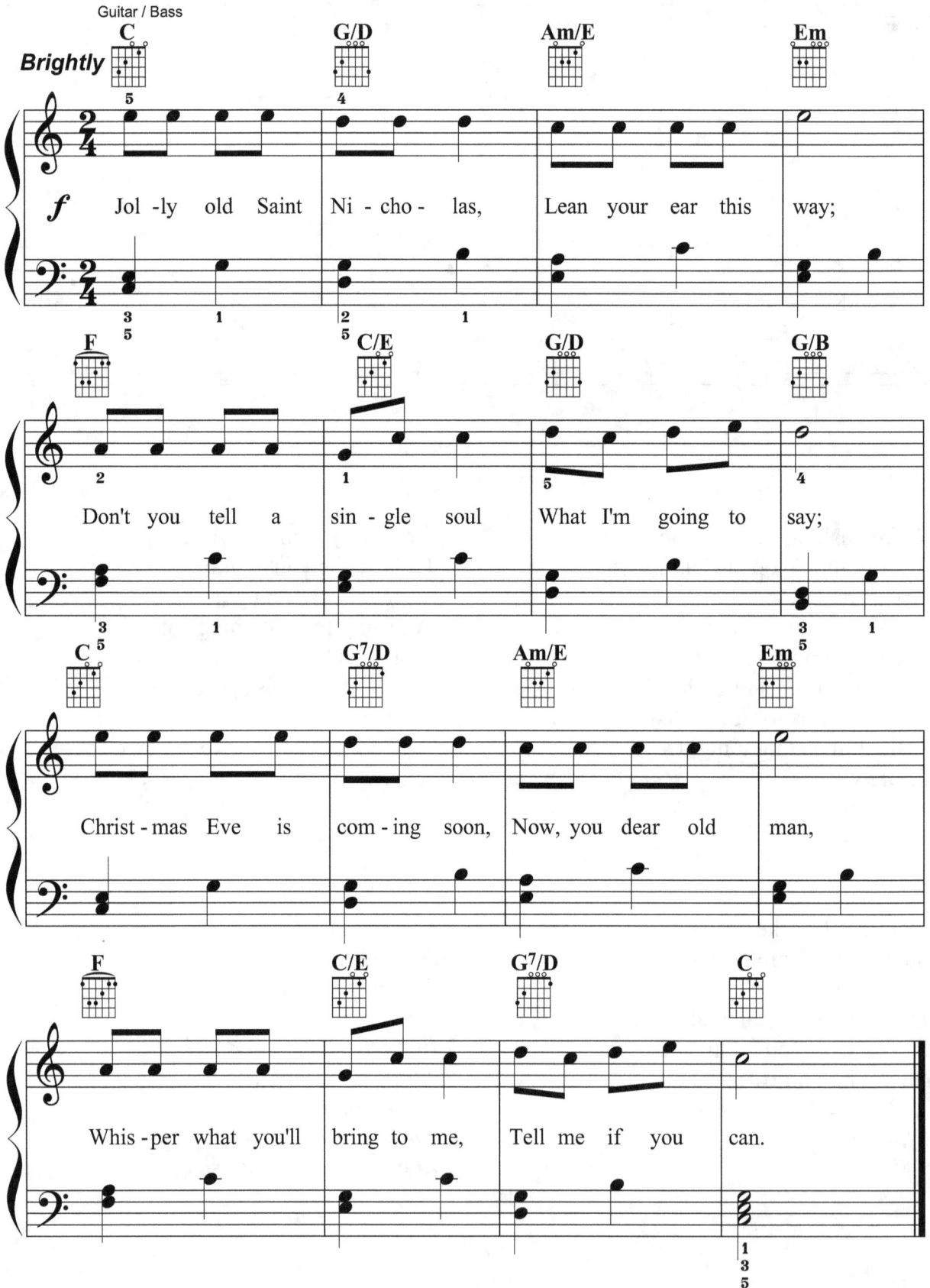

Jolly Old Saint Nicholas

Jolly Old Saint Nicholas,
Lean your ear this way,
Don't you tell a single soul,
What I'm going to say,
Christmas Eve is coming soon,
Now you dear old man,
Whisper what you'll bring to me,
Tell me, if you can.

When the clock is striking twelve,
When I'm fast asleep,
Down the chimney broad and black,
With your pack you'll creep,
All the stockings you will find,
Hanging in a row,
Mine will be the shortest one,
You'll be sure to know.

Johnny wants a pair of skates,
Susy wants a sled,
Nellie wants a picture book,
Yellow, blue and red,
Now I think I'll leave to you,
What to give the rest,
Choose for me, dear Santa Claus,
You will know the best.

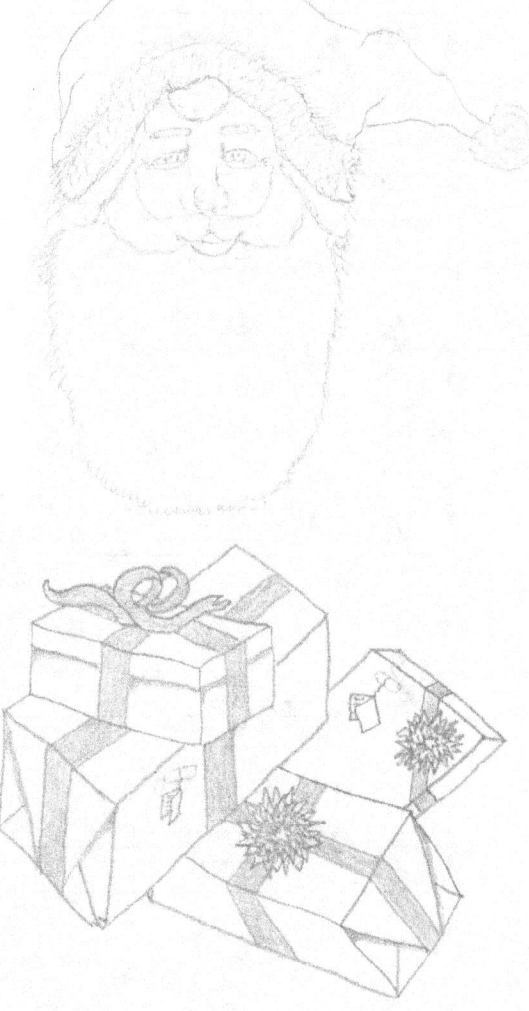

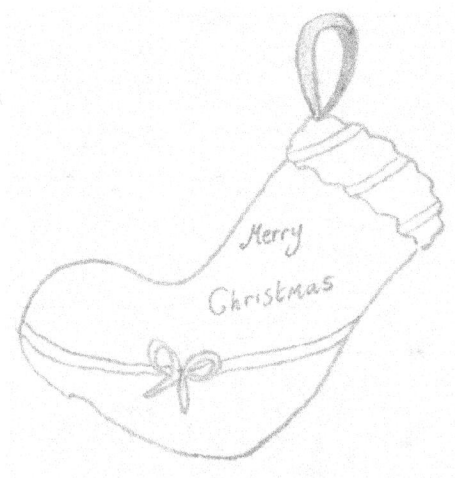

Joy To The World

Arr. Claire

Maestoso

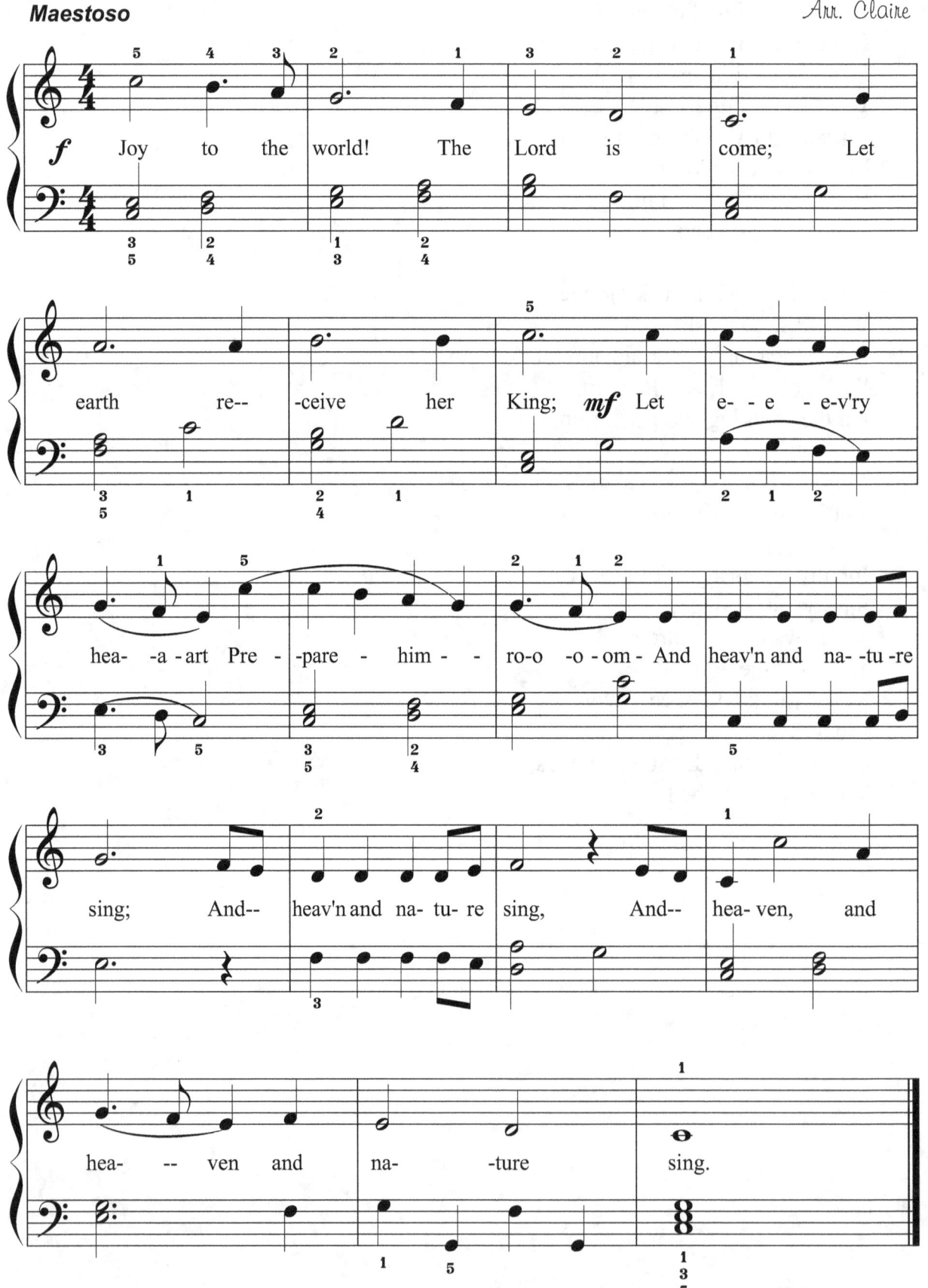

Joy To The World

Joy to the world, The Lord is come,
Let earth receive her King.
Let every heart,
Prepare him room,
And heav'n and nature sing,
And heav'n and nature sing,
And heav'n and heav'n and nature sing.

Joy to the world ! The Saviour reigns,
Let men their songs employ,
While fields and floods, rocks, hills, and plains
Repeat the sounding joy, repeat the sounding joy,
Repeat, repeat the sounding joy.

He rules the world with truth and grace,
And makes the nations prove,
The glories of His righteousness,
And wonders of His love, and wonders of His love.
And wonders, and wonders of His love.

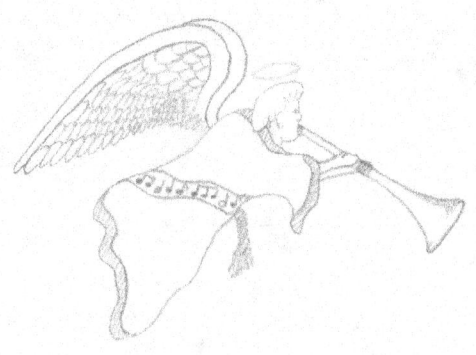

Little Donkey

Arr. Claire

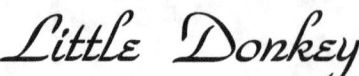

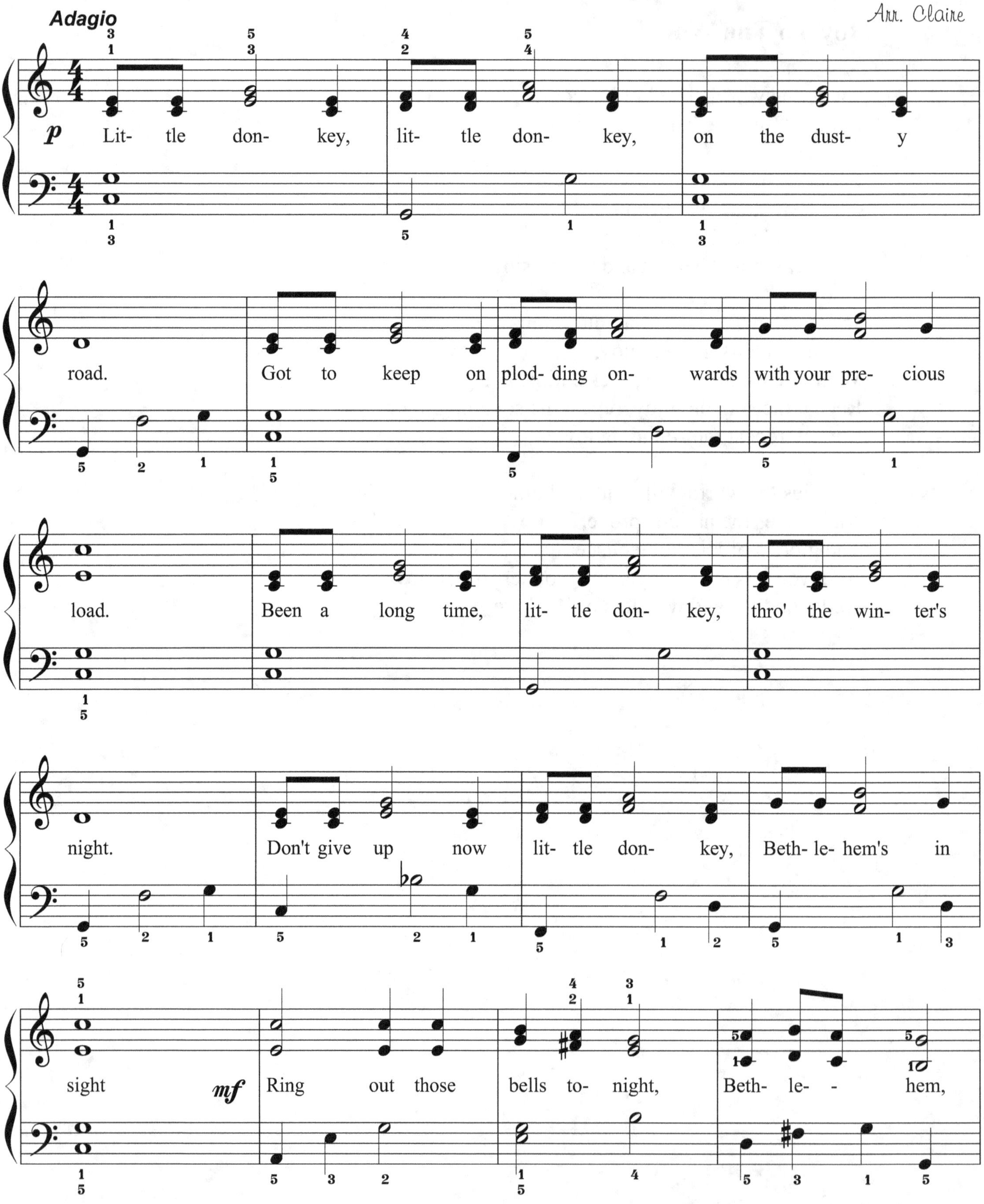

Adagio

p Lit- tle don- key, lit- tle don- key, on the dust- y

road. Got to keep on plod- ding on- wards with your pre- cious

load. Been a long time, lit- tle don- key, thro' the win- ter's

night. Don't give up now lit- tle don- key, Beth- le- hem's in

sight *mf* Ring out those bells to- night, Beth- le- - hem,

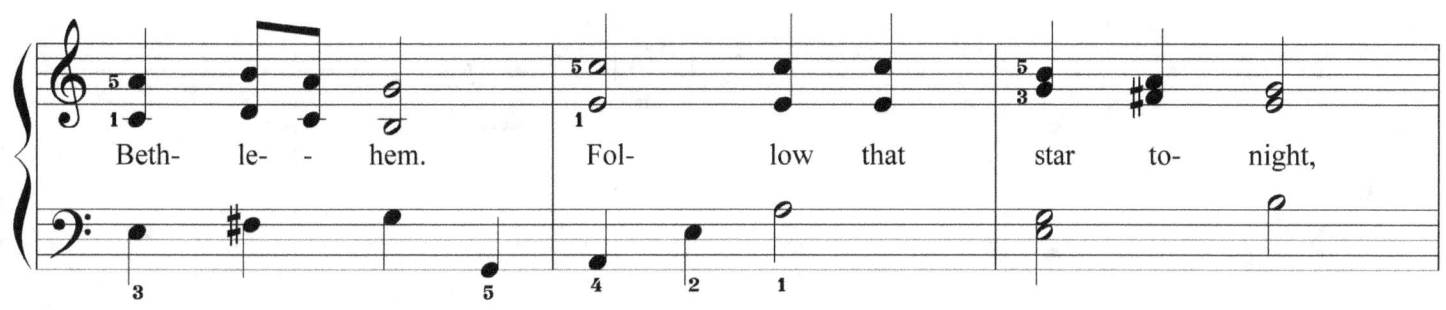

Beth- le - hem. Fol- low that star to- night,

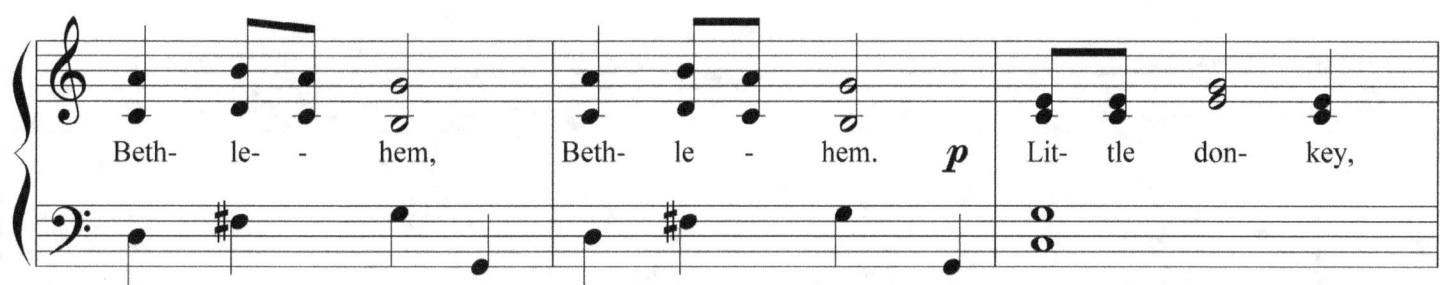

Beth- le - hem, Beth- le - hem. *p* Lit- tle don- key,

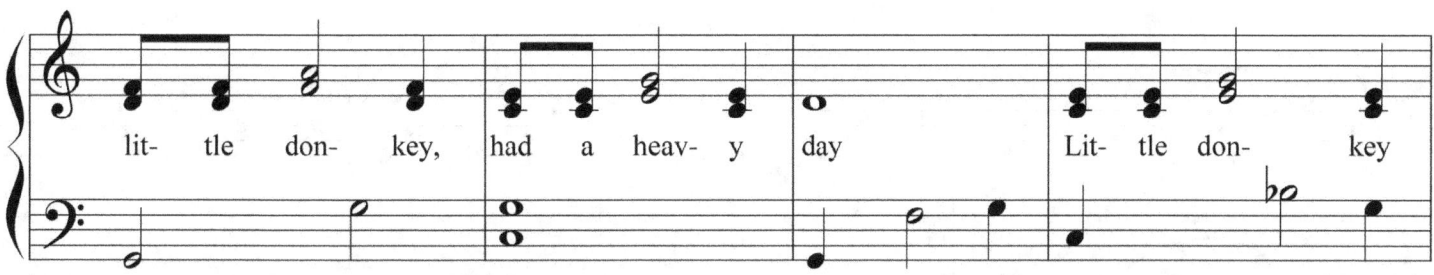

lit- tle don- key, had a heav- y day Lit- tle don- key

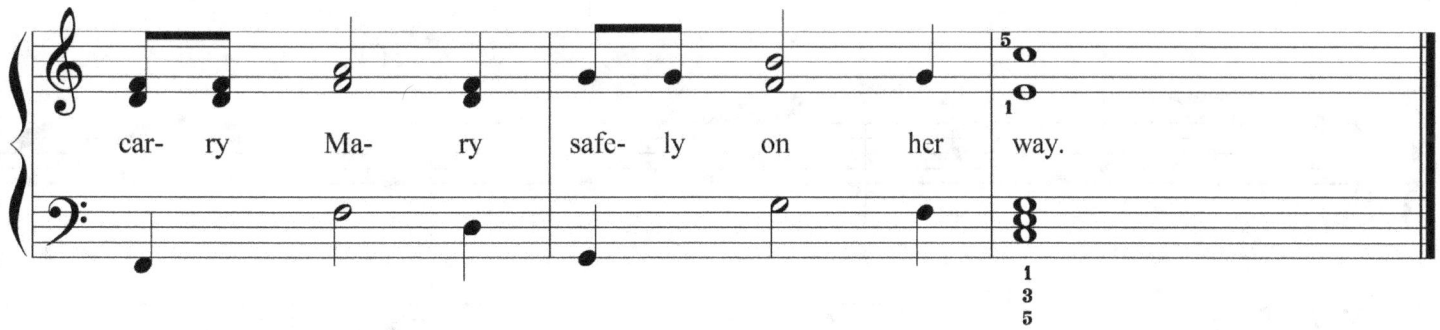

car- ry Ma- ry safe- ly on her way.

1 Little donkey, little donkey,
  On the dusty road;
  Got to keep on plodding onwards
  With your precious load.

2 Been a long time, little donkey,
  Thro' the winter's night;
  Don't give up now little donkey,
  Bethlehem's in sight.

3 Ring out those bells tonight,
  Bethlehem, Bethlehem;
  Follow that star tonight,
  Bethlehem, Bethlehem.

4 Little donkey, little donkey,
  Had a heavy day;
  Little donkey, carry Mary
  Safely on her way.

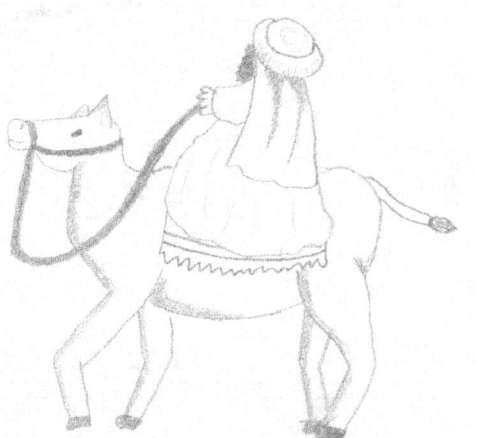

March of the Three Kings

Provencal 13th Century
Arr. Eros

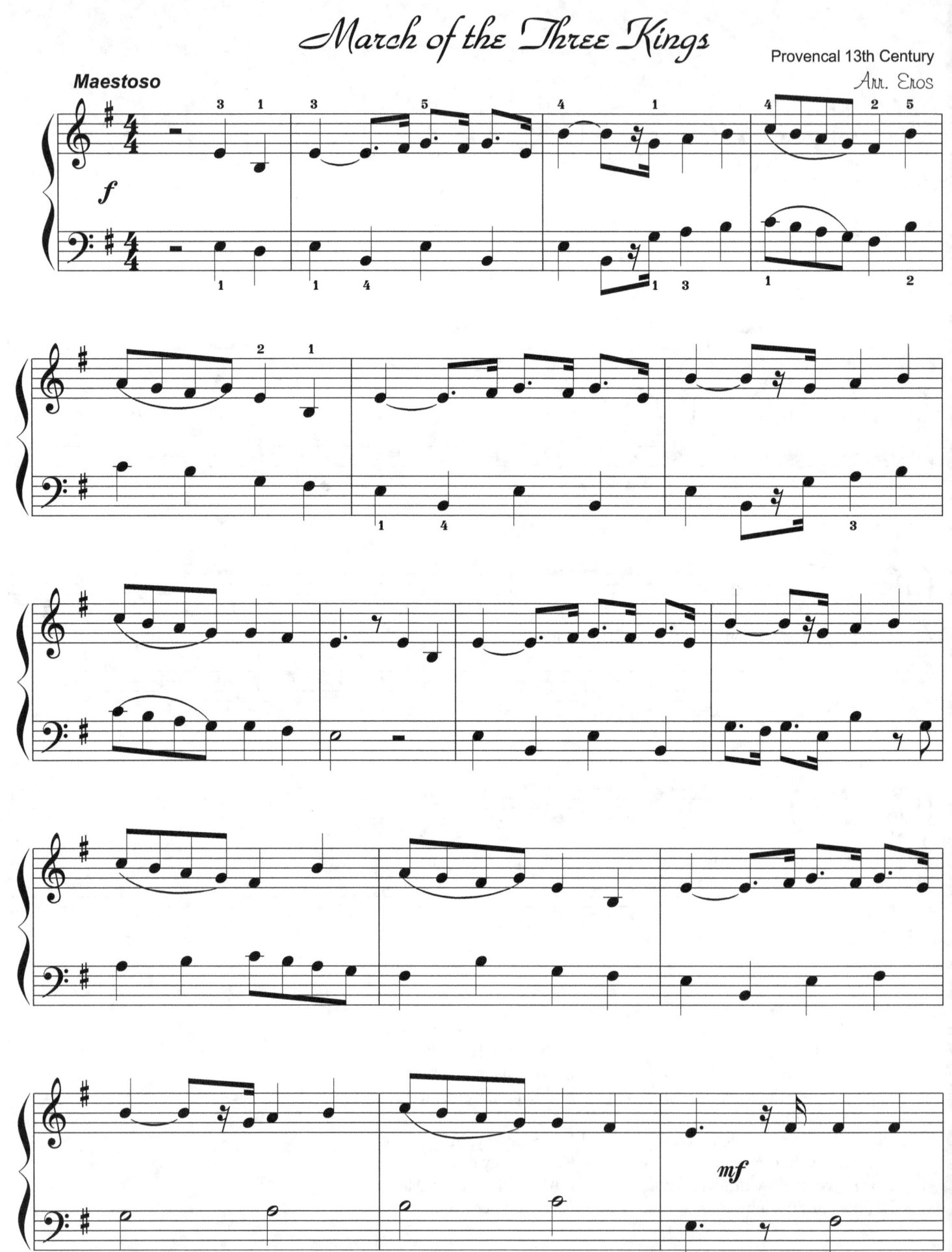

March of the Three Kings

Provencal 13th Century
Arr. Eros

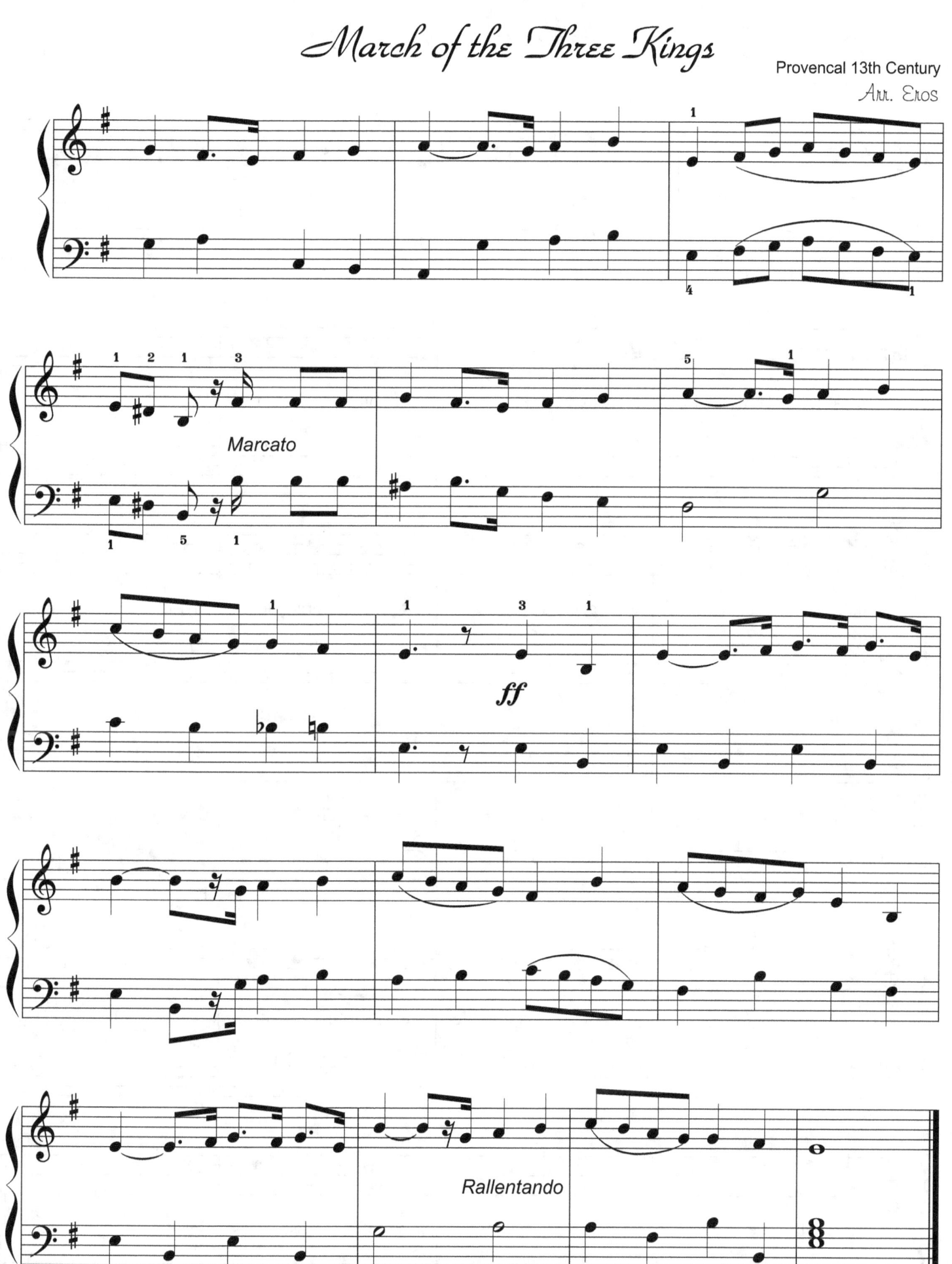

Mary's Boy Child

Traditional West Indian
Arr. Claire

Andante

Long time a- go in Beth-le-hem so the Ho- ly Bi- ble say_____ ,

Ma- ry's Boy Child, Je- sus Christ, was born on Christ- mas Day_____ .

Hark, now hear the an- gels sing, a new King born to- day, And

Man will live for ev- er more, Be- cause of Christ- mas Day_____ . *ff*

Trum- pets sound and an- gels sing, *mp* lis- ten to what they say_____ , *p* That

Man will live for ev- er- more, Be- cause of Christ- mas Day_____ .

Mary's Boy Child.

Long time ago, in Bethlehem,
So the Holy Bible say;
Mary's boy child, Jesus Christ,
Was born, on Christmas day.

Hark, now hear the Angels sing,
A new king born today.
And man will live for ever more,
Because of Christmas day.

Trumpets sound and angels sing,
Listen to what they say:
That man will live for ever more,
Because of Christmas day.

While shepherds watch their flocks by night,
Them see a bright new shining star;
Them hear a choir sing,
The music seemed to come from afar.

How Joseph and his wife, Mary,
Come to Bethlehem that night;
Them find no place to born she Child,
Not a single room was in sight.

By and by they find a little nook,
A stable all forlorn;
And in a manger cold and dark,
Mary's little boy was born.

Long time ago, in Bethlehem,
So the Holy Bible say;
Mary's boy child, Jesus Christ,
Was born, on Christmas day.

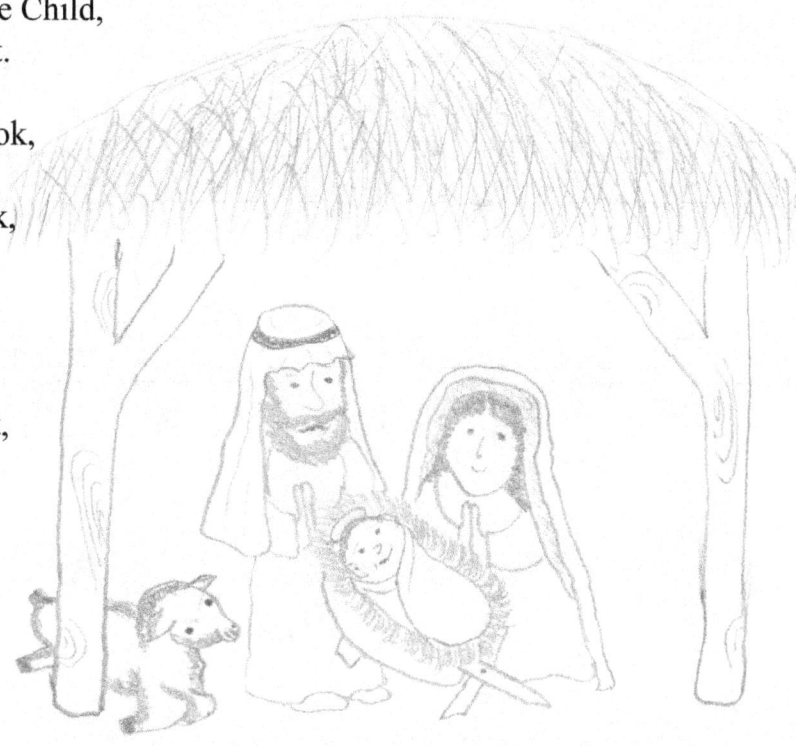

Mary had a Baby

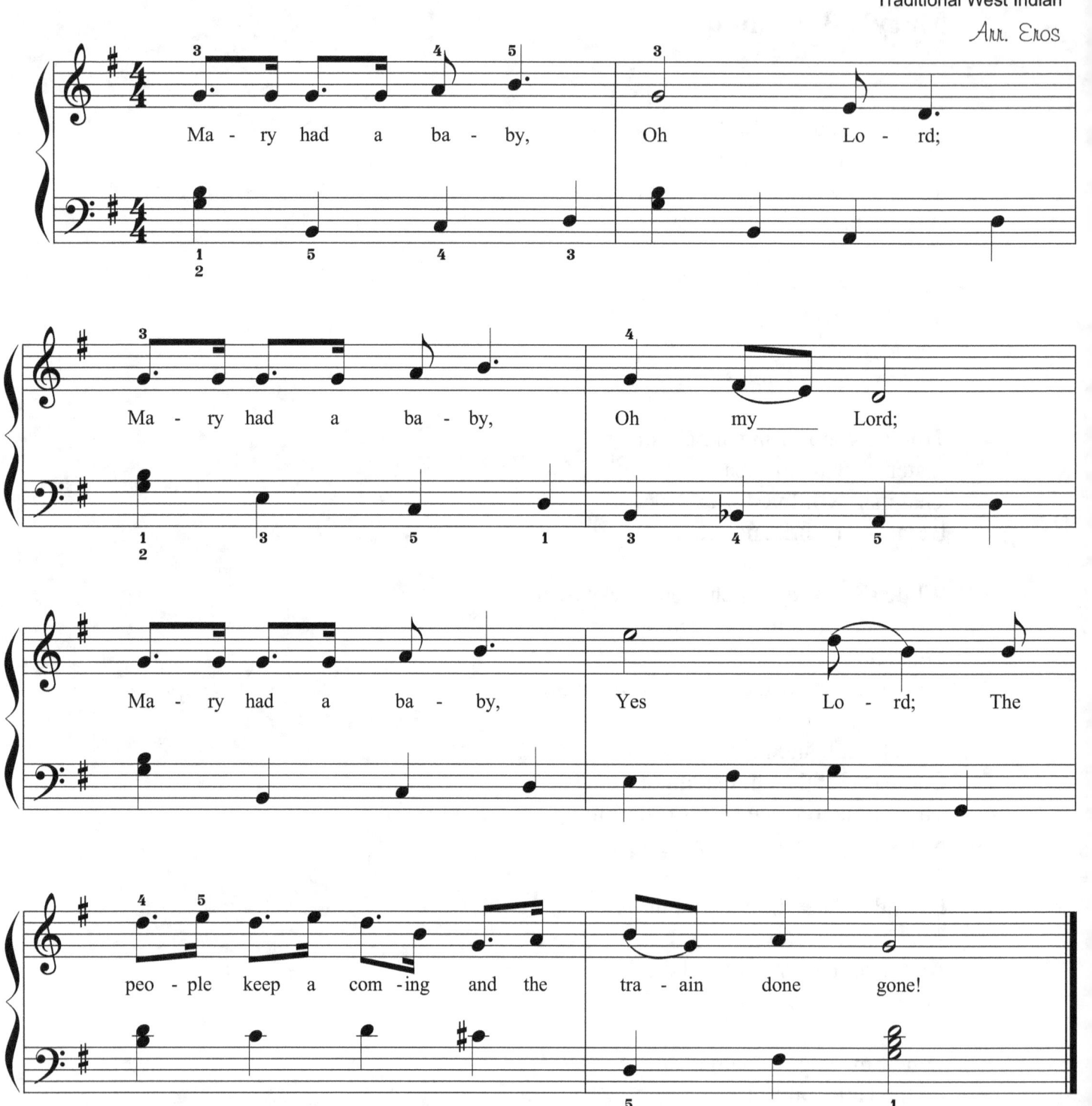

Traditional West Indian
Arr. Eros

Ma - ry had a ba - by,   Oh   Lo - rd;

Ma - ry had a ba - by,   Oh   my_____ Lord;

Ma - ry had a ba - by,   Yes   Lo - rd;   The

peo - ple keep a com -ing and the   tra - ain   done   gone!

Mary had a Baby

1. Mary had a baby, Oh Lord;
   Mary had a baby, Oh my Lord;
   Mary had a baby, Oh Lord;
   The people keep a-comin'
   And the train done gone.

2. What did she name him, Oh Lord?
   What did she name him, Oh my Lord?
   What did she name him, Oh, Lord?
   The people keep a-comin'
   But the train long gone.

3. She called him Jesus, Oh, Lord,
   She called him Jesus, Yes, My Lord;
   She called him Jesus, Oh, Lord,
   The people keep a-comin'
   And the train done gone.

4. Where was He born, Oh, Lord?
   Where was He born, Oh, my Lord?
   Where was He born, Oh, Lord?
   The people keep a-comin'
   But the train long gone.

5. Born in a stable, Oh, Lord,
   Born in a stable, Yes, my Lord;
   Born in a stable, Oh, Lord,
   The people keep a-comin'
   And the train done gone.

6. Where did they lay Him, Oh, Lord?
   Where did they lay Him, Oh, My Lord?
   Where did they lay Him, Oh, Lord?
   The people keep a-comin'
   But the train long gone.

7. Laid Him in a manger, Oh, Lord,
   Laid Him in a manger, Yes, My Lord;
   Laid Him in a manger, Oh, Lord,
   The people keep a-comin'
   And the train done gone.

8. Who came to see Him, Oh, Lord?
   Who came to see Him, Oh, My Lord?
   Who came to see Him, Oh, Lord?
   The people keep a-comin'
   But the train long gone.

9. Shepherds came to see Him, Oh, Lord,
   Shepherds came to see Him, Yes, my Lord;
   Shepherds came to see Him, Oh, Lord,
   The people keep a-comin'
   And the train done gone.

10. Wise men kneeled before Him, Oh, Lord,
    Wise men kneeled before Him, Oh, my Lord;
    Wise men kneeled before Him, Yes, Lord,
    The people keep a-comin'
    But the train long gone.

11. King Herod tried to find Him, Oh, Lord,
    Kind Herod tried to find Him, Yes, my Lord;
    King Herod tried to find Him, Oh, Lord,
    The people keep a-comin'
    And the train done gone.

12. They went away to Egypt, Oh, Lord,
    They went away to Egypt, Yes, my Lord,
    They went away to Egypt, Oh, Lord,
    The people keep a-comin'
    But the train long gone.

13. Angels watching over Him, Oh, Lord,
    Angels watching over Him, Yes, my Lord;
    Angels watching over Him, Oh, Lord,
    The people keep a-comin'
    And the train done gone.

14. Mary had a baby, Yes, Lord;
    Mary had a baby, Yes, my Lord;
    Mary had a baby, Oh Yes, Lord;
    The people keep a-coming'
    But the train long gone.

Masters in this Hall

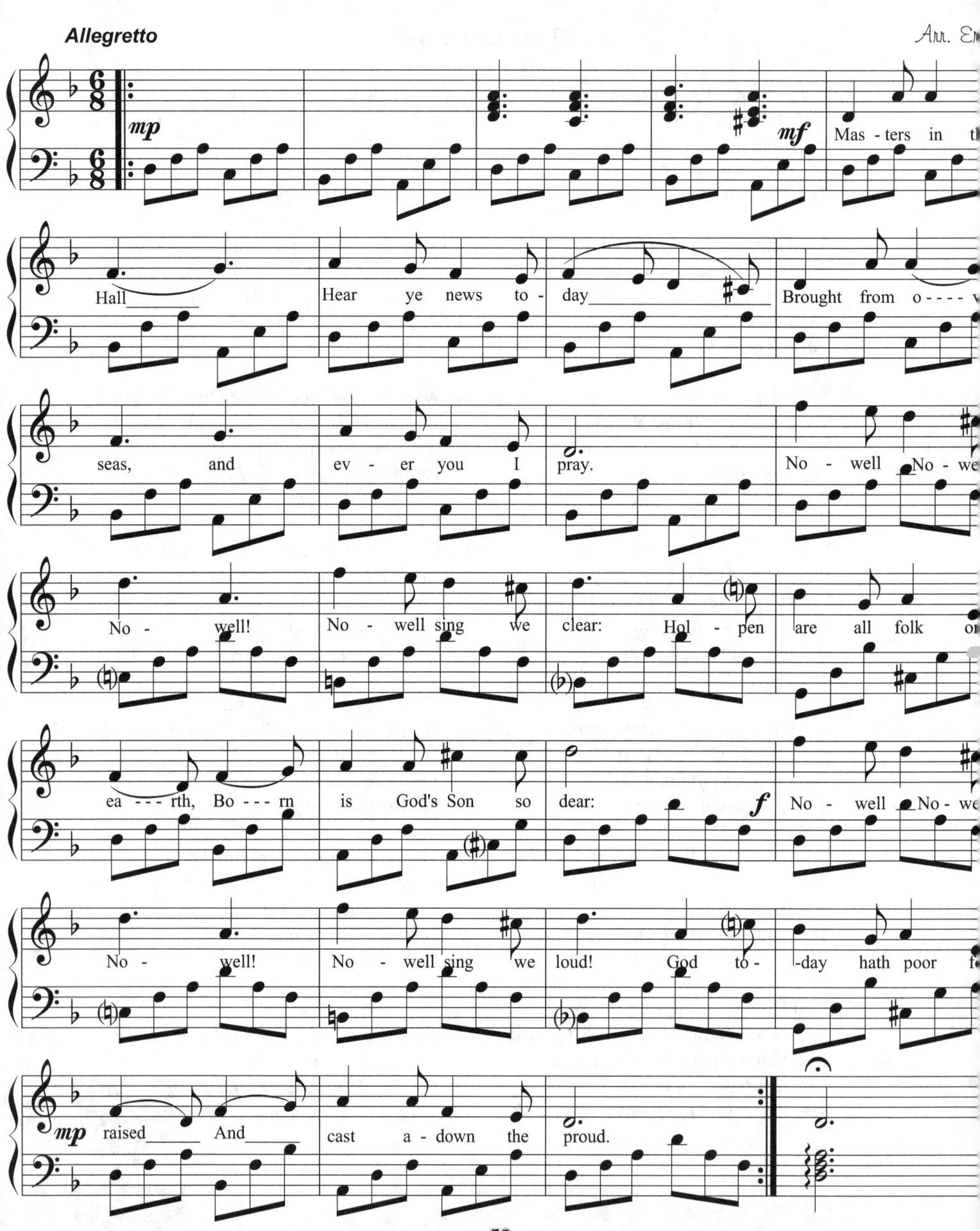

Masters in this Hall

1. Masters in this Hall,
   Hear ye news today -
   Brought from overseas,
   And ever you I pray.

   Chorus:

   Nowell! Nowell! Nowell!
   Nowell sing we clear,
   Holpen are all folk on earth,
   Born is God's Son so dear:
   No - well! No - well! No - well!
   No - well sing we loud!
   God to - day hath poor folk raised
   And cast a - down the proud.

2. Going o'er the hills;
   Through the milk-white snow,
   Heard I ewes bleat
   While the wind did blow.
   Chorus: *Nowell! Nowell! Nowell!...*

3. Shepherds many and one
   Sat among the sheep,
   No man spake more word
   Than they had been asleep.
   Chorus: *Nowell! Nowell! Nowell!...*

4. Quoth I, "Fellows mine,
   Why this guise sit ye?
   Making but dull cheer
   Shepherds though you be?"
   Chorus: *Nowell! Nowell! Nowell!...*

5. "Shepherds should of right
   Leap and dance and sing,
   Thus to see ye sit,
   Is a right strange thing."
   Chorus: *Nowell! Nowell! Nowell!...*

6. Quoth those fellows then,
   "To Bethlehem Town we go,
   To see a Mighty Lord
   Lie in manger low."
   Chorus: *Nowell! Nowell! Nowell!...*

7. "How name ye this Lord
   Shepherds?", then said I
   "Very God," they said,
   "Come from Heaven high."
   Chorus: *Nowell! Nowell! Nowell!...*

8. Then to Bethlehem Town
   We went two by two,
   And in a sorry place
   Heard the oxen low.
   Chorus: *Nowell! Nowell! Nowell!...*

9. Therein did we see
   A sweet and goodly May
   And a fair old man,
   Upon the straw She lay.
   Chorus: *Nowell! Nowell! Nowell!...*

10. And a little Child
    On Her arm had She
    "Wot ye Who this is?",
    Said the hinds to me.
    Chorus: *Nowell! Nowell! Nowell!...*

11. Ox and ass Him know,
    Kneeling on their knee,
    Wondrous joy had I
    This little Babe to see.
    Chorus: *Nowell! Nowell! Nowell!...*

12. This is Christ the Lord,
    Masters be ye glad!
    Christmas has come in,
    And no folk should be sad.
    Chorus: *Nowell! Nowell! Nowell!...*

O Christmas Tree

Arr. Claire

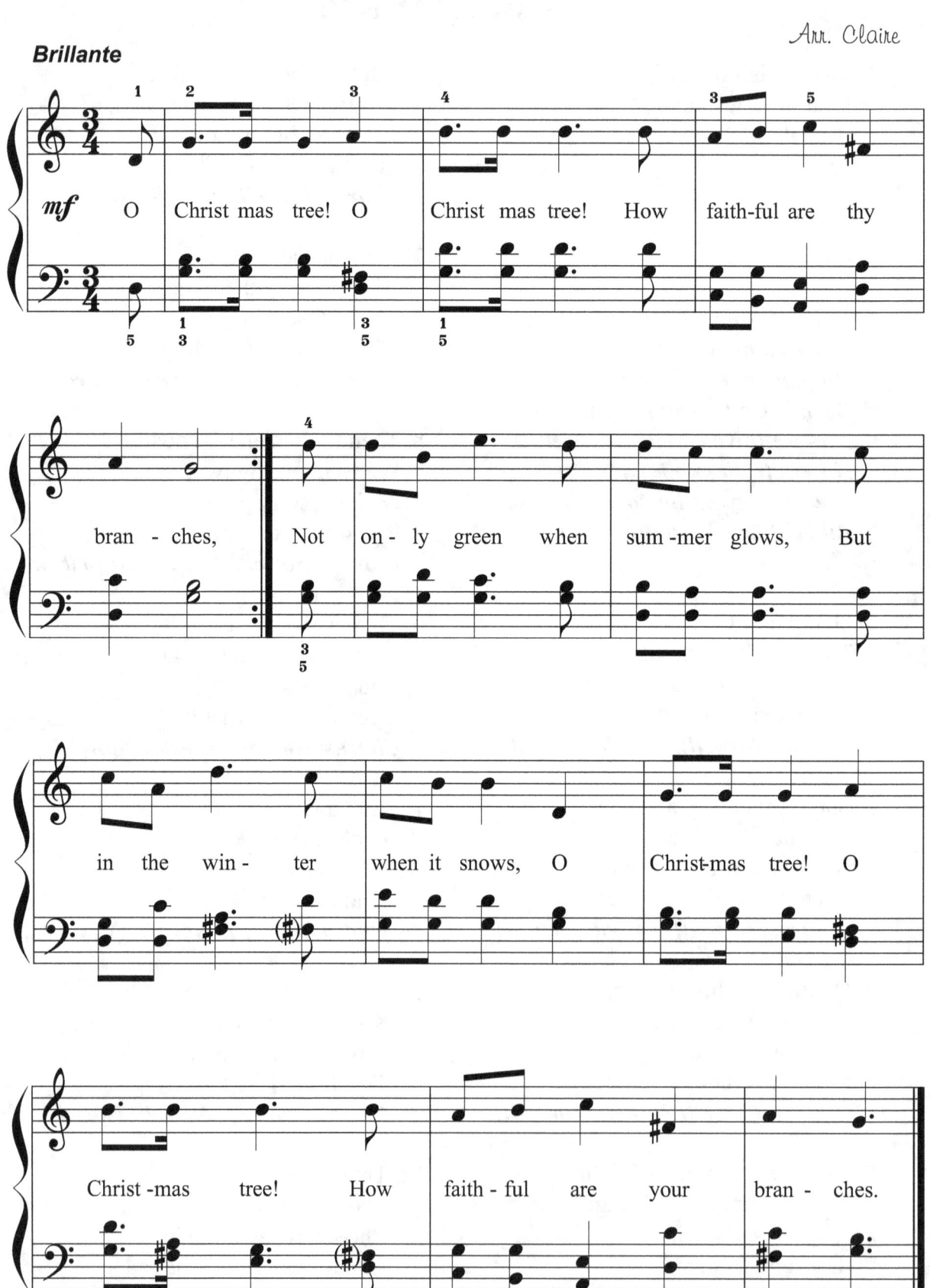

O Christmas Tree

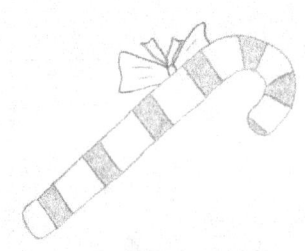

O Christmas tree, O Christmas tree,
How lovely are your branches,
In beauty green they'll always grow,
Through summer sun and winter snow.
O Christmas tree, O Christmas tree
How lovely are your branches.

O Christmas tree, O Christmas tree,
Of all the trees most lovely,
Each year you bring to me delight,
Shining bright on Christmas night,
O Christmas tree, O Christmas tree,
Of all the trees most lovely.

O Christmas tree, O Christmas tree,
Your beauty green will teach me,
That hope and joy will ever be,
The way to joy and peace for me,
O Christmas tree, O Christmas tree,
Your beauty green will teach me.

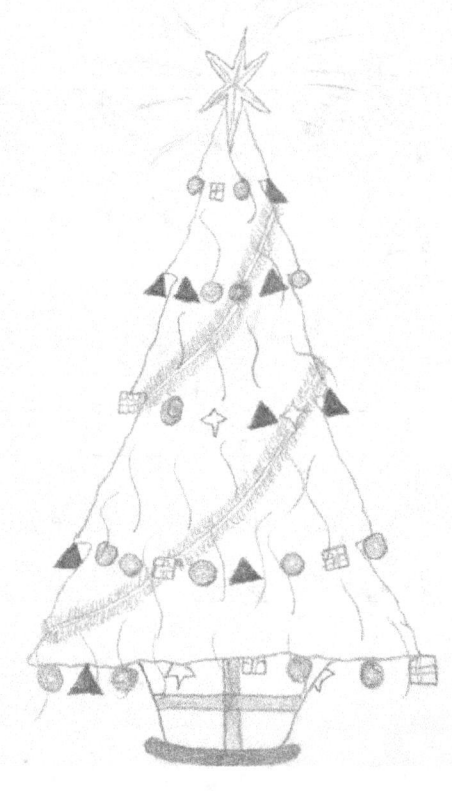

O Come All Ye Faithful

Arr. Claire

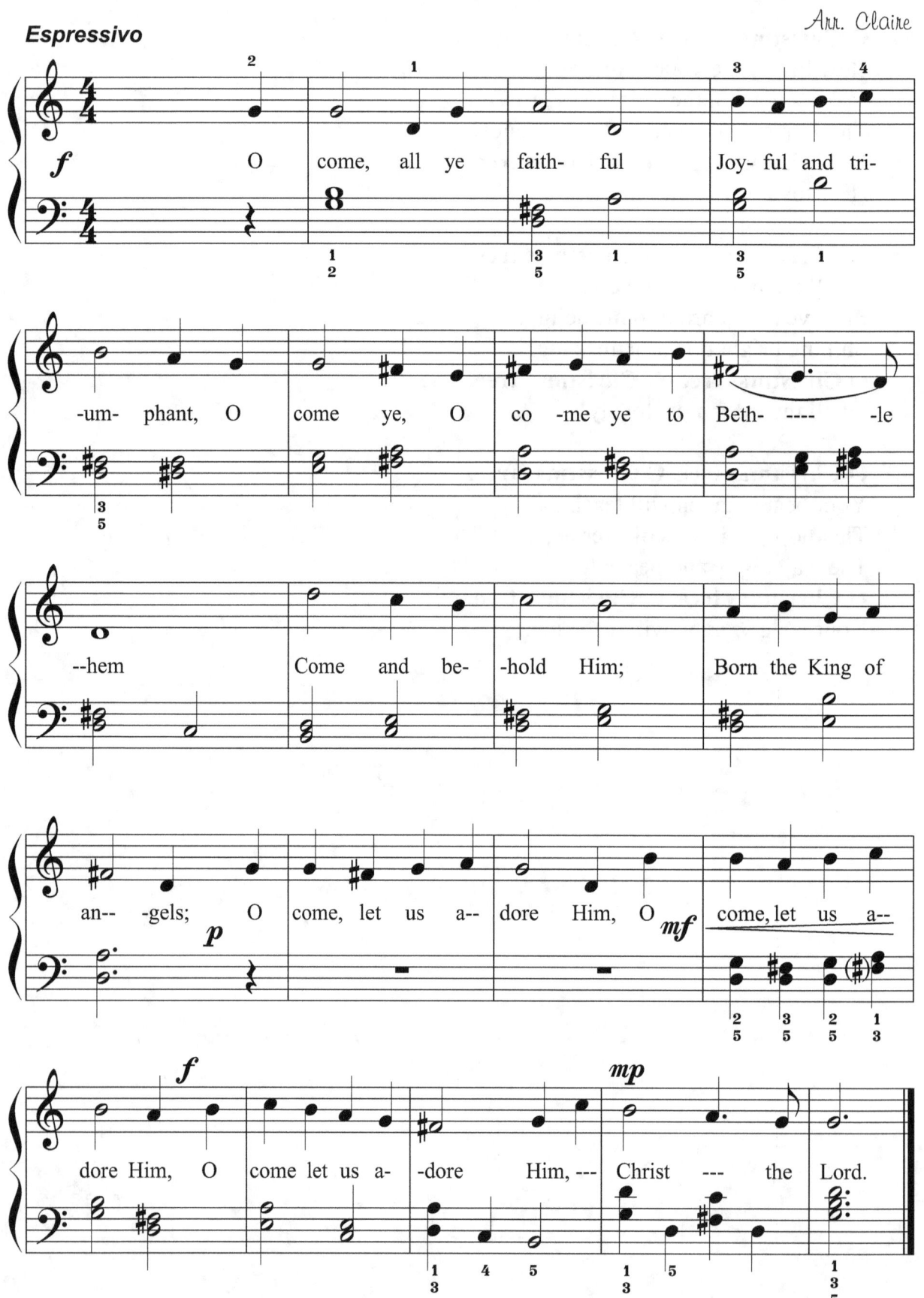

O Come All Ye Faithful.

1. O come all ye faithful,
   Joyful and triumphant,
   O come ye, O come ye to Bethlehem;
   Come and behold him,
   Born the king of angels.

   O come, let us adore him,
   O come, let us adore him,
   O come, let us adore him,
   Christ, the Lord.

2. God of God,
   Light of light,
   Lo, He adhors not the Virgin's womb;
   Very God,
   Begotten, not created.

3. Sing, choir of angels,
   Sing in exhultation,
   Sing, all ye citizens of Heaven above;
   Glory to God,
   In the highest!

4. Yea, Lord we greet thee,
   Born this happy morning,
   Jesus, top thee be glory given;
   Word of the father,
   Now in flesh appearing.

O Come, O Come, Emmanuel

15th Century

Arr. Eros

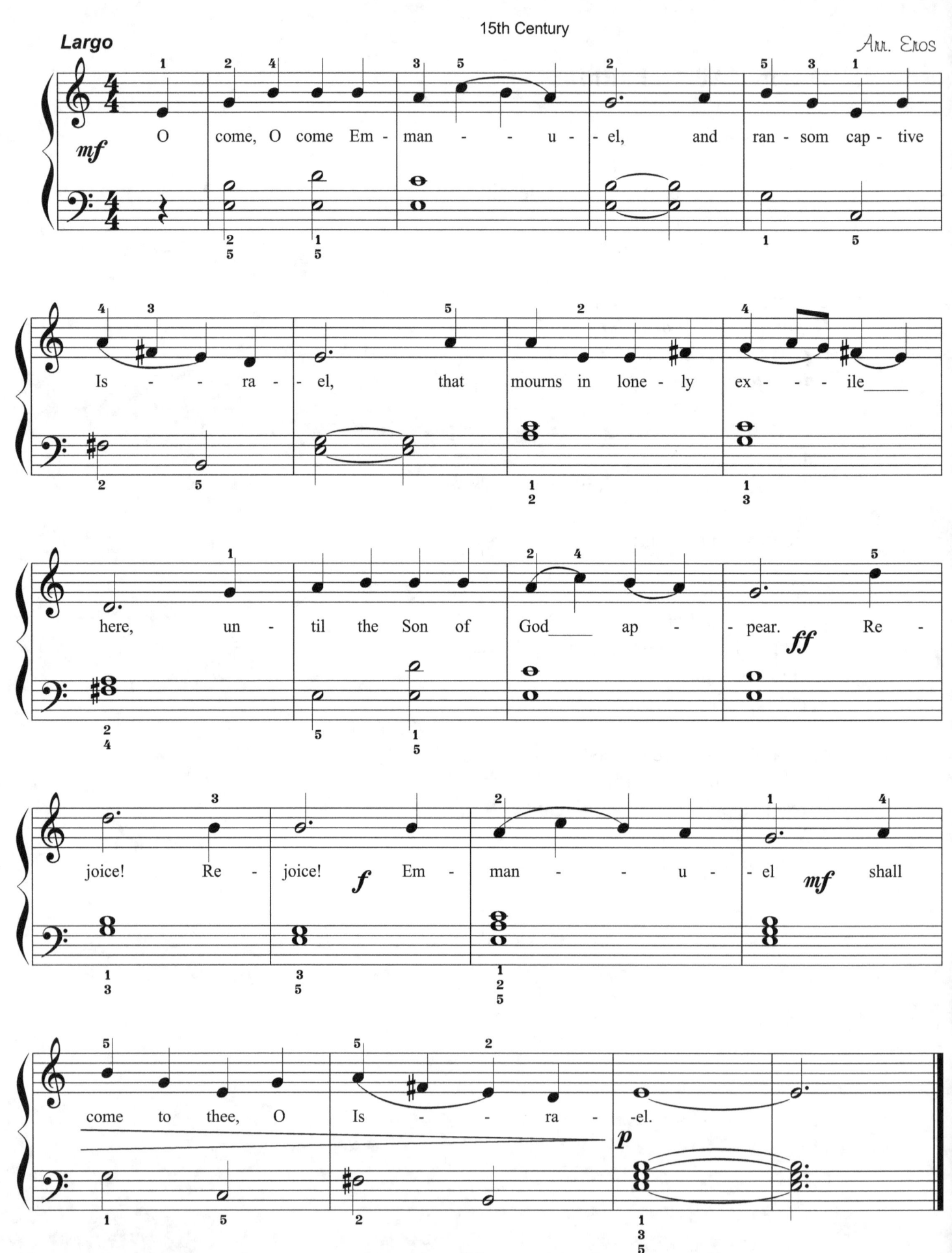

O Come, O Come, Emmanuel

O come, O come Emmanuel,
And ransom captive Israel,
That mourns in lonely exile here,
Until the Son of God appear.
Rejoice! Rejoice! Emmanuel shall come to thee, O Israel.

O come, O come, Thou Lord of might,
Who to Thy tribes, on Sinai's height,
In ancient times didst give the law
In cloud, and majesty, and awe.

O come, Thou Rod of Jesse, free
Thine own from Satan's tyranny;
From depths of hell Thy people save.
And give them victory o'er the grave.

O come, Thou Day-spring, come and cheer
Our spirits by Thine advent here;
Disperse the gloomy clouds of night,
And death's dark shadows put to flight.

O come, Thou Key of David, come,
And open wide our heavenly home;
Make safe the way that leads on high,
And close the path to misery.

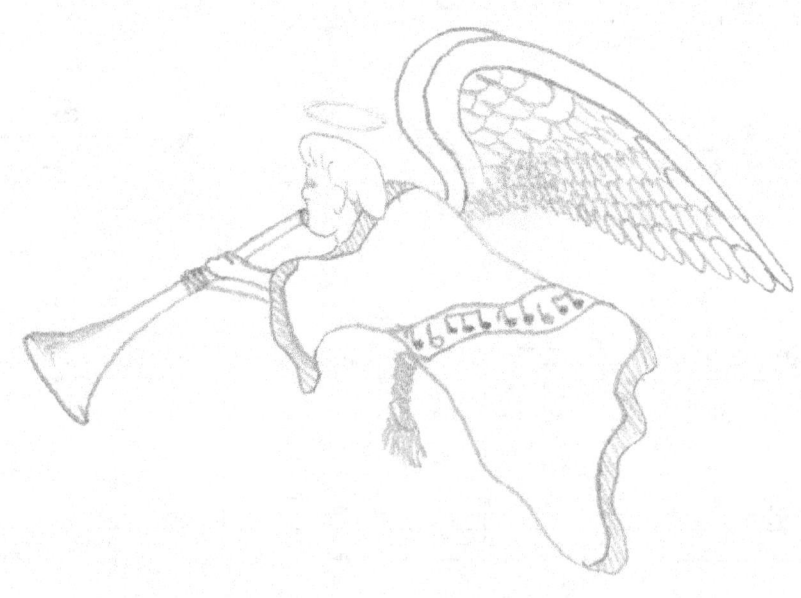

O Holy Night

Maestoso

Cantique de Noel

Arr. Eros

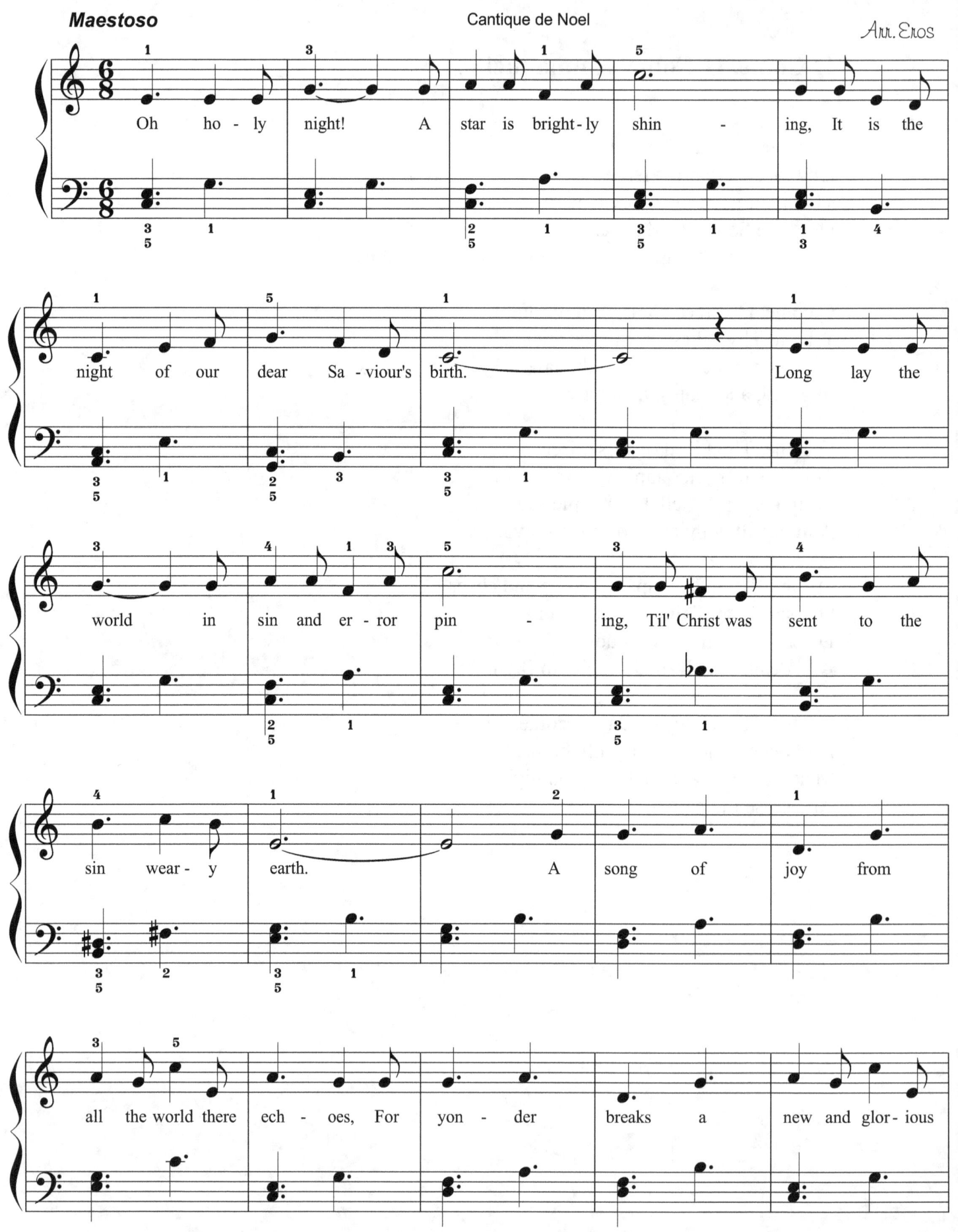

Oh ho - ly night! A star is bright - ly shin - ing, It is the

night of our dear Sa - viour's birth. Long lay the

world in sin and er - ror pin - ing, Til' Christ was sent to the

sin wear - y earth. A song of joy from

all the world there ech - oes, For yon - der breaks a new and glor - ious

O Holy Night

Arr. Eros

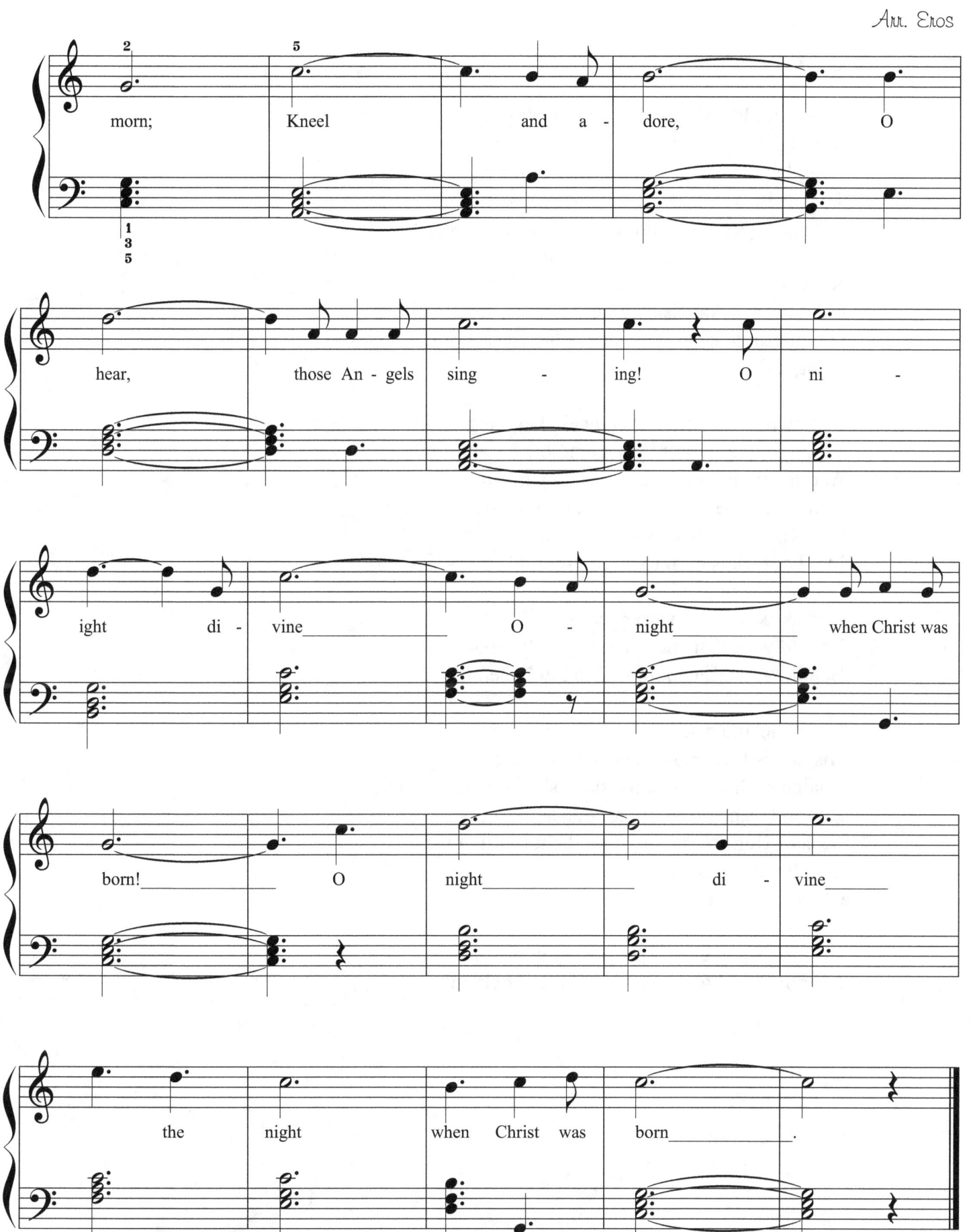

O Holy Night

O holy night! A star was brightly shining,
It was the night of the dear Saviour's birth.
Long lay the world in sin and error pining,
Till Christ was sent to the sin-weary earth.
A song of joy from all the world there echoes,
For now there breaks a new glorious morn;
Kneel and adore,
O hear those Angels singing!
O night divine; O night when Christ was born!
O night divine the night our Christ was born.

Led by the light of faith serenely beaming,
With glowing hearts by his cradle we stand.
And led by light of star so sweetly gleaming,
Here came the wise men from Orient land.
The King of Kings lay thus in lowly manger,
In all our trials born to be our friend;
He knows our need,
Our weakness is no stranger!
Behold your King before Him lowly bend!
Behold your King before Him lowly bend!

Love one another, He did truly teach us,
His law is love and His gospel is peace.
Chains shall He break for slave shall be our brother,
And in His name all oppression shall cease.
Sweet hymns of joy in grateful chorus sing we,
Let all within us praise His holy name:
Christ is our Lord,
O praise His name forever!
His pow'r and glory Forever more proclaim!
His pow'r His glory Forever more proclaim!

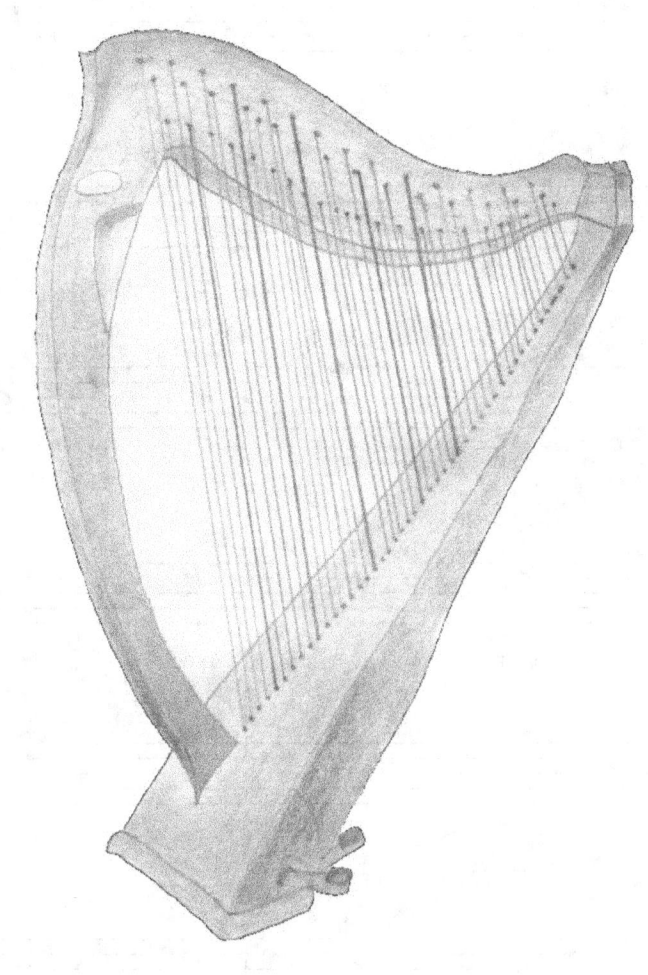

O Little One Sweet

O Jesulein süss

Arr. Eros

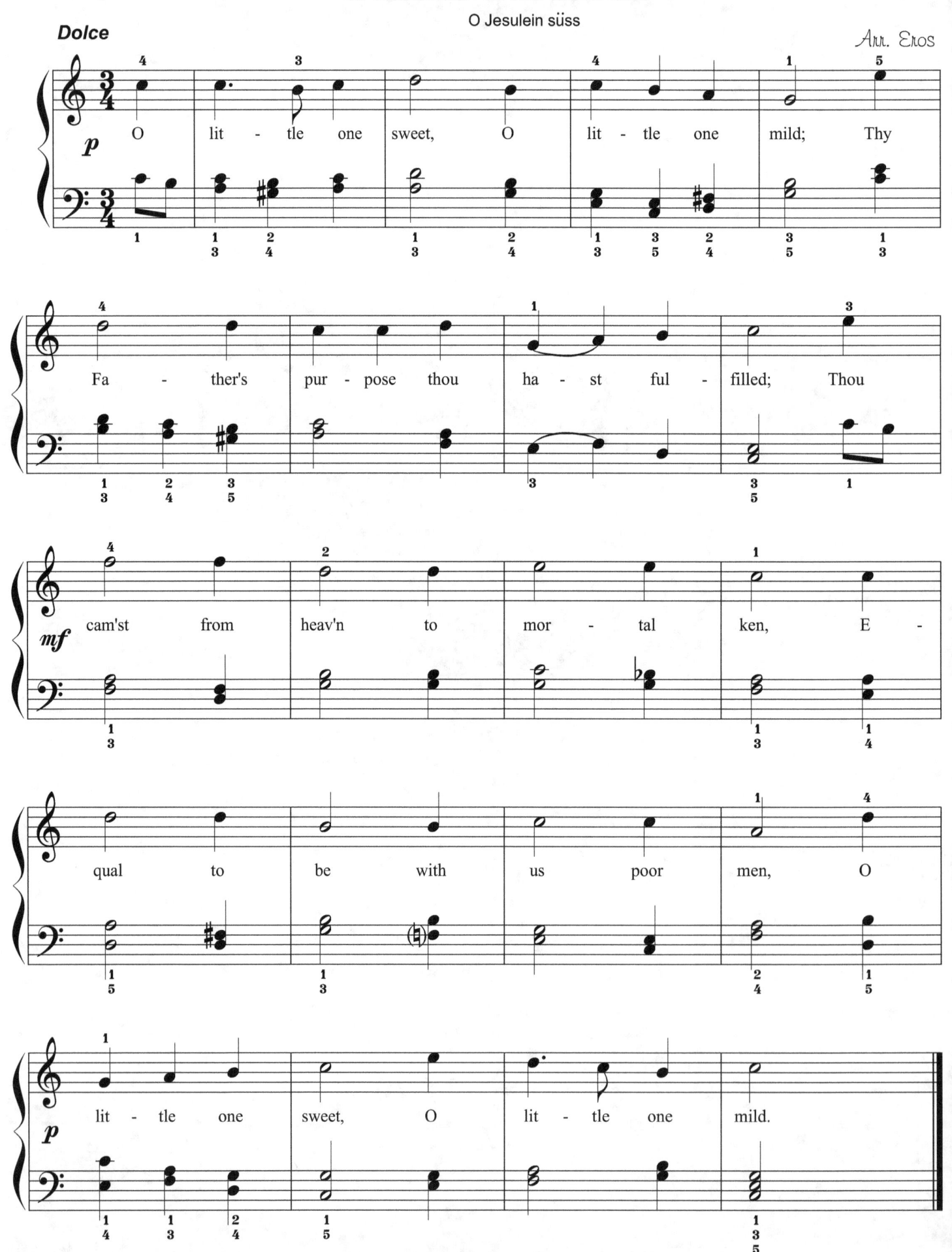

O Little One Sweet

O little one sweet, O little one mild,
Thy Father's purpose thou hast fulfillled;
Thou cam'st from heav'n to mortal ken,
Equal to be with us poor men,
O little one sweet, O little one mild.

O little one sweet, O little one mild,
With joy thou hast the whole world filled:
Thou camest here from heaven's domain,
To bring us comfort in our pain,
O little one sweet, O little one mild.

O little one sweet, O little one mild,
In thee love's beauties are all distilled;
Then light in us thy love's bright flame,
That we may give thee back the same,
O little one sweet, O little one mild.

O little one sweet, O little one mild,
Help us to do as thou hast willed.
Lo, all we have belongs to thee!
Ah, keep us in our fealty!
O little one sweet, O little one mild.

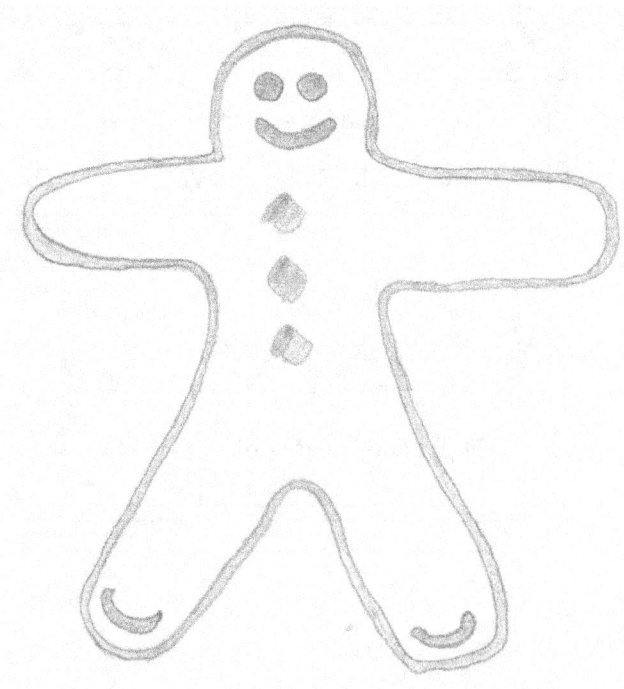

O Little Town Of Bethlehem

Version One

Dolce

Arr. Claire

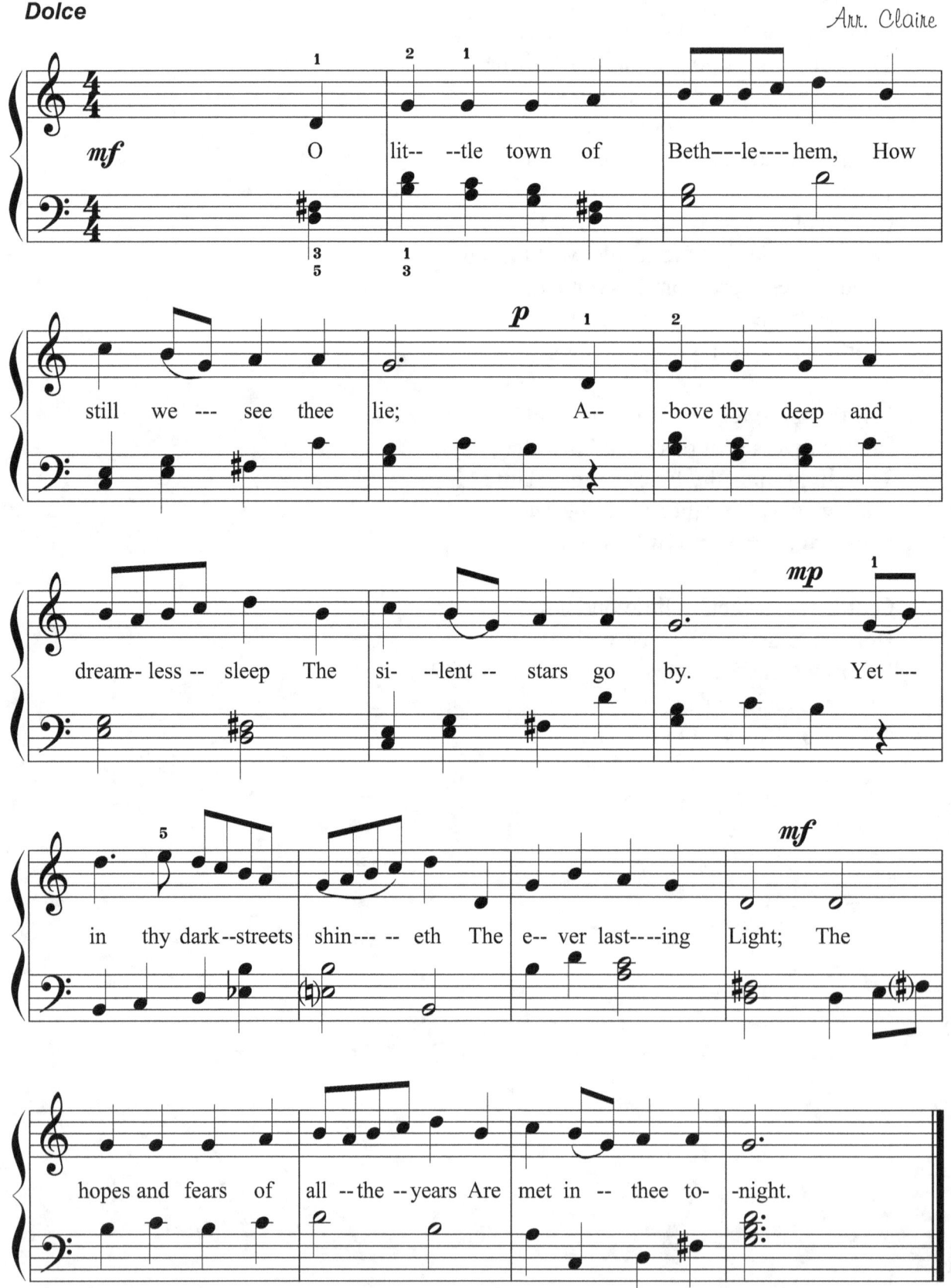

O Little Town Of Bethlehem

O little Town of Bethlehem,
How still we see thee lie!
Above thy deep and dreamless sleep
The silent stars go by.
Yet in thy dark streets shineth
The everlasting light;
The hopes and fears of all the years,
Are met in thee to night.

For Christ is born of Mary,
And gather'd all above;
While mortals sleep, the angels keep
Their watch of wond'ring love.
O morning stars, together
Proclaim the Holy birth,
And praises sing to God the King,
And peace to men on earth.

O morning stars, together,
Proclaim the Holy birth;
And praises sing to God the King,
And peace to men on Earth;
For Christ is born of Mary;
And gathered all above,
While mortals sleep, the angels keep
Their watch of wondering love.

How silently, how silently,
The wondrous gift is given!
So God imparts to human hearts
The blessings of His heaven.
No ear may hear His coming;
But in this world of sin,
Where meek souls will receive Him still,
The dear Christ enters in.

O Holy Child of Bethlehem,
Descend to us we pray;
Cast out our sin, and enter in,
Be born in us to-day.
We hear the Christmas Angels
The great glad tidings tell:
O come to us, abide with us,
Our Lord Emmanuel.

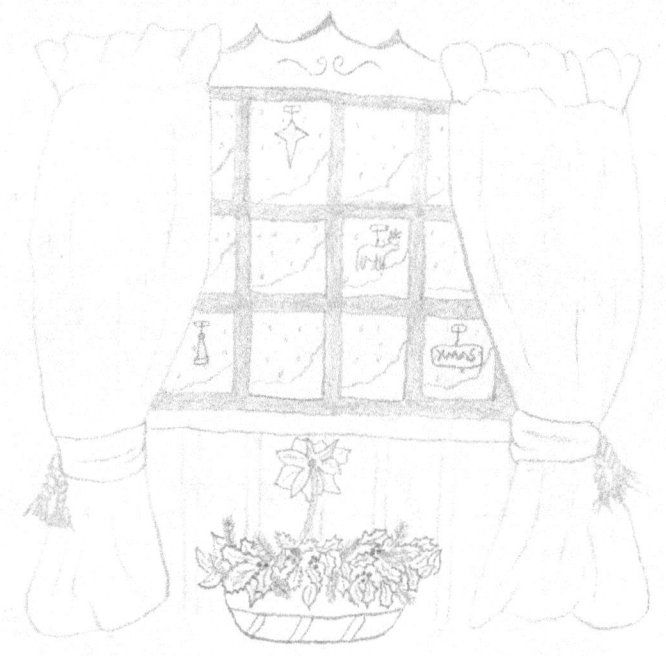

O Little Town Of Bethlehem

Version Two

Traditional American

Arr. Claire

Dolce

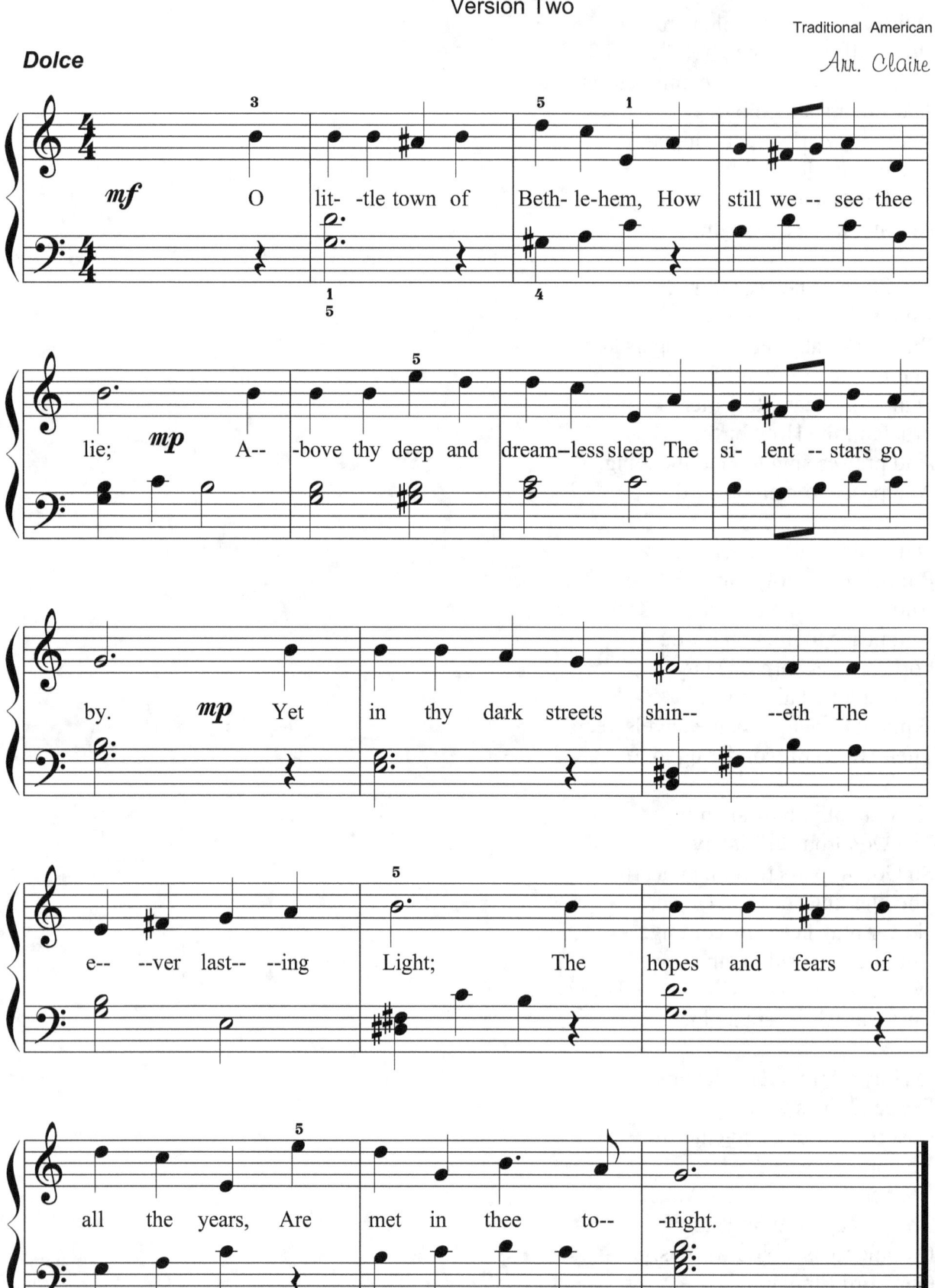

O Little Town Of Bethlehem

O little Town of Bethlehem,
How still we see thee lie!
Above thy deep and dreamless sleep
The silent stars go by.
Yet in thy dark streets shineth
The everlasting light;
The hopes and fears of all the years,
Are met in thee to night.

O morning stars, together,
Proclaim the Holy birth;
And praises sing to God the King,
And peace to men on Earth;
For Christ is born of Mary;
And gathered all above,
While mortals sleep, the angels keep
Their watch of wondering love.

How silently, how silently,
The wondrous gift is given!
So God imparts to human hearts
The blessings of His heaven.
No ear may hear His coming,
But in this world of sin,
Where meek souls will receive Him still,
The dear Christ enters in.

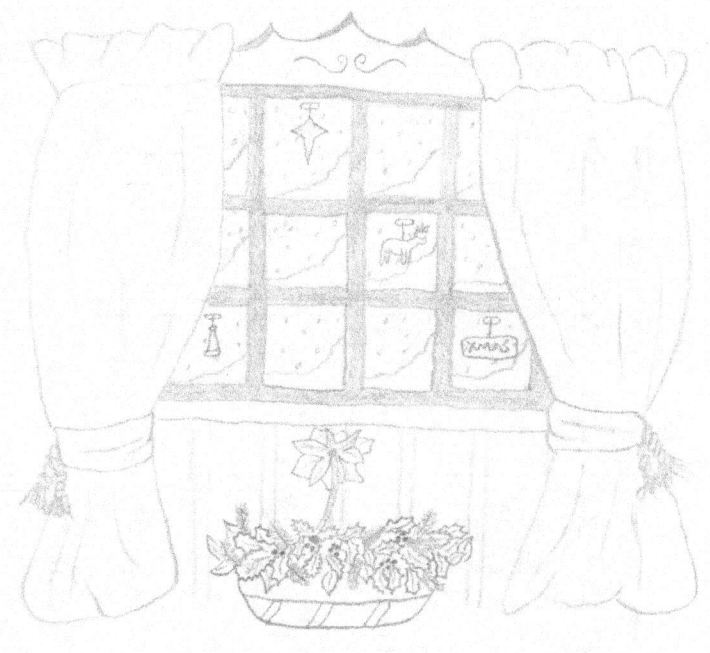

Where children pure and happy
Pray to the blessed Child;
Where misery cries out to thee,
Son of the mother mild;
Where charity stands watching
And Faith holds wide the door,
The dark night wakes, the glory breaks,
And Christmas comes once more.

O Holy Child of Bethlehem,
Descend to us we pray;
Cast out our sin, and enter in,
Be born in us to-day.
We hear the Christmas Angels
The great glad tidings tell:
O come to us, abide with us,
Our Lord Emmanuel.

Once In Royal David's City

Arr. Claire

Maestoso

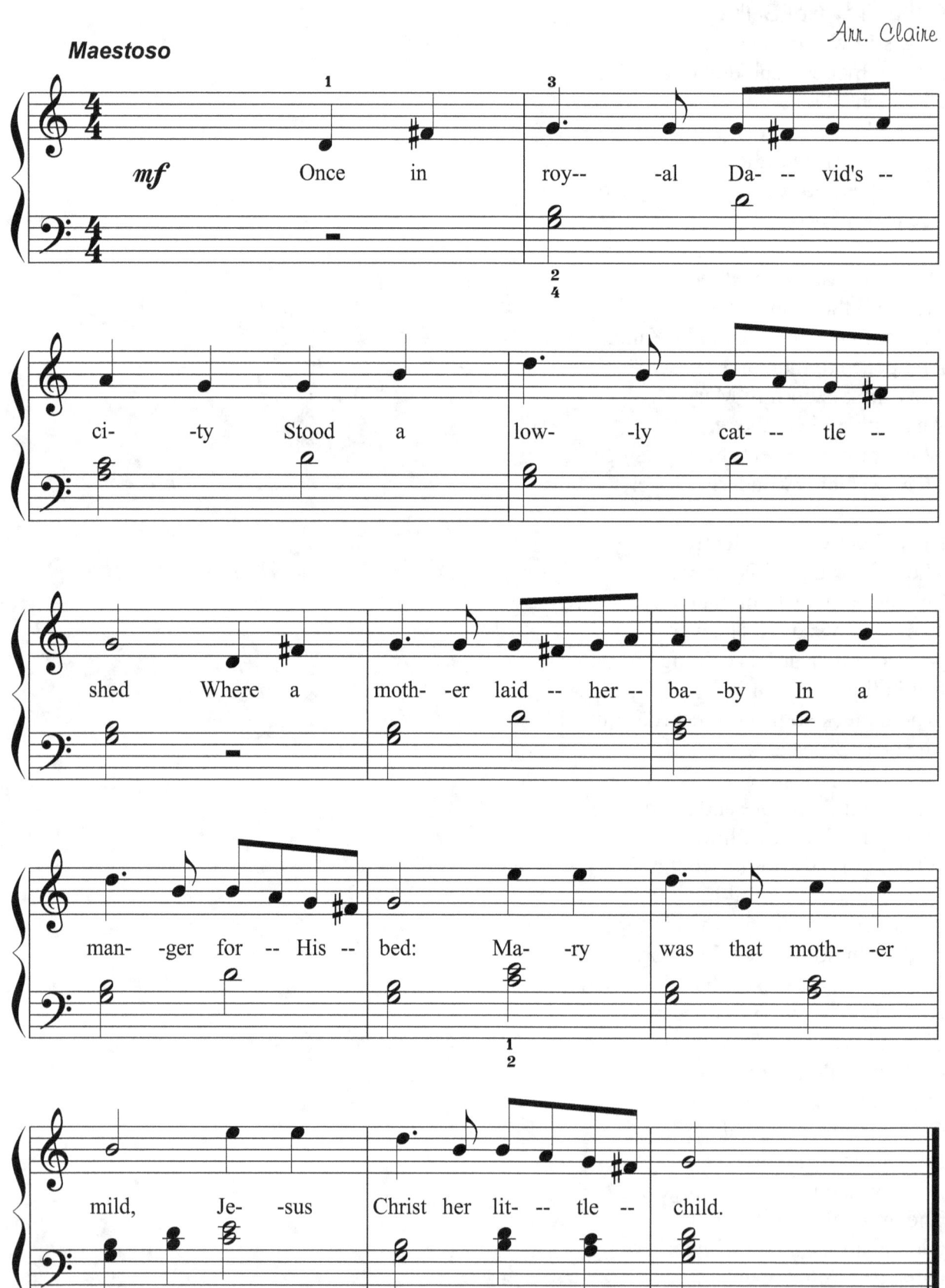

Once In Royal David's City

Once in royal David'd city,
Stood a lowly cattle shed,
Where a mother laid her baby,
In a manger for his bed,
Mary was that mother mild
Jesus Christ her little child.

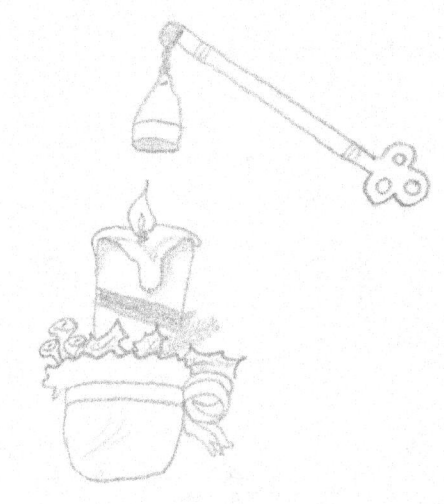

He came down to earth from heaven,
Who is God and Lord of all,
And his shelter was a stable,
And his cradle was a stall,
With the poor, and mean, and lowly,
Lived on earth our Saviour holy.

And through all his wondrous childhood,
He would honour and obey,
Love and watch the lowly mother,
In whose gentle arms he lay,
Christian children all must be,
Mild, obedient, good as he.

For he is our childhood's pattern,
Day by day like us he grew,
He was little, weak, and helpless,
Tears and smiles like us he knew,
And he feeleth for our sadness,
And he shareth in our gladness.

And our eyes at last shall see him,
Through his own redeeming love,
For that child so dear and gentle,
Is our Lord in heaven above,
And he leads his children on,
To the place where he has gone.

Not in that poor lowly stable,
With the oxen standing by,
We shall see him, but in heaven,
Set at God's right hand on high,
When like stars his children crowned,
All in white shall wait around.

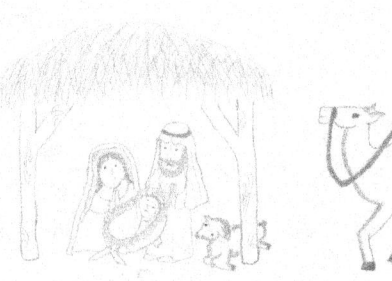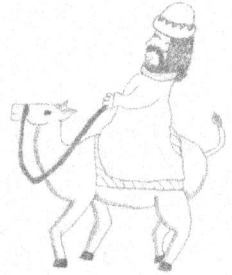

See Amid The Winter Snow

Arr. Claire

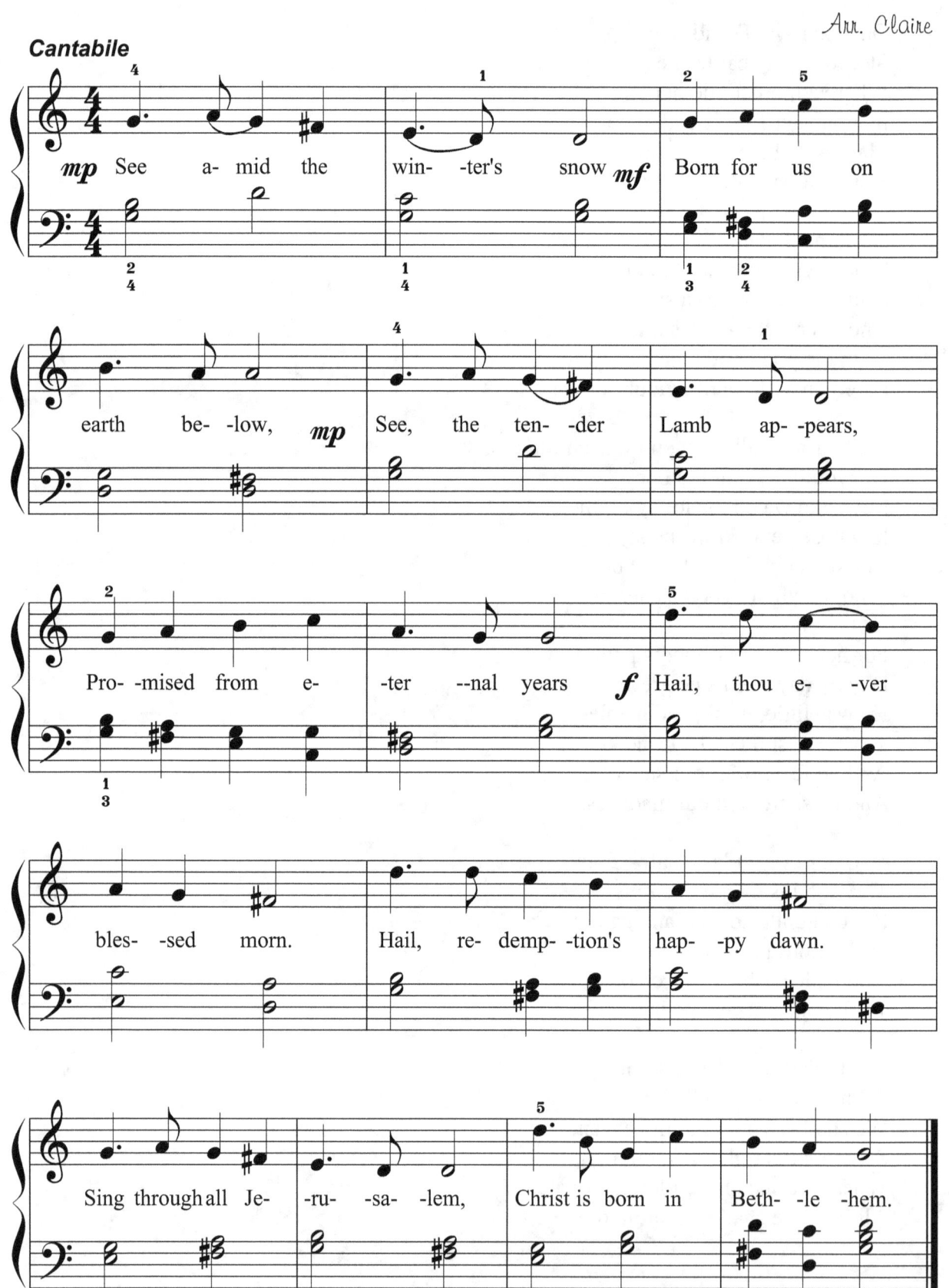

See amid the winter's snow.

See amid the winter's snow,
Born for us on earth below,
See! the tender Lamb appears,
Promised from eternal years.

CHORUS

Hail, thou ever-blessed morn,
Hail, redemption's happy dawn,
Sing through all Jerusalem,
Christ is born in Bethlehem.

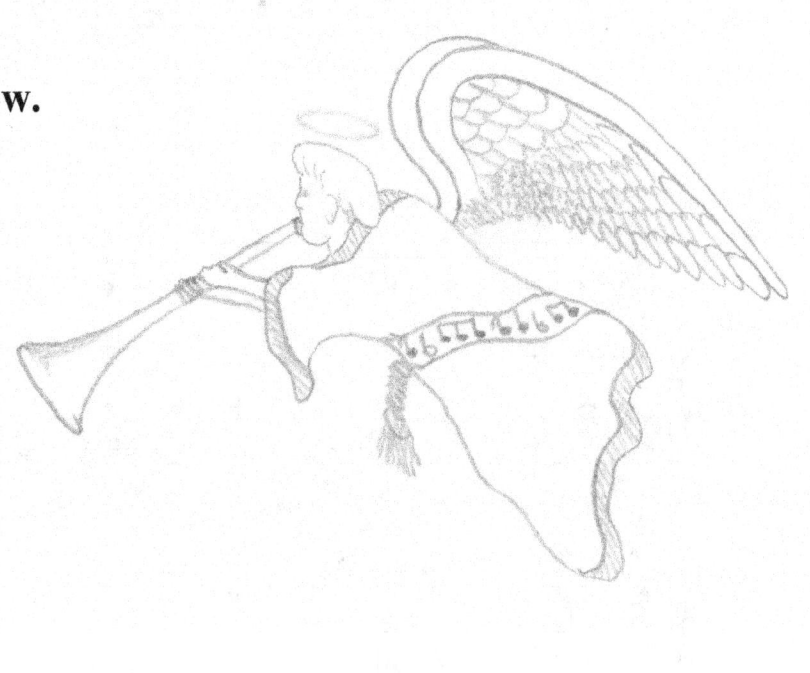

Lo! Within a manger lies,
He who built the starry skies,
He who throned in heights sublime,
Sits amid the Cherubim.

CHORUS

Say, ye holy shepherds say,
What your joyful news to-day,
Wherefore have ye left your sheep,
On the lonely mountain steep?

CHORUS

"As we watched at dead of night,
Lo! We saw a wondrous light,
Angels, singing peace on earth,
Told us of a Saviour's birth."

CHORUS

Sacred Infant, all Divine,
What a tender love was Thine,
Thus to come from highest bliss,
Down to such a world as this.

CHORUS.

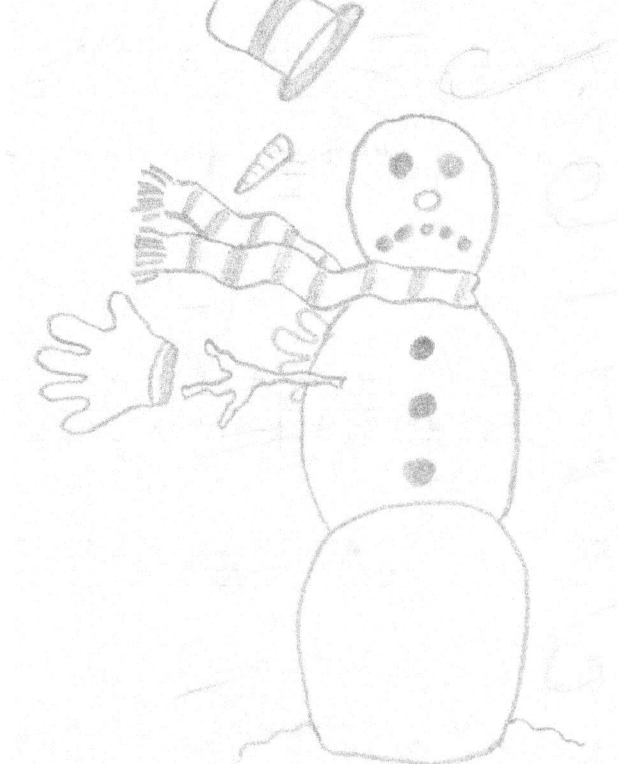

Silent Night

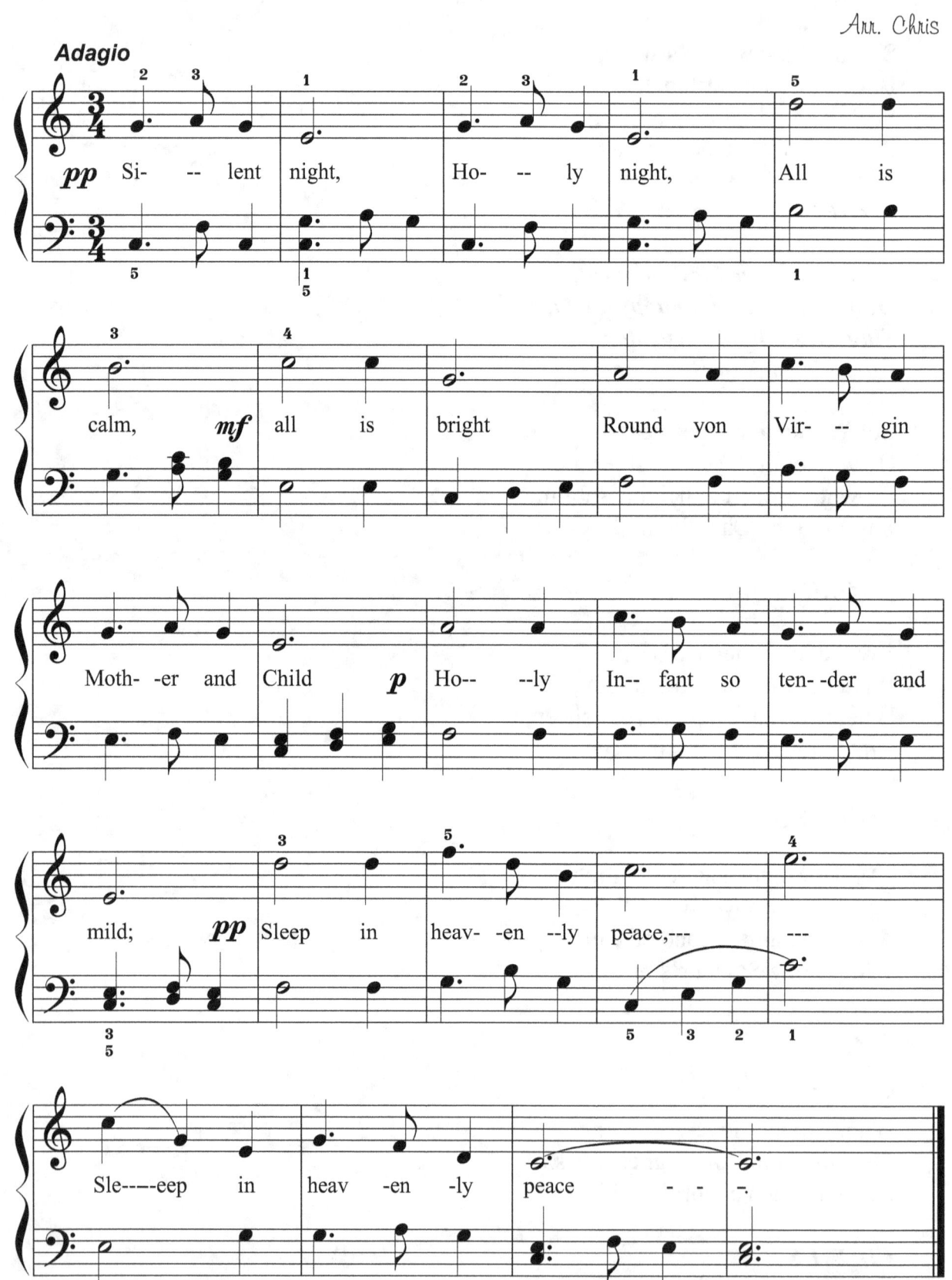

Silent Night

Silent night, holy night,
All is calm, all is bright,
Round yon Virgin Mother and Child,
Holy infant so tender and mild,
Sleep in heavenly peace !
Sleep in heavenly peace !

Silent night, holy night,
Shepherds wake at the sight;
Glory streams from heaven afar,
Heavenly hosts sing Alleluia.
Christ the Saviour is born !
Christ the Saviour is born !

Silent night, holy night,
Son of God, love's pure light;
Radiance beams from thy holy face,
With the dawn of redeeming grace,
Jesus, Lord at thy birth,
Jesus, Lord at thy birth.

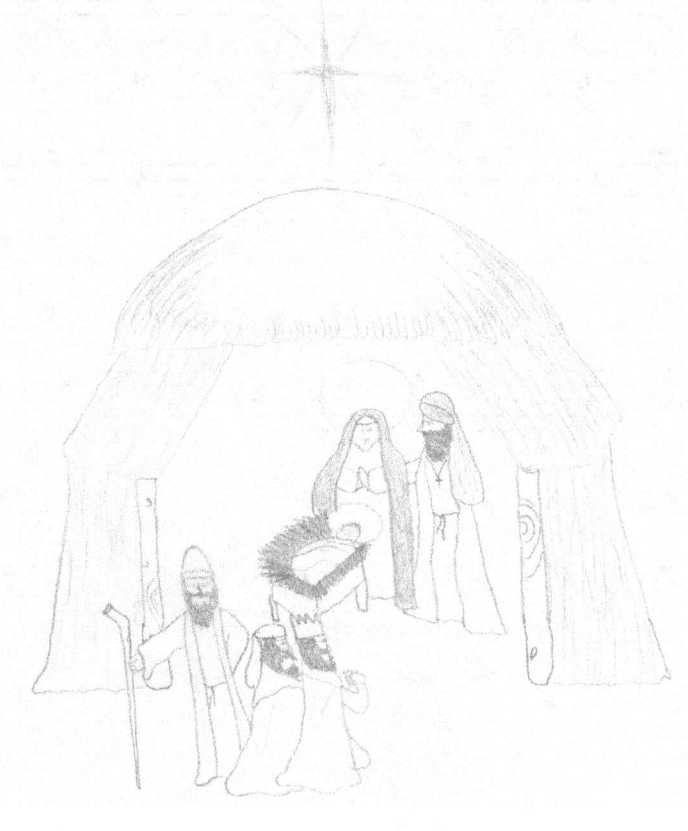

Sussex Carol

Arr. Claire

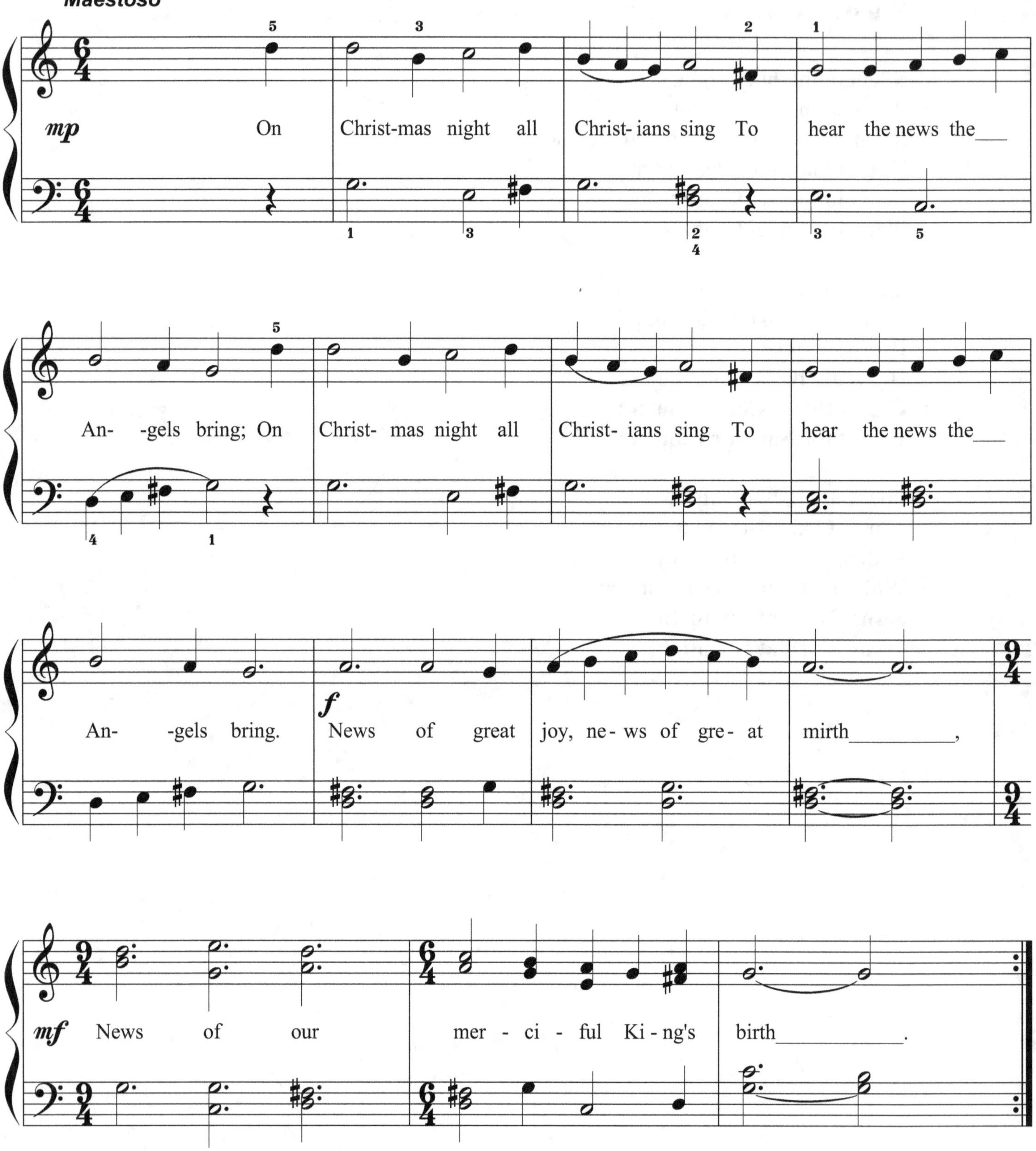

Maestoso

mp

On Christ-mas night all Christ-ians sing To hear the news the___

An- -gels bring; On Christ- mas night all Christ- ians sing To hear the news the___

An- -gels bring. *f* News of great joy, ne-ws of gre- at mirth_____,

mf News of our mer - ci - ful Ki- ng's birth_____.

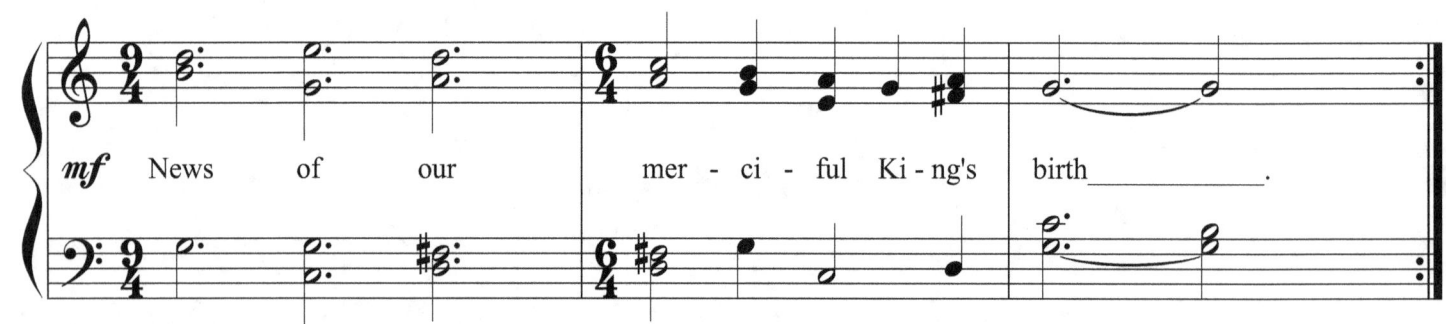

Sussex Carol

On Christmas night all Christians sing,
To hear the news the Angels bring
On Christmas night all Christians sing,
To hear the news the Angels bring
News of great joy, news of great mirth,
News of our merciful King's birth.

Then why should men on earth be sad,
Since our Redeemer made us glad,
Then why should men on earth be sad,
Since our Redeemer made us glad,
When from our sin He set us free,
All for to gain our liberty.

When sin departs before his grace,
Then life and health come in its place;
When sin departs before his grace,
Then life and health come in its place;
Angels and men with joy may sing,
All for to see the new-born King

All out of darkness we have light,
Which made the Angels sing this night;
All out of darkness we have light,
Which made the Angels sing this night;
Glory to God and peace to men,
Now and for evermore, *Amen.*

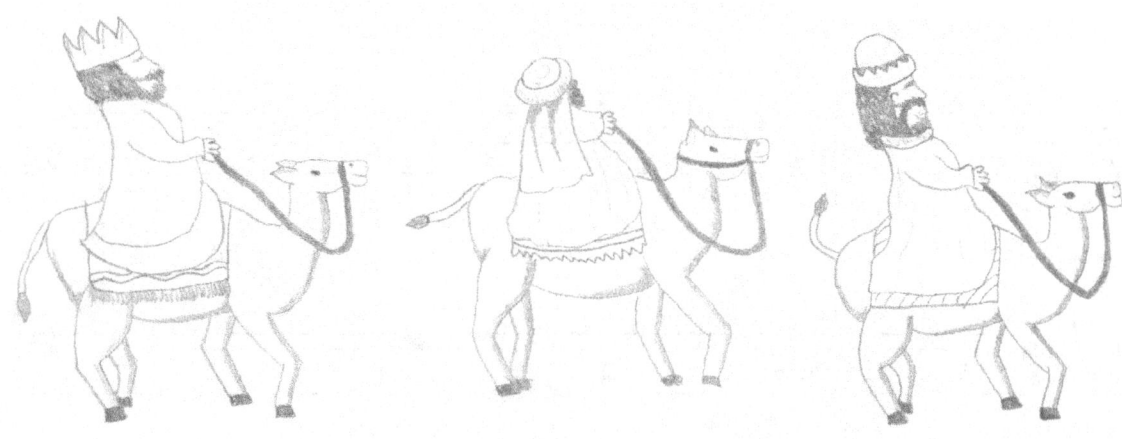

The Coventry Carol

Arr. Claire

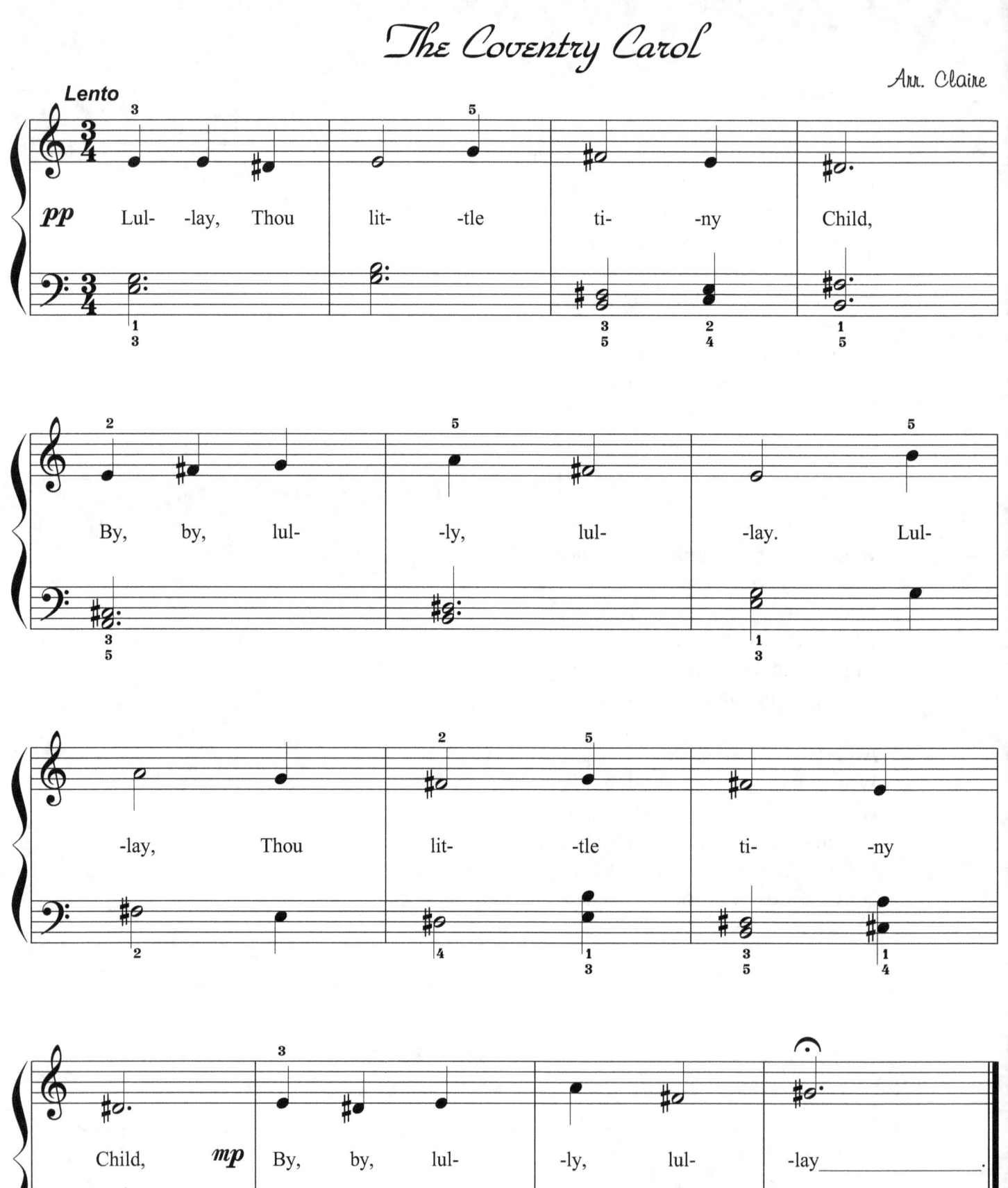

The Coventry Carol

Lullay, Thou little tiny Child,
By, by, lully, lullay.
Lullay, Thou little tiny Child.
By, by, lully, lullay.

Oh sisters, too, how may we do,
For to preserve this day,
This poor Youngling for whom we sing,
By, by, lully, lullay.

Herod the King in his raging,
Charged he hath this day,
His men of might, in his own sight,
All children young to slay.

Then woe is me, poor child, for Thee,
And ever mourn and say,
For Thy parting nor say, nor sing,
By, by, lully, lullay.

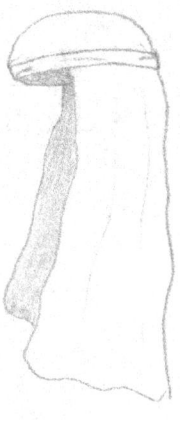

The First Noel

Arr. Claire

Andante

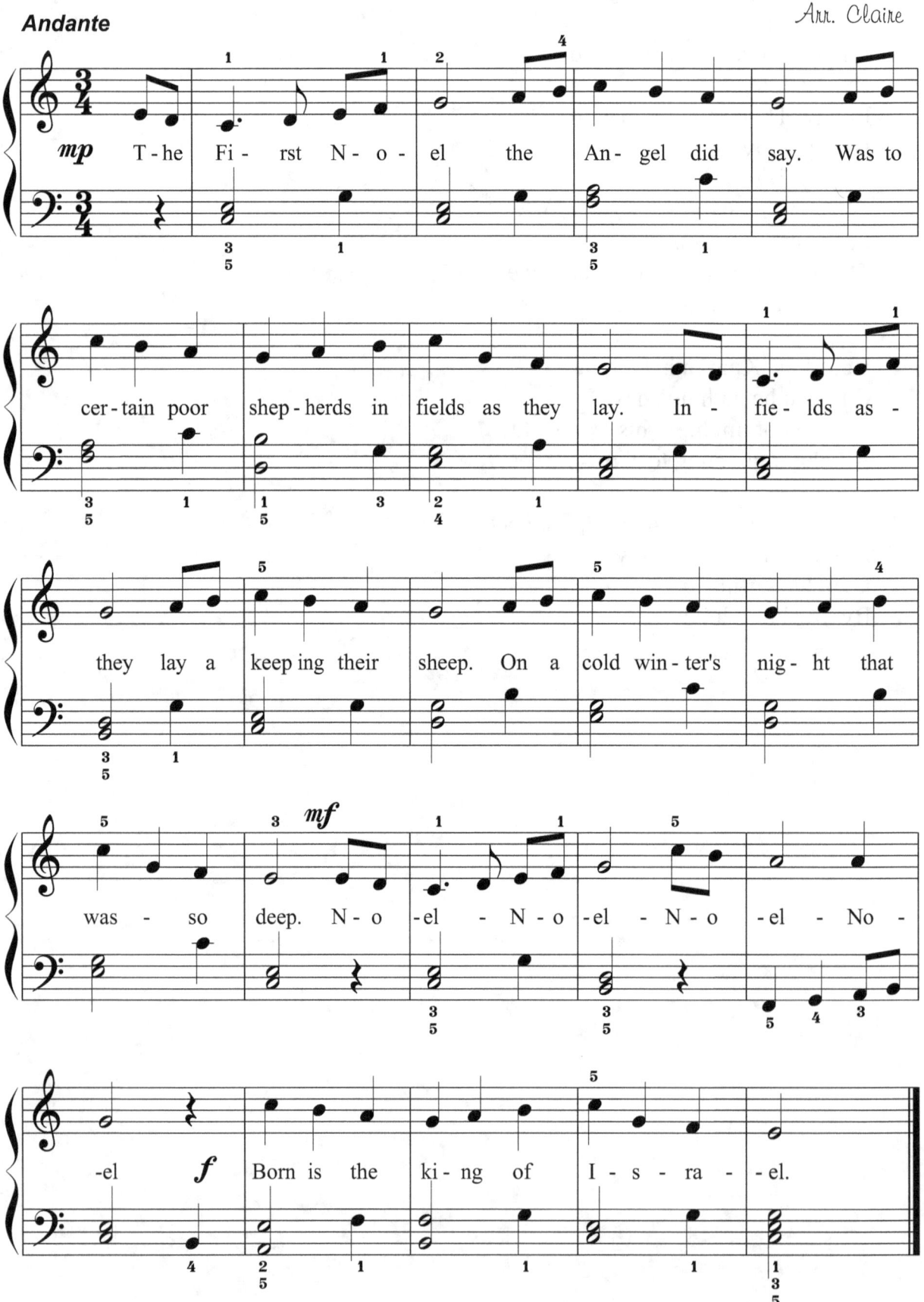

The First Noel

The First Noel the angel did say,
Was to certain poor shepherds in fields as they lay;
In fields where they lay keeping their sheep
On a cold winter's night that was so deep.

Chorus: Noel, Noel, Noel, Noel
Born is the King of Israel.

They looked up and saw a star,
Shining in the East beyond them afar,
And to the earth it gave great light,
And so it continued both day and night.

Chorus

And by the light of that same star,
Three wise men came from country far:
To seek for a King was their intent,
And to follow the star wherever it went.

Chorus

This star drew nigh to the north-west,
O'er Bethlehem it took its rest,
And there it did both stop and stay
Right over the place where Jesus lay.

Chorus

Then entered in those wise men three,
Full reverently upon their knee,
And offered there in His presence,
Their gold and myrrh and frankincense.

Chorus

Then let us all with one accord,
Sing praises to our Heavenly Lord,
That hath made Heaven and earth of nought,
And with His blood mankind hath bought.

Chorus

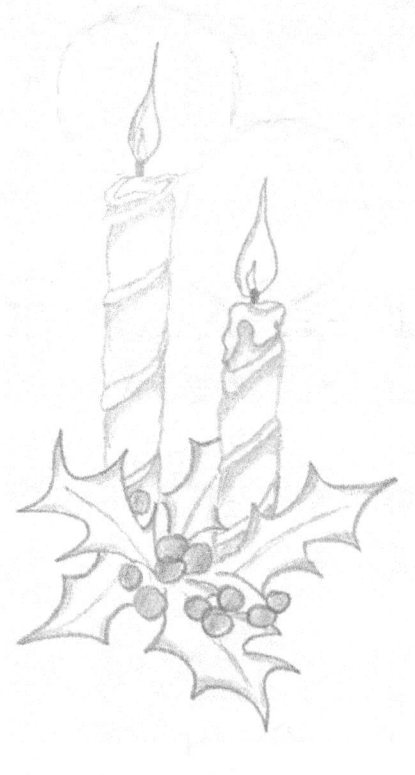

Holly And The Ivy

Arr. Claire

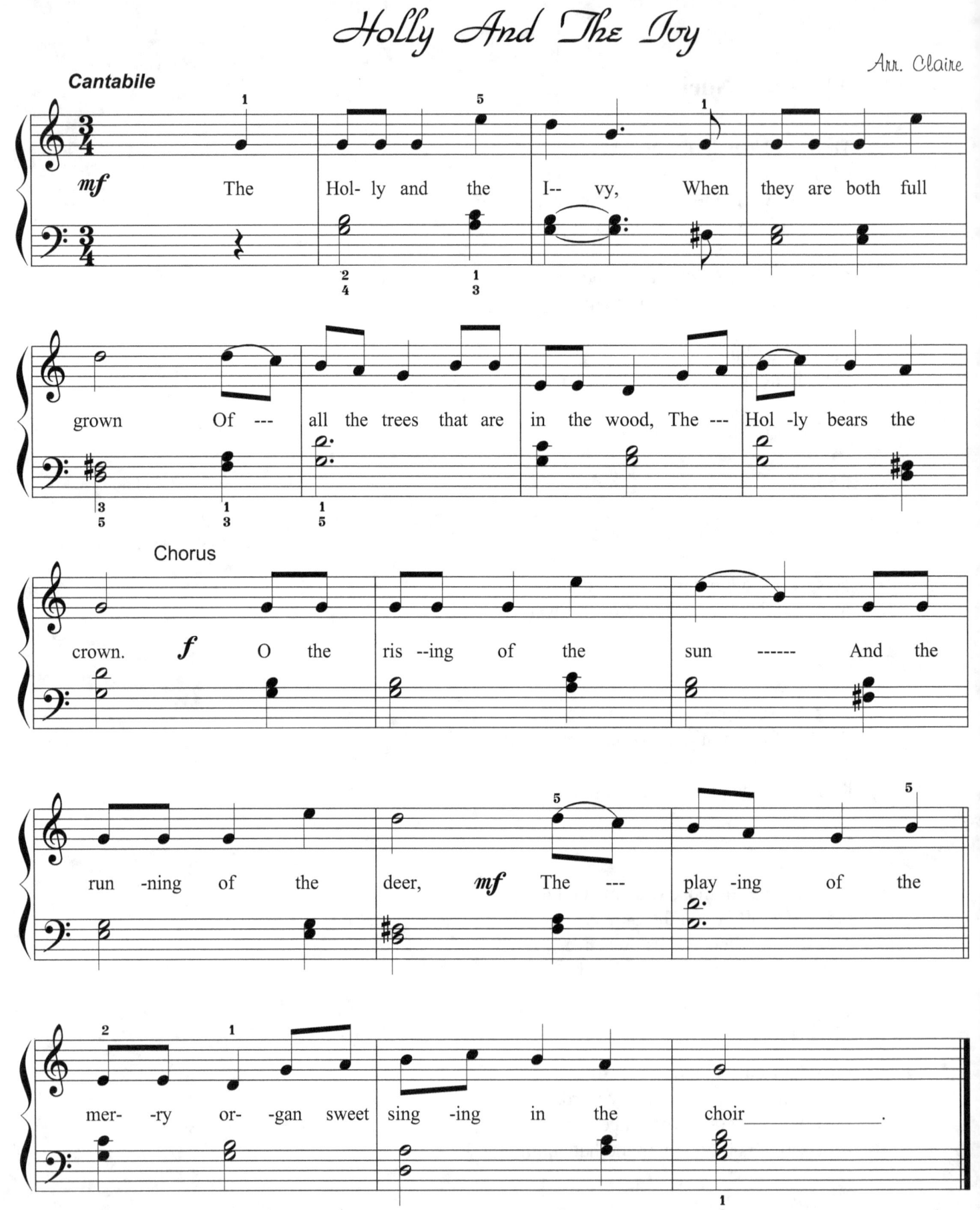

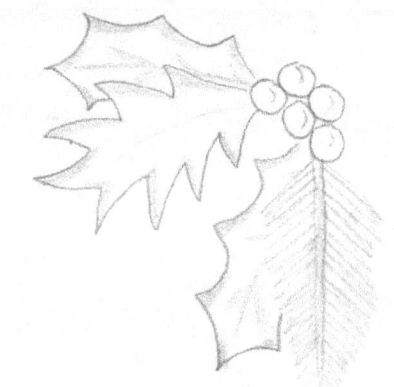

The Holly and the Ivy.

The holly and the ivy,
When they are both full grown,
Of all the trees that are in the wood,
The holly bears the crown:

**Chorus: The rising of the sun,
and the running of the deer,
The playing of the merry organ
Sweet singing in the choir.**

The holly bears a blossom,
As white as the lily flower,
And Mary bore sweet Jesus Christ
To be our Saviour:
Chorus:
The holly bears a berry
As red as any blood,
And Mary bore sweet Jesus Christ
To do poor sinners good:
Chorus:
The holly bears a prickle
As sharp as any thorn,
And Mary bore sweet Jesus Christ
In Christmas day in the morn.
Chorus:
The holly hears a hark
As bitter as any gall,
And Mary bore sweet]esus Christ
For to redeem us all.
Chorus:
The holly and the ivy,
When they are both full grown,
Of all the trees that are in the wood,
The holly bears the crown.

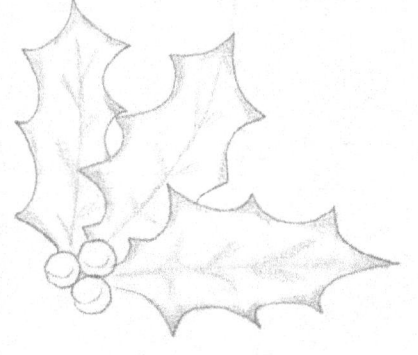

The Twelve Days of Christmas

Arr. Claire

Brillante

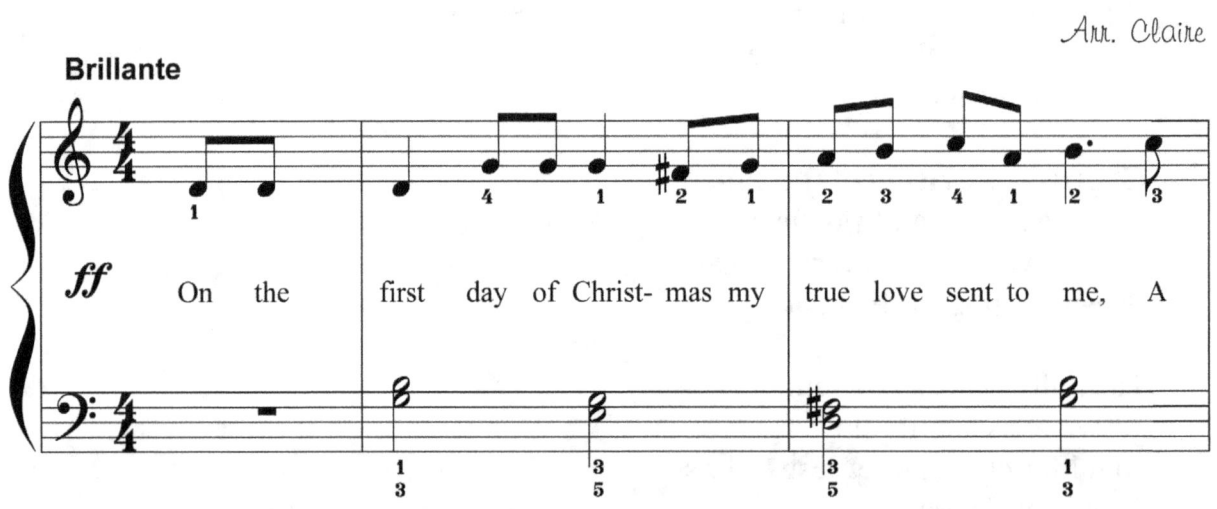

ff On the first day of Christ- mas my true love sent to me, A

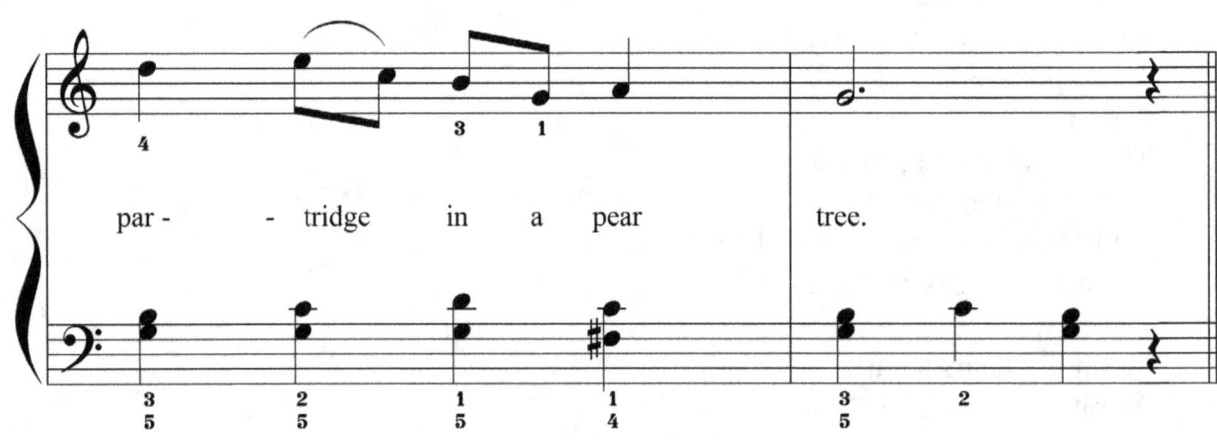

par - - tridge in a pear tree.

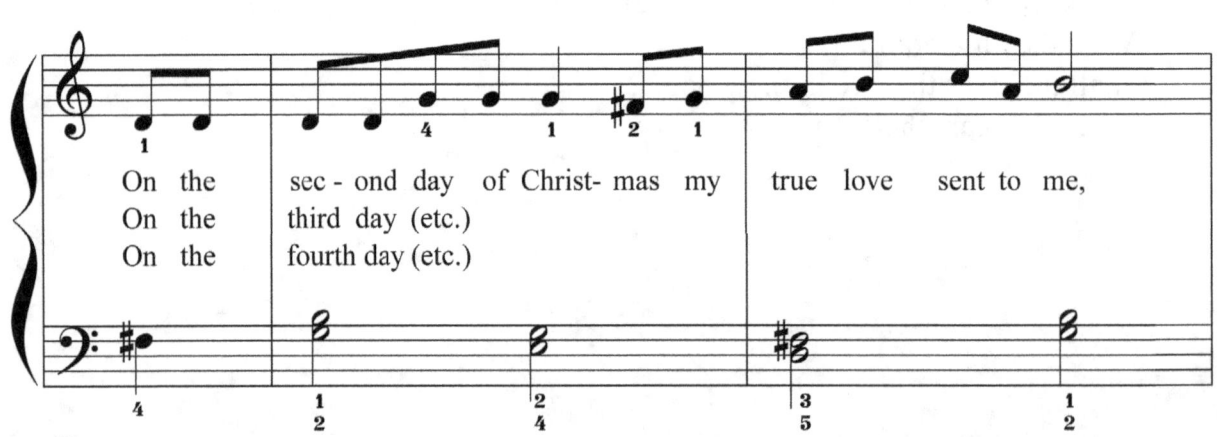

On the sec - ond day of Christ- mas my true love sent to me,
On the third day (etc.)
On the fourth day (etc.)

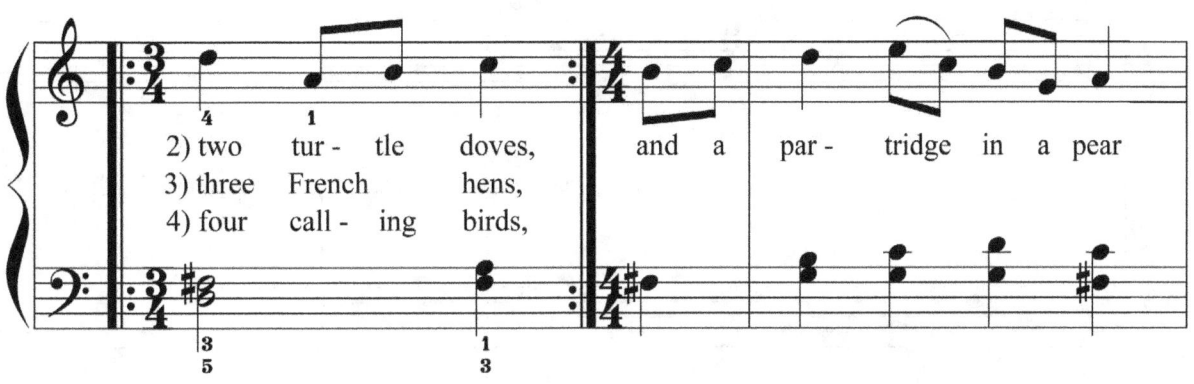

2) two tur - tle doves,
3) three French hens,
4) four call - ing birds,

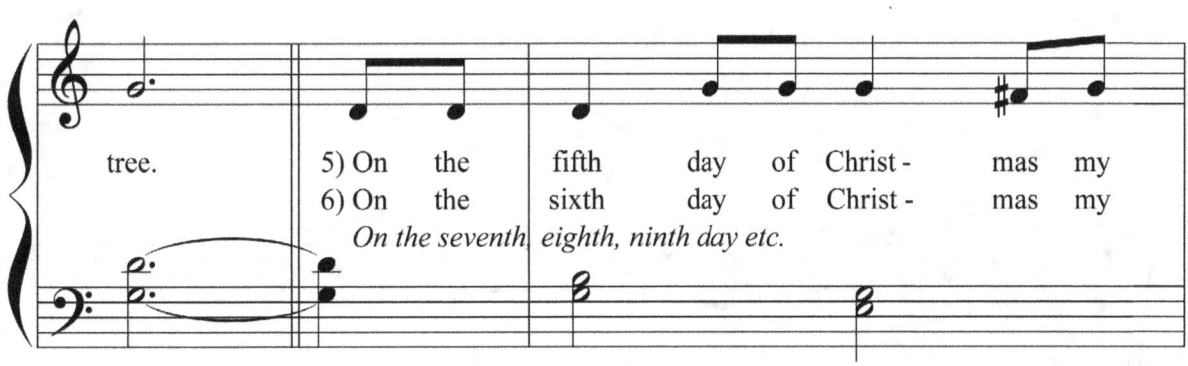

tree.
5) On the fifth day of Christ - mas my
6) On the sixth day of Christ - mas my
On the seventh, eighth, ninth day etc.

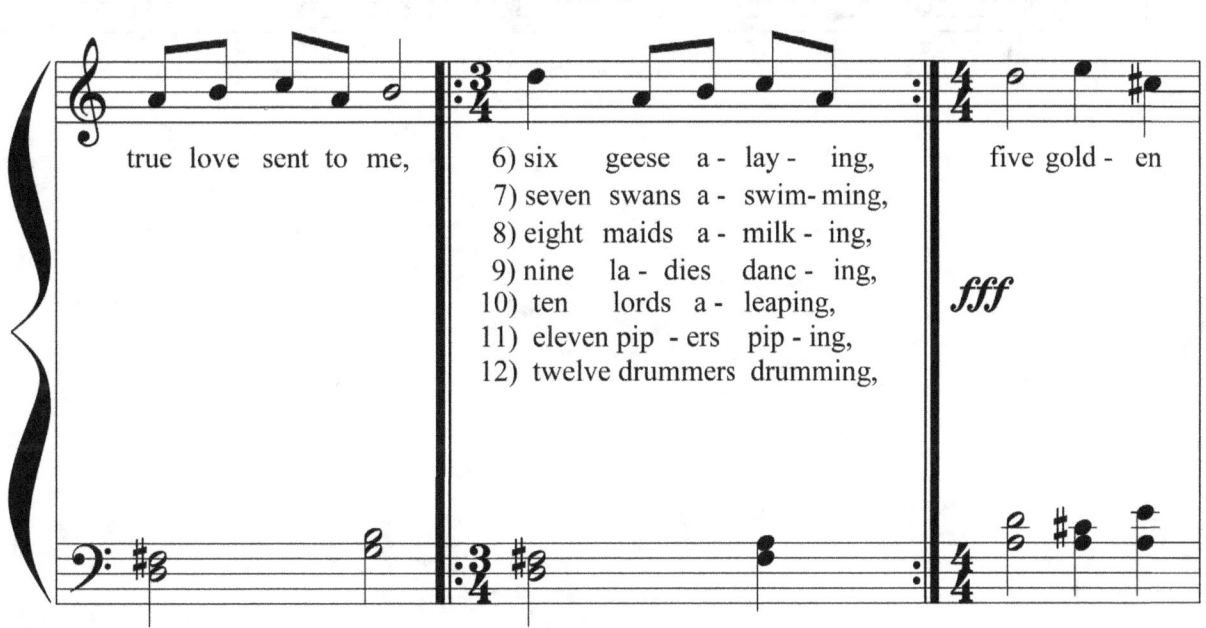

true love sent to me,
6) six geese a - lay - ing,
7) seven swans a - swim - ming,
8) eight maids a - milk - ing,
9) nine la - dies danc - ing,
10) ten lords a - leaping,
11) eleven pip - ers pip - ing,
12) twelve drummers drumming,

five gold - en

fff

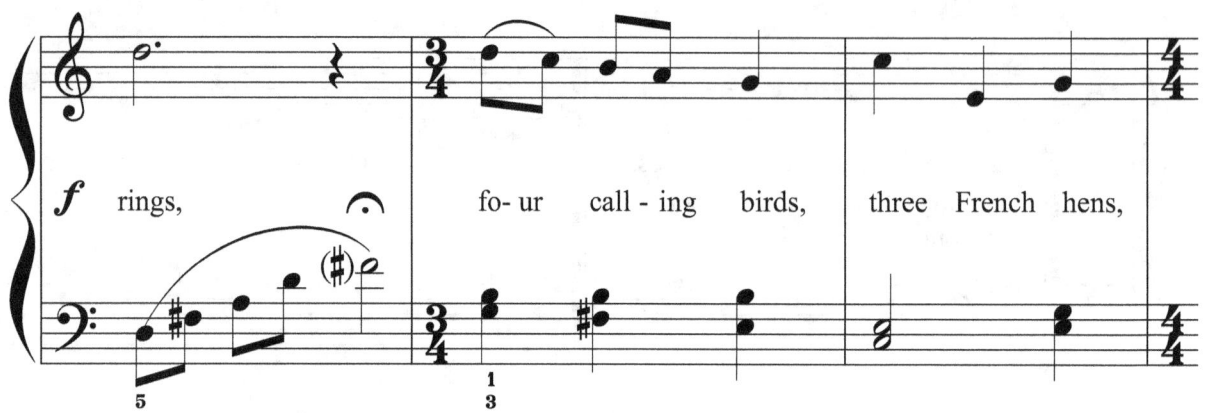

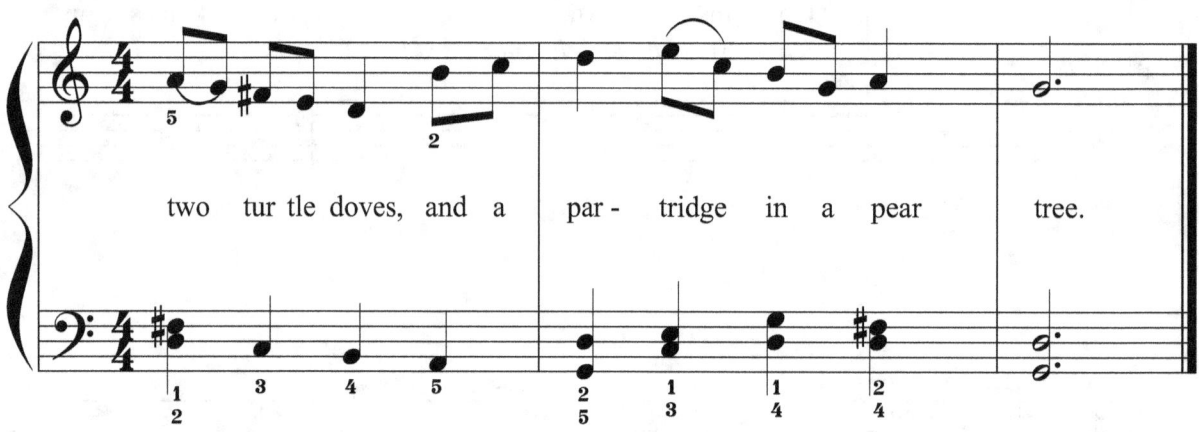

The Twelve Days of Christmas.

1. The first day of Christmas,
   My true love sent to me,
   A partridge in a pear tree.

2. The second day of Christmas,
   My true love sent to me,
   Two turtle doves... *

3. The third day of Christmas,
   My true love sent to me,
   Three french hens... *

4. The fourth day of Christmas,
   My true love sent to me,
   Four calling birds... *

5. The fifth day of Christmas,
   My true love sent to me,
   Five gold rings... *

6. The sixth day of Christmas,
   My true love sent to me,
   Six geese a-laying... *

7. The seventh day of Christmas,
   My true love sent to me,
   Seven swans a-swimming... *

8. The eighth day of Christmas,
   My true love sent to me,
   Eight maids a-milking... *

9. The ninth day of Christmas,
   My true love sent to me,
   Nine ladies dancing... *

10. The tenth day of Christmas,
    My true love sent to me,
    Ten lords a-leaping... *

11. The eleventh day of Christmas,
    My true love sent to me,
    Eleven pipers piping... *

12. The twelfth day of Christmas,
    My true love sent to me,
    Twelve drummers drumming.. *

Repeat the last line of each preceding verse in reverse
order after the verse is completed.

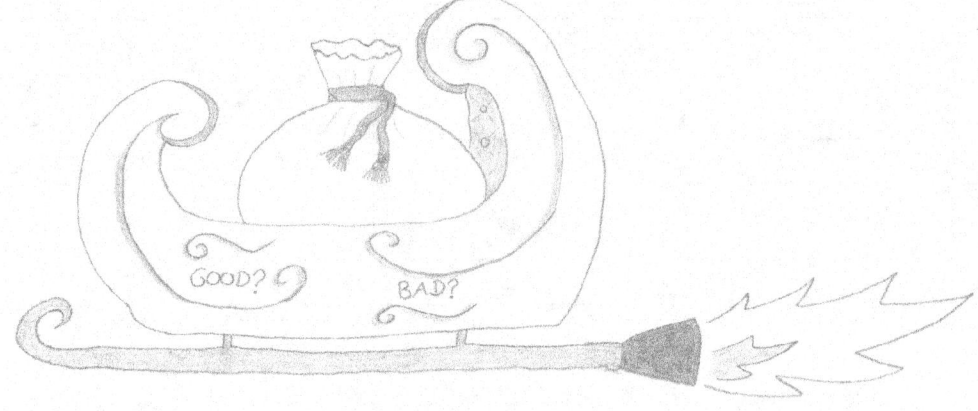

The Virgin Mary had a Baby Boy

Traditional West Indian
Arr. by Eros

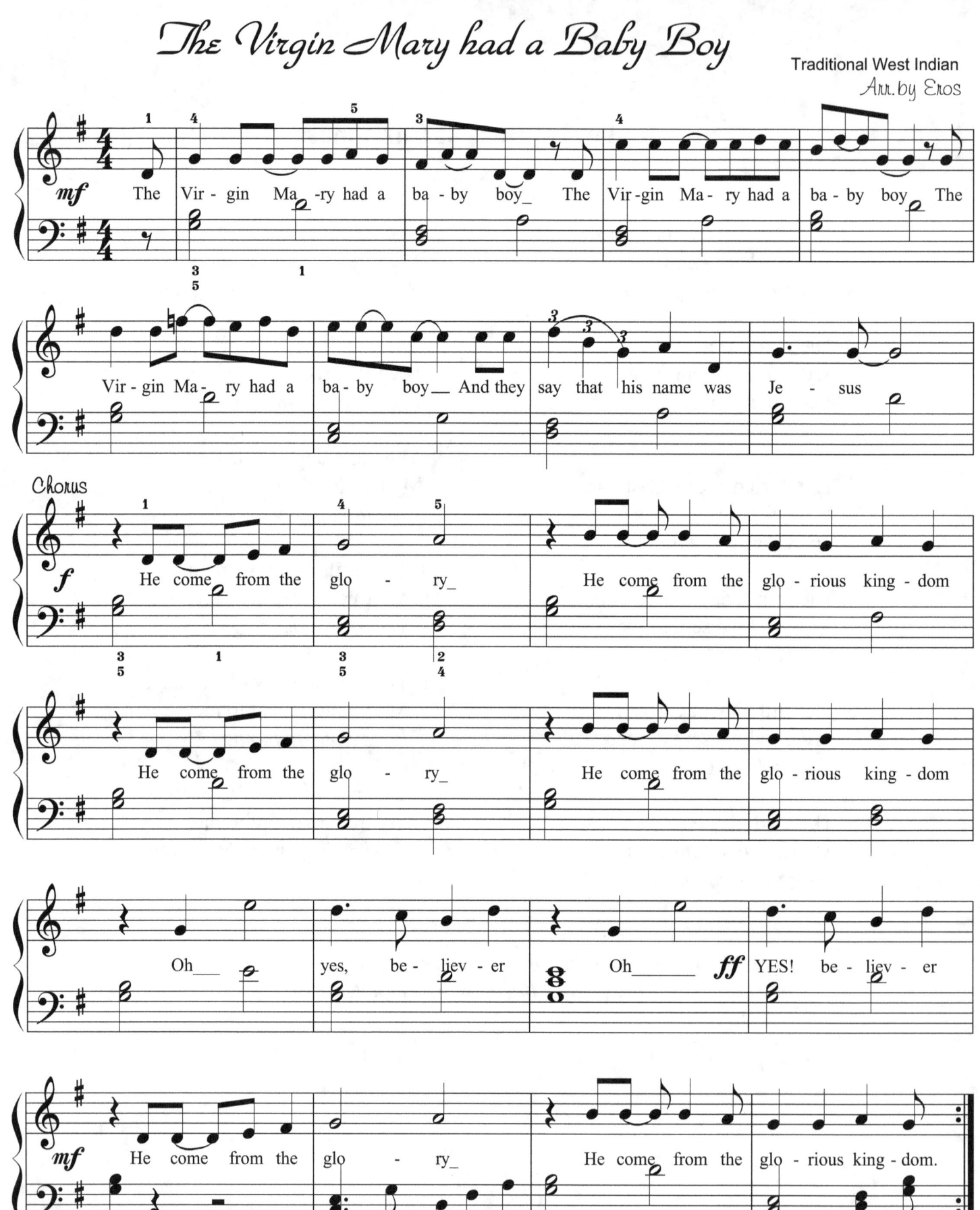

The Virgin Mary had a baby boy

The Virgin Mary had a baby boy,
The Virgin Mary had a baby boy,
The Virgin Mary had a baby boy,
And they say that his name was Jesus.

He come from the glory,
He come from the glorious king-dom.
Oh yes, believer,
Oh yes, believer!
He come from the glory,
He come from the glorious king-dom.

The angels sang when the baby born,
The angels sang when the baby born,
The angels sang when the baby born,
And proclaimed him the Saviour Jesus.

He come from the glory,
He come from the glorious kingdom.

The wise men saw where the baby born,
The wise men saw where the baby born,
The wise men saw where the baby born,
And they say that his name was Jesus.

He come from the glory,
He come from the glorious kingdom.

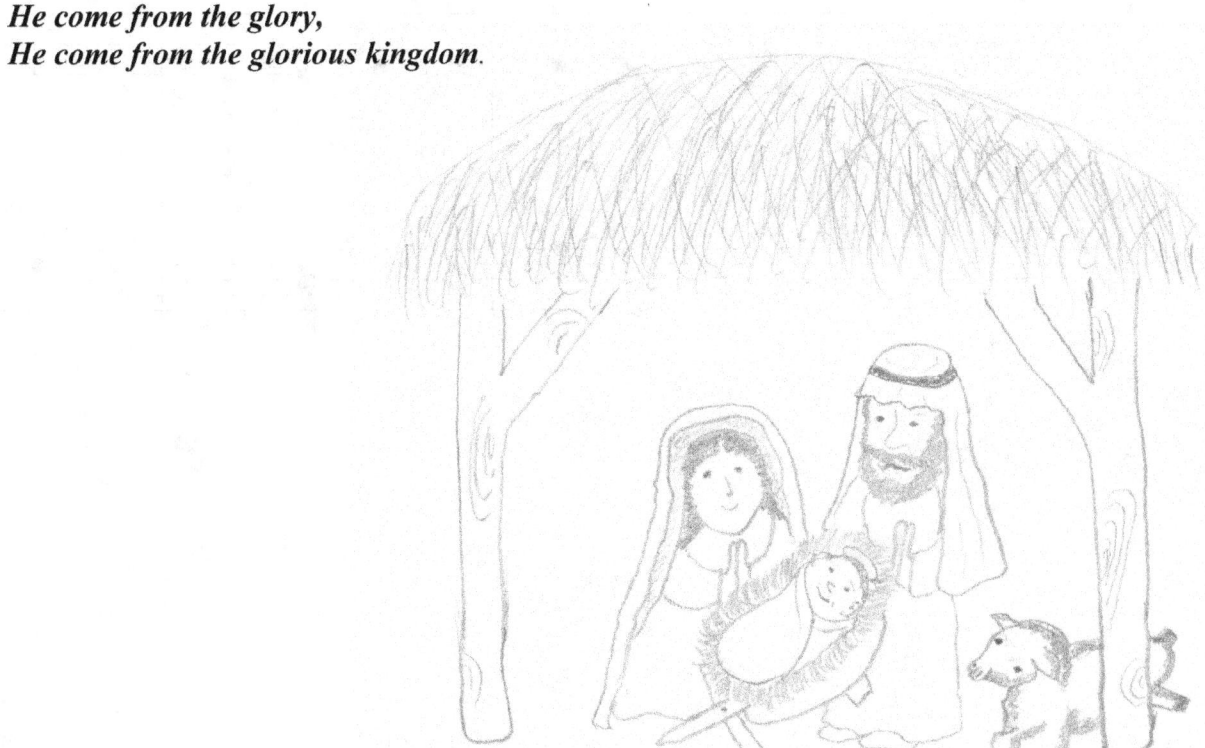

Unto us a Boy is Born

Puer Nobis

Arr. Eros

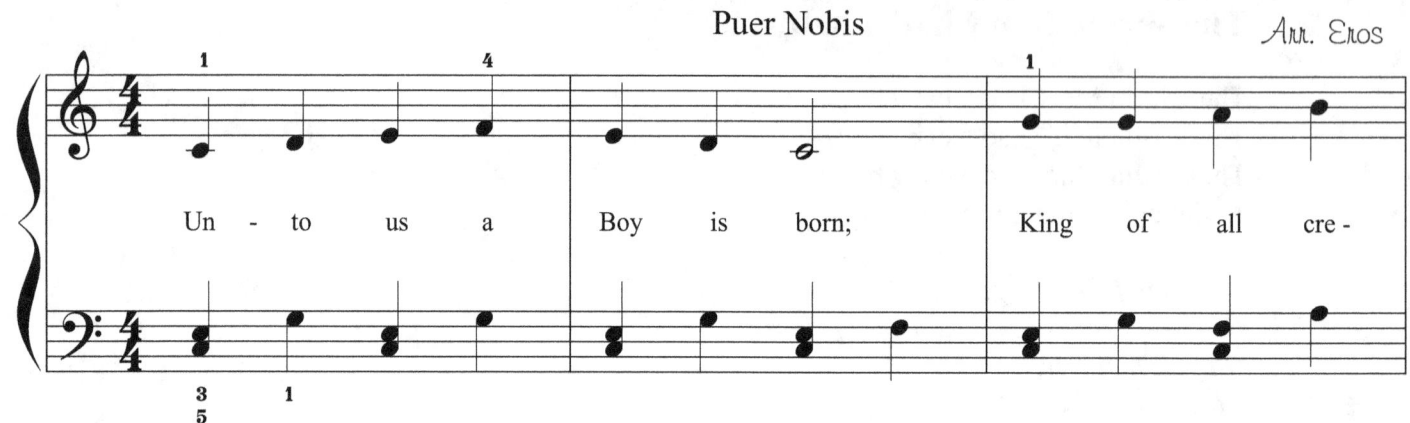

Un - to us a Boy is born; King of all cre -

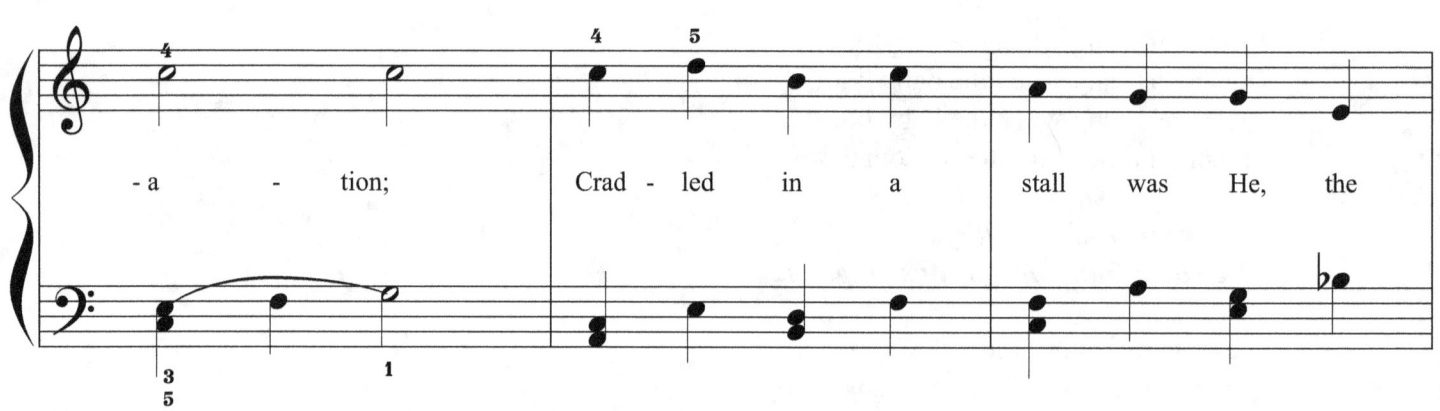

- a - tion; Crad - led in a stall was He, the

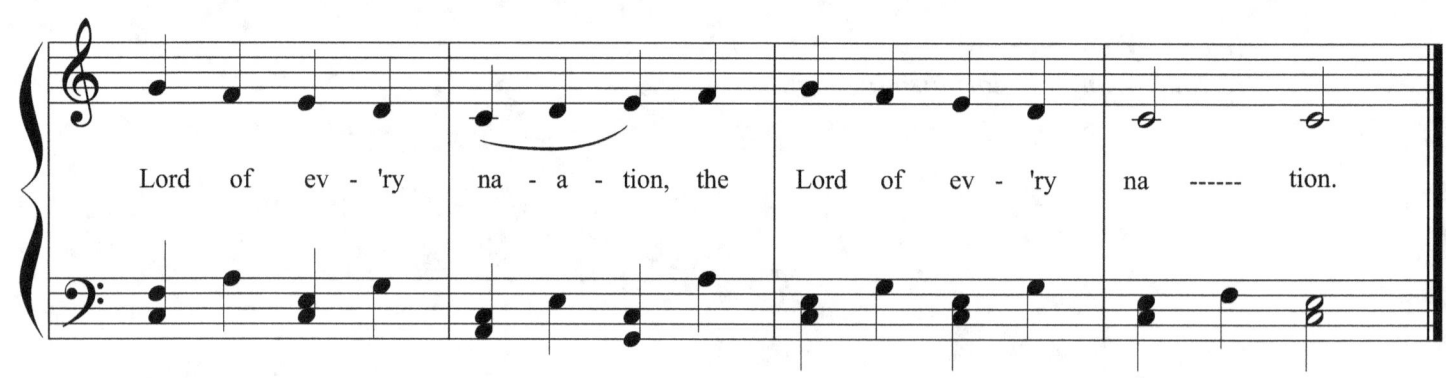

Lord of ev - 'ry na - a - tion, the Lord of ev - 'ry na ------ tion.

Unto Us a Boy is Born

Un to us a boy is born
King of all creation,
Came He to a world forlorn,
The Lord of every nation,
The Lord of every nation.

Cradled in a stall was He
With sleepy cows and asses;
But the very beasts could see
That he all men surpasses,
That he all men surpasses.

Herod then with fear was filled;
'A prince', he said, 'in Jewry!',
All little boys he killed
At Bethl'em in his fury,
At Bethl'em in his fury.

Now may Mary's son, who came
So long ago to love us,
Lead us all with hearts aflame
Unto the joys above us,
Unto the joys above us.

Omega and Alpha He!
Let the organ thunder,
While the choir with peals of glee
Shall rend the air asunder,
Shall rend the air asunder.

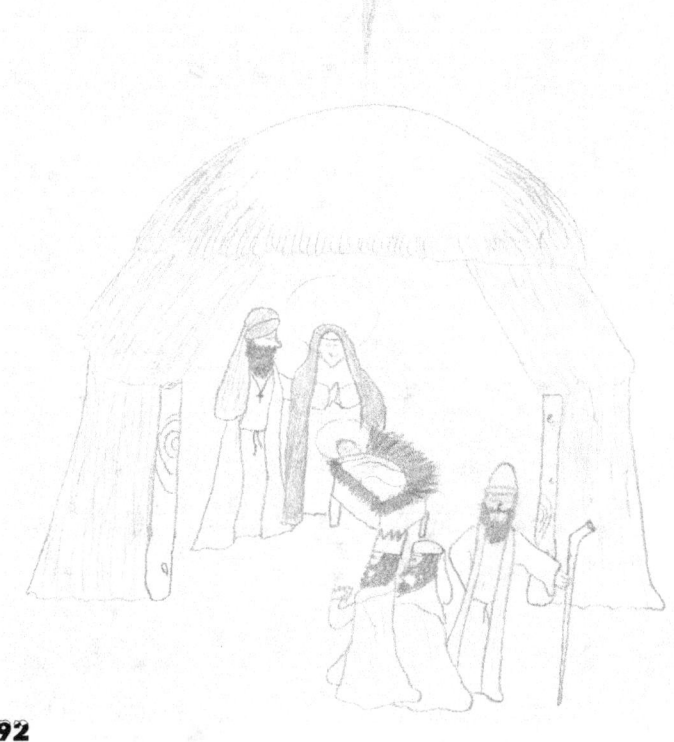

We Wish You A Merry Christmas

Arr. Claire

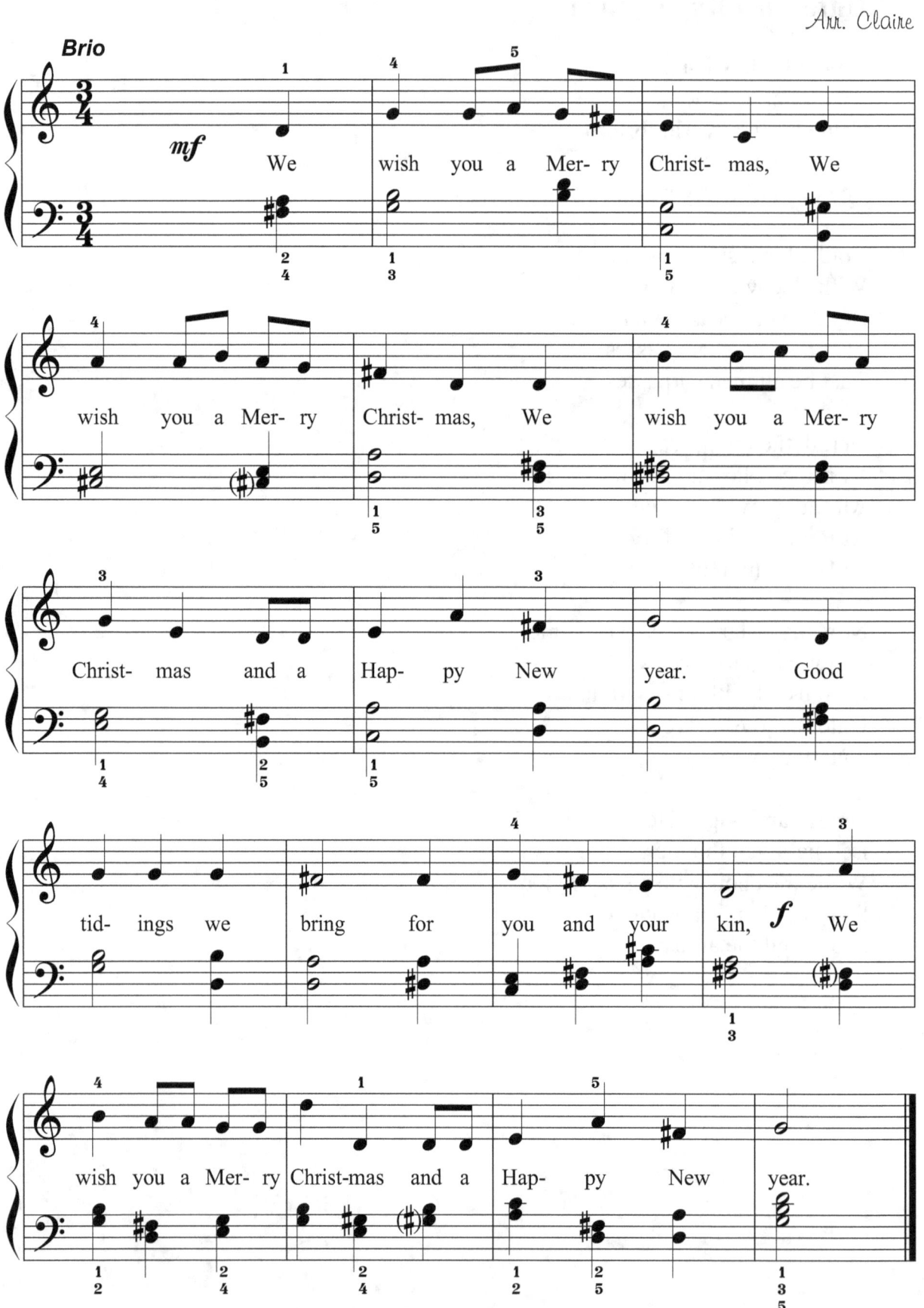

We Wish You A Merry Christmas.

We wish you a merry Christmas,
We wish you a merry Christmas,
We wish you a merry Christmas,
And a happy new year.

Good tidings we bring,
To you and your kin,
We wish you a merry Christmas,
And a happy new year.

Now bring us some figgy pudding,
Now bring us some figgy pudding,
Now bring us some figgy pudding,
And bring some out here.

For we all love some figgy pudding,
For we all love some figgy pudding,
For we all love some figgy pudding,
So bring some out here.

And we won't go till we've got some,
We won't go till we've got some,
And we won't go till we've got some,
So bring some out here.

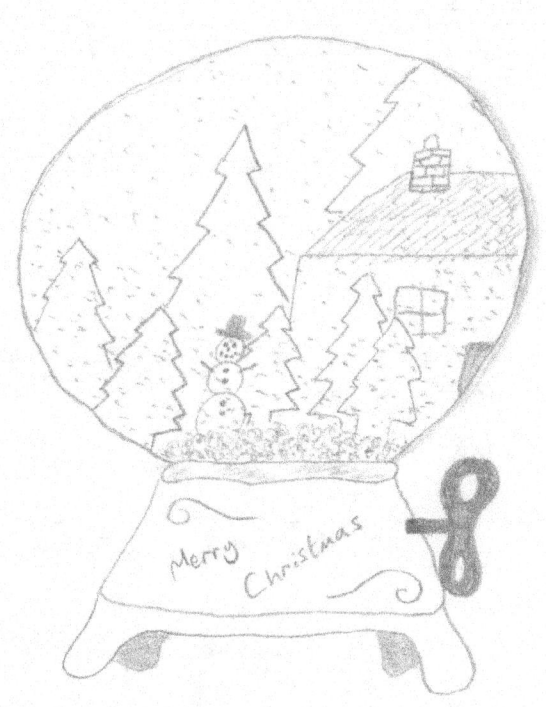

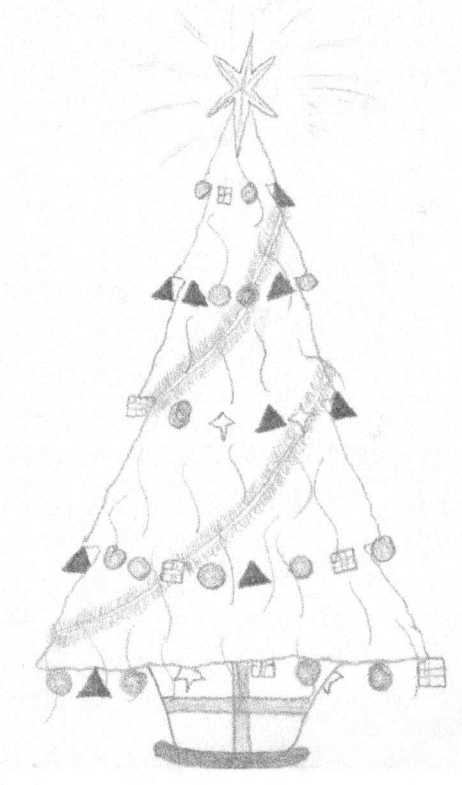

We Three Kings of Orient Are

Traditional American

Arr. Claire

Maestoso

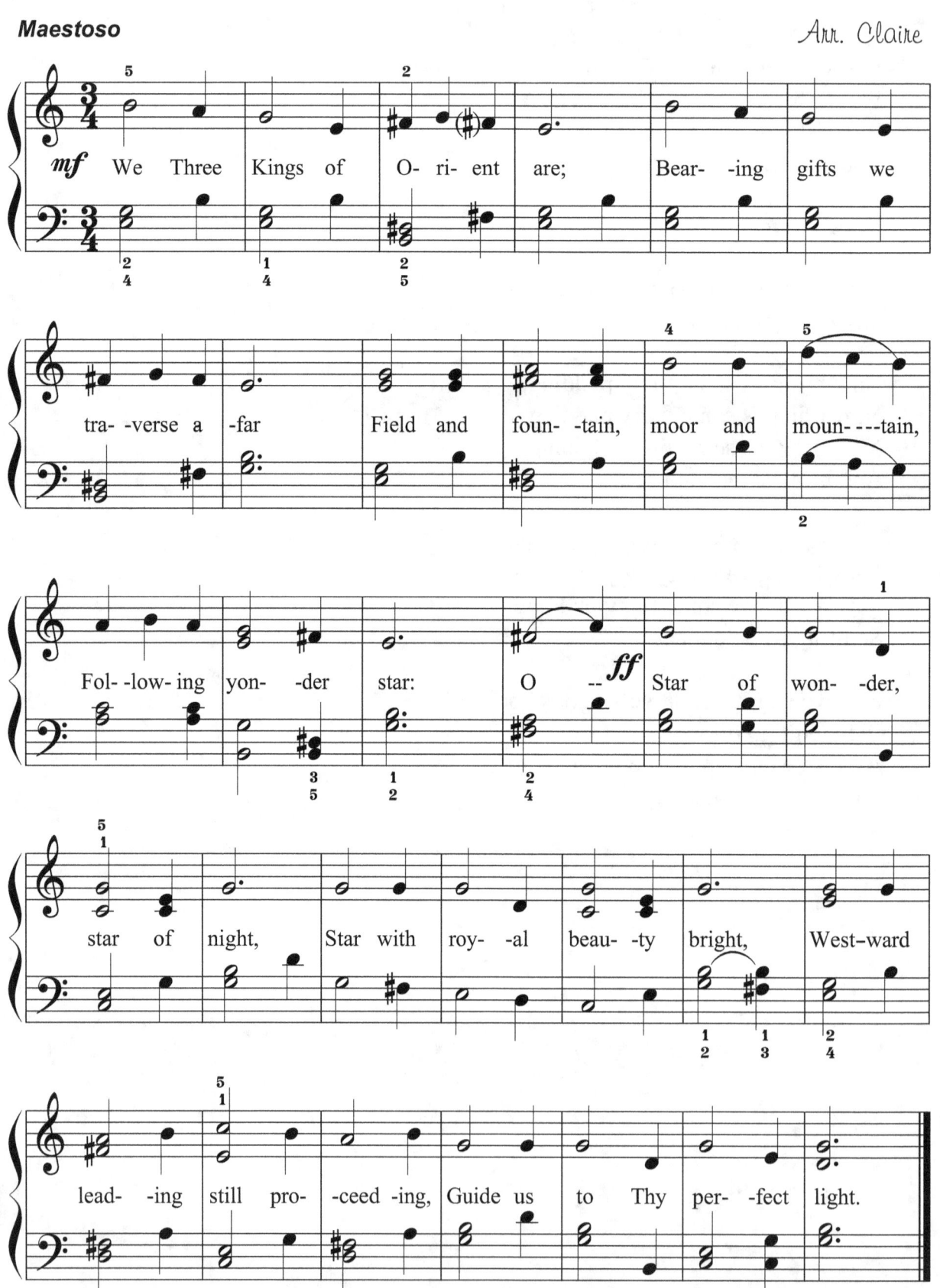

We Three Kings.

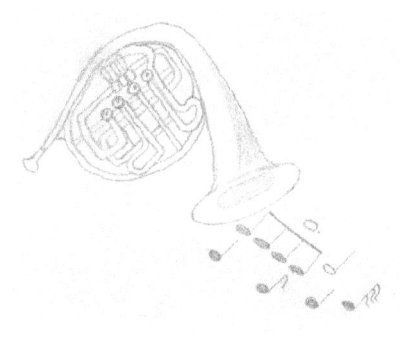

We three Kings of Orient are,
Bearing gifts we traverse afar,
Field and fountain, moor and mountain,
Following yonder star.

Chorus

O star of wonder, star of night,
Star with royal beauty bright,
Westward leading, still proceeding,
Guide us to Thy perfect light.

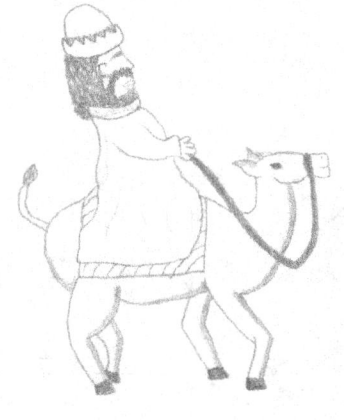

Melchoir:
Born a King on Bethlehem's plain,
Gold I bring to crown Him again,
King for ever, ceasing never,
Over us all to reign.

Caspar:
Frankincense to offer have I,
Incense owns a Deity nigh,
Prayer and praising, all men raising,
Worship Him, God most High.

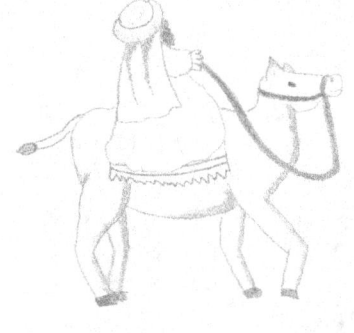

Balthazar:
Myrrh is mine, it's bitter perfume,
Breathes a life of gathering gloom,
Sorrowing, sighing, bleeding, dying,
Sealed in the stone-cold tomb.

All:
Glorious now behold Him arise,
King and God and sacrifice,
Alleluia, Alleluia,
Earth to the heavens replies.

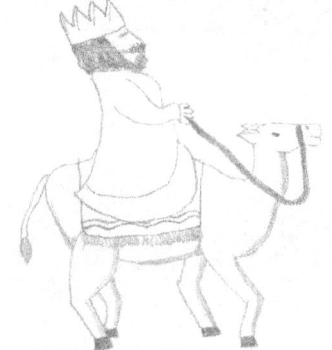

Melchoir, Caspar, Balthazar: The Three Wise Men.

While Shepherds

Version One

Arr. Claire

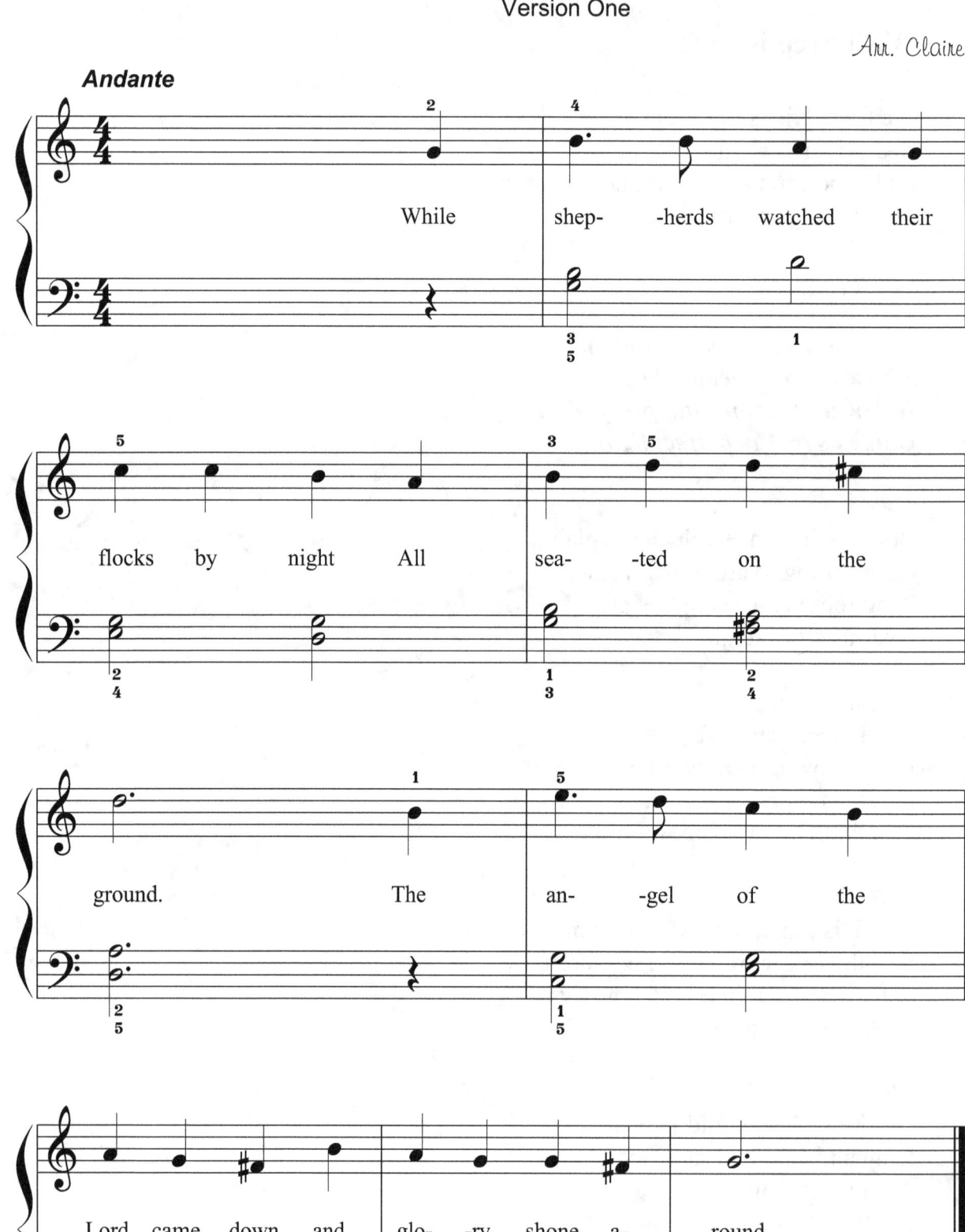

While Shepherds Watched their Flocks by Night.

While shepherds watched their flocks by night,
All seated on the ground,
The Angel of the Lord came down,
And glory shone around.

"Fear not", said he (for mighty dread
Had seized their troubled mind);
"Glad tidings of great joy I bring,
To you and all mankind".

"To you, in David's town, this day,
Is born, of David's line,
A Saviour, who is Christ the Lord;
And this shall be the sign".

"The heavenly Babe you there shall find,
To human view displayed,
All meanly wrapped in swathing bands
And in a manger laid".

Thus spake the seraph; and forthwith
Appeared a shining throng
Of angels, praising God, and thus
Addressed their joyful song:

"All glory be to God on high,
And to the earth be peace;
Goodwill henceforth from heaven to men,
Begin, and never cease!"

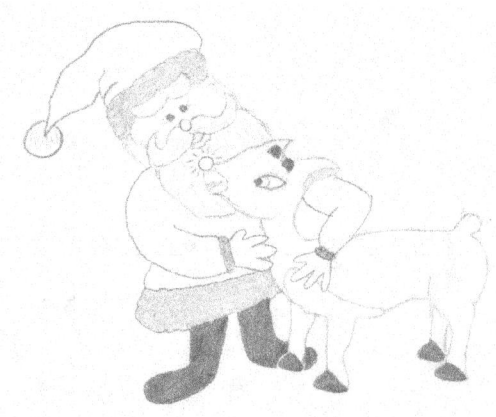

While Shepherds

Version Two

Arr. Claire

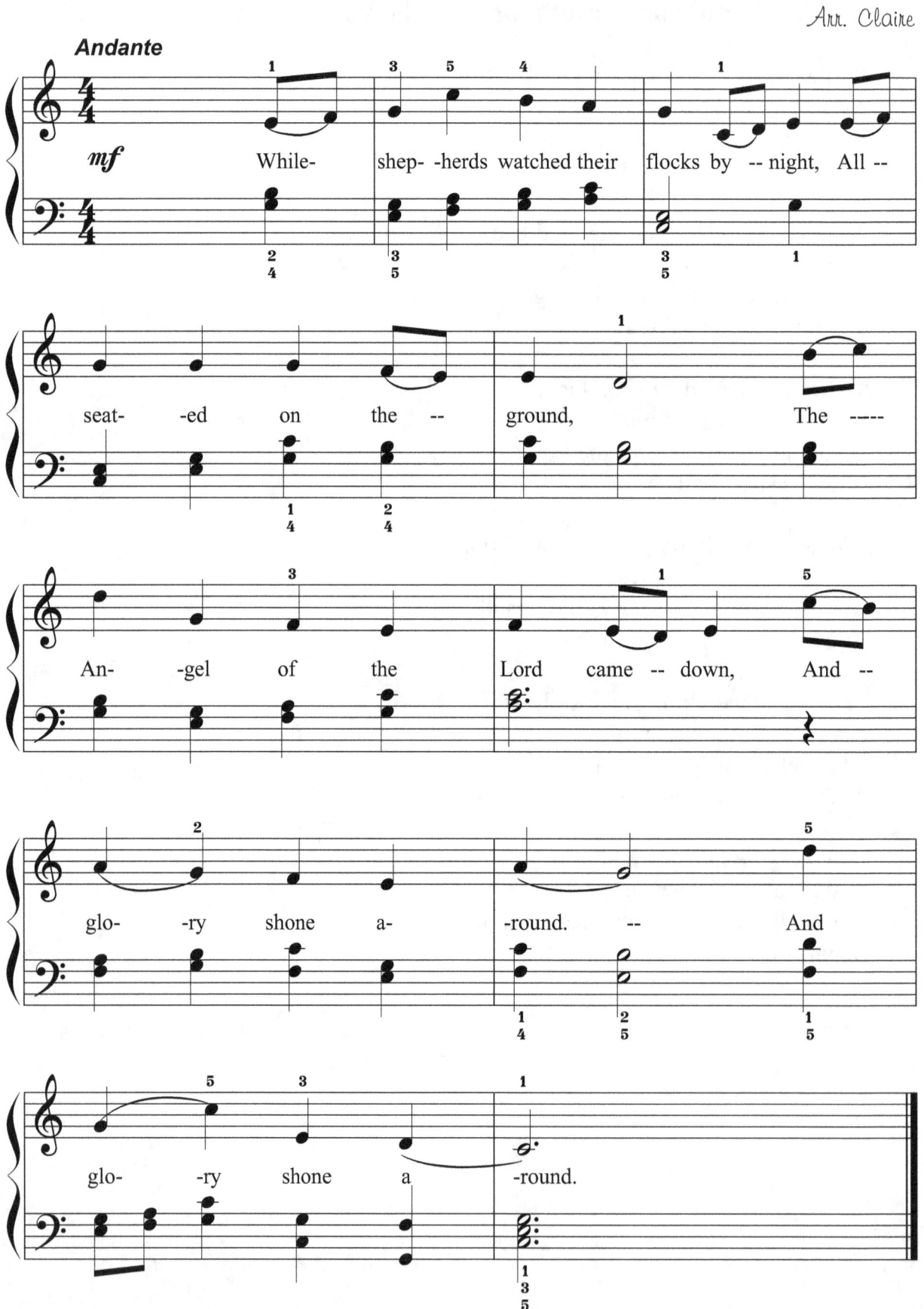

While Shepherds Watched their Flocks by Night.

While shepherds watched their flocks by night,
All seated on the ground,
The Angel of the Lord came down,
And glory shone around.

"Fear not", said he (for mighty dread
Had seized their troubled mind);
"Glad tidings of great joy I bring,
To you and all mankind".

"To you, in David's town, this day,
Is born, of David's line,
A Saviour, who is Christ the Lord;
And this shall be the sign".

"The heavenly Babe you there shall find,
To human view displayed,
All meanly wrapped in swathing bands
And in a manger laid".

Thus spake the seraph; and forthwith
Appeared a shining throng
Of angels, praising God, and thus
Addressed their joyful song:

"All glory be to God on high,
And to the earth be peace;
Goodwill henceforth from heaven to men,
Begin, and never cease!"

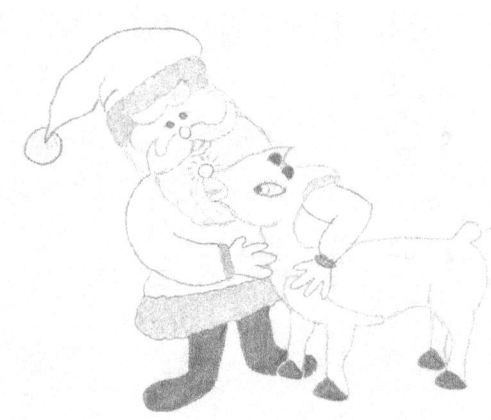

Little Angels

Eros Mungal

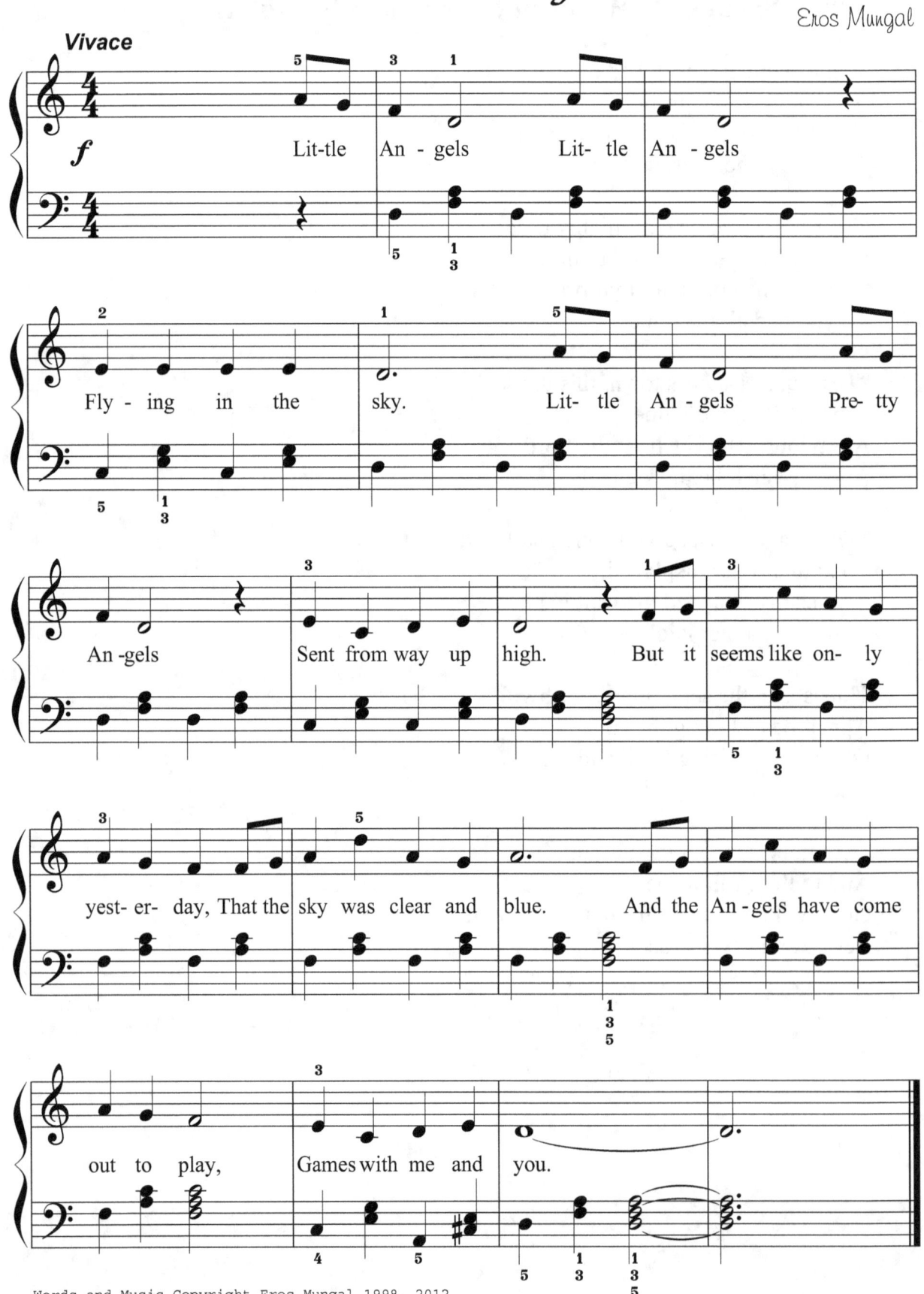

Little Angels.

Little angels, little angels.
Flying in the sky,
Little angels, pretty angels,
Sent from way up high.

But it seems like only yesterday,
That the sky was clear and blue.
And the angels have come out to play,
Games with me and you.

Little raindrops, tiny raindrops,
Coming from the sky,
Little raindrops, little raindrops
Sprinkling from on high.

But it seems like only yesterday,
That the sky was clear and blue,
And the raindrops have come out to play,
Games with me and you.

Little rainbows, little rainbows,
Curving 'cross the sky,
Little rainbows, sparkling rainbows,
Bowing from on high.

But it seems like only yesterday,
That the sky was clear and blue.
Now that all the clouds have gone away,
With the rainbows too.

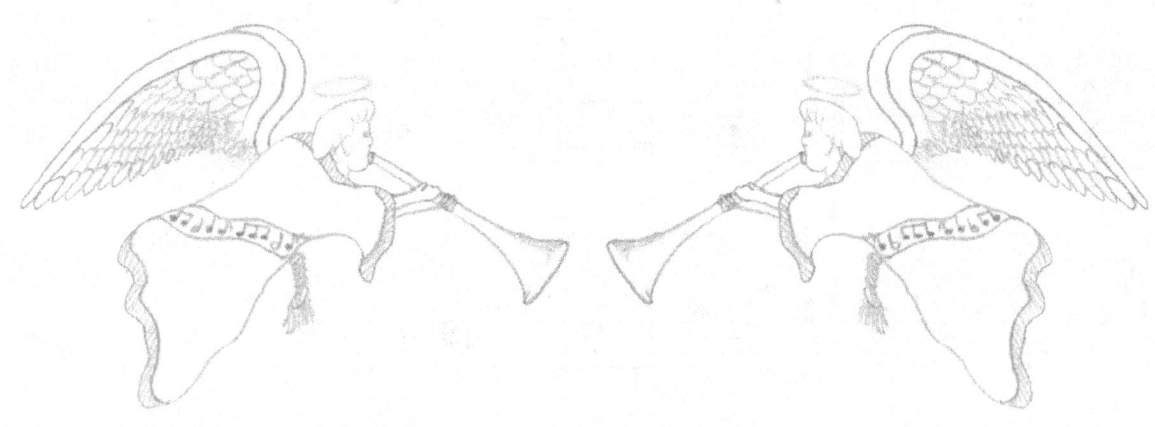

Auld Lang Syne

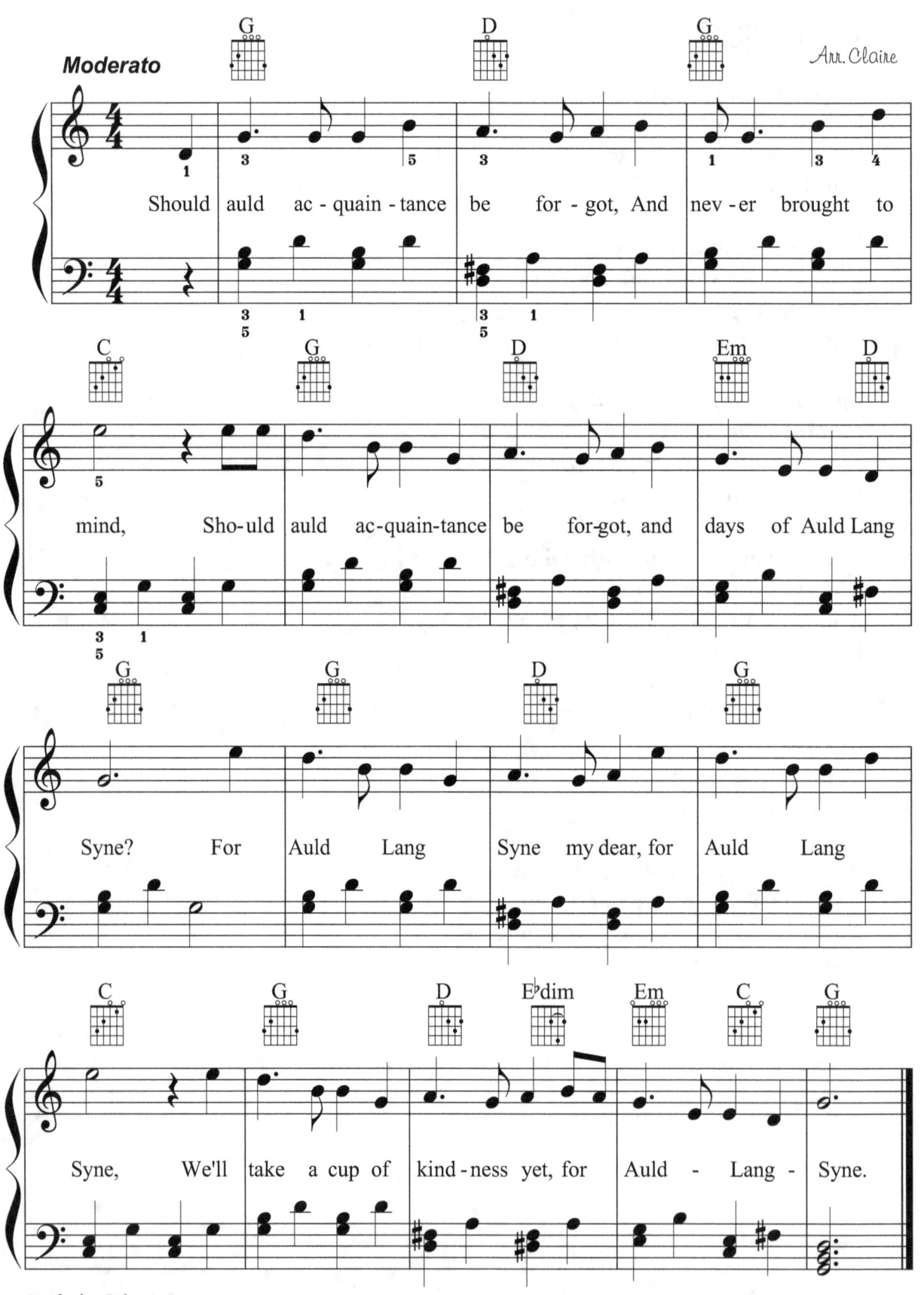

Words by Robert Burns

103

Auld Lang Syne

Should auld acquaintance be forgot,
And never brought to mind ?
Should auld acquaintance be forgot,
And days of Auld Lang Syne ?

Chorus:
For Auld Lang Syne, my dear,
For Auld Lang Syne,
We'll take a cup of kindness yet
For Auld Lang Syne.

We will have run about the braes,
And pou'd the gowans fine;
We've wandered many a weary mile,
Since Auld Lang Syne.

Chorus

We will have paid it in the braes,
Frae morning sun till dine;
But seas between us braid hae roar'd,
Since Auld Lang Syne.

Chorus

And surely you'll be your favourite
And surely I'll be mine,
And we'll take a cup of kindness yet
For the sake of Auld Lang Syne.

Words by Robert Burns

Hymn for Christmas

Eros Mungal

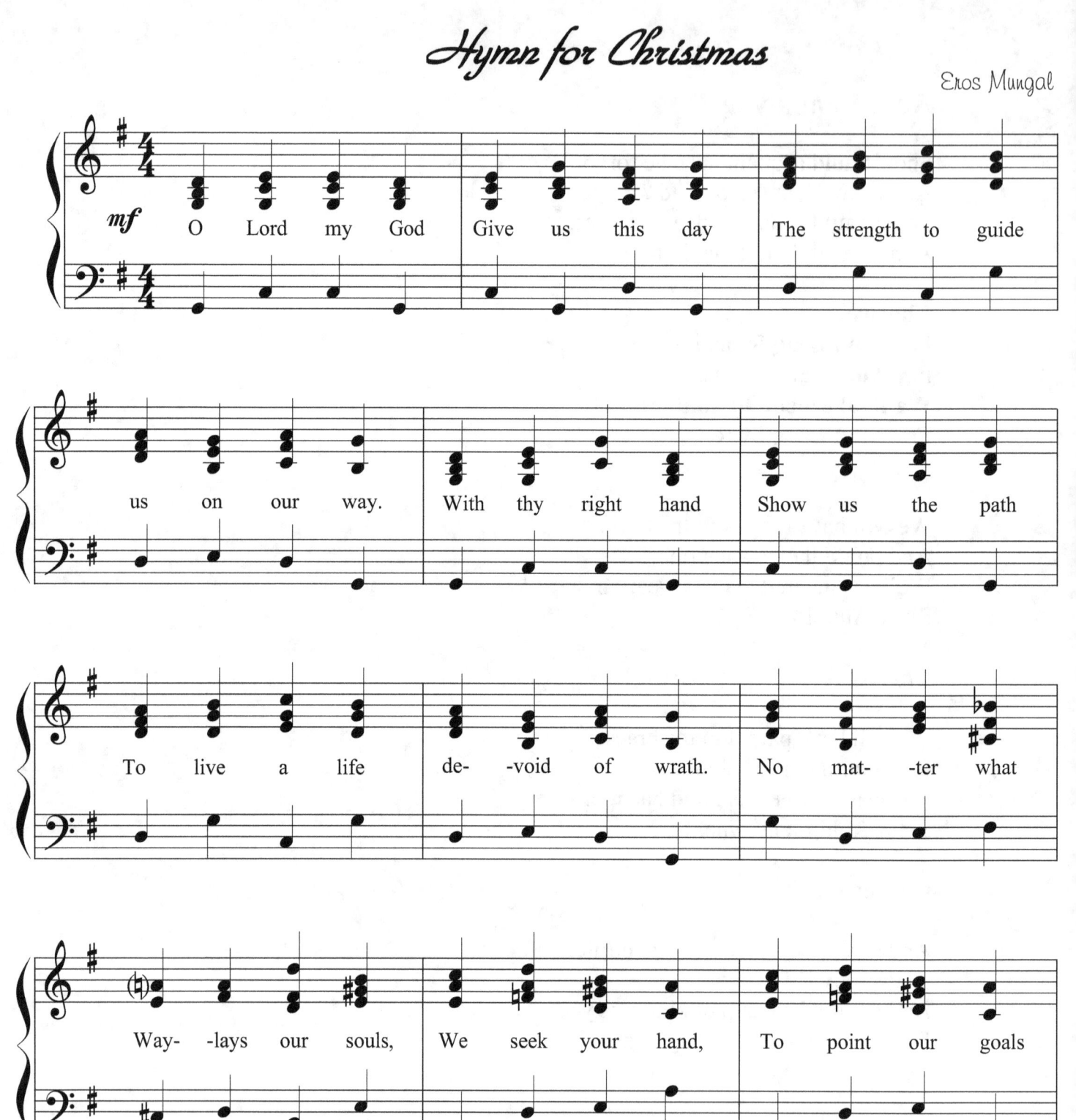

Hymn for Christmas

Eros Mungal

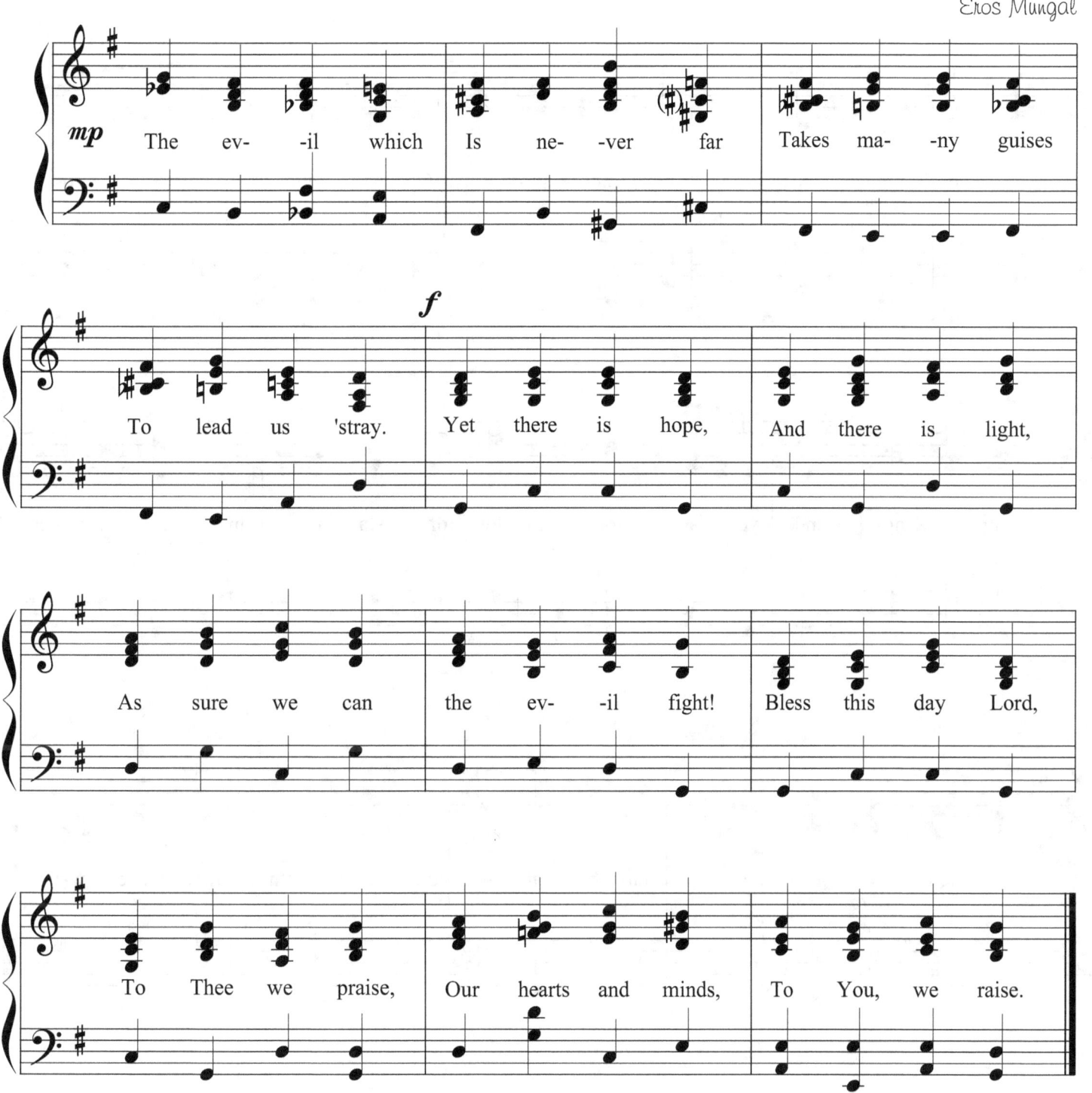

Guide Us By A Star.

Evan Gumbs Choir
Arr. Eros M.

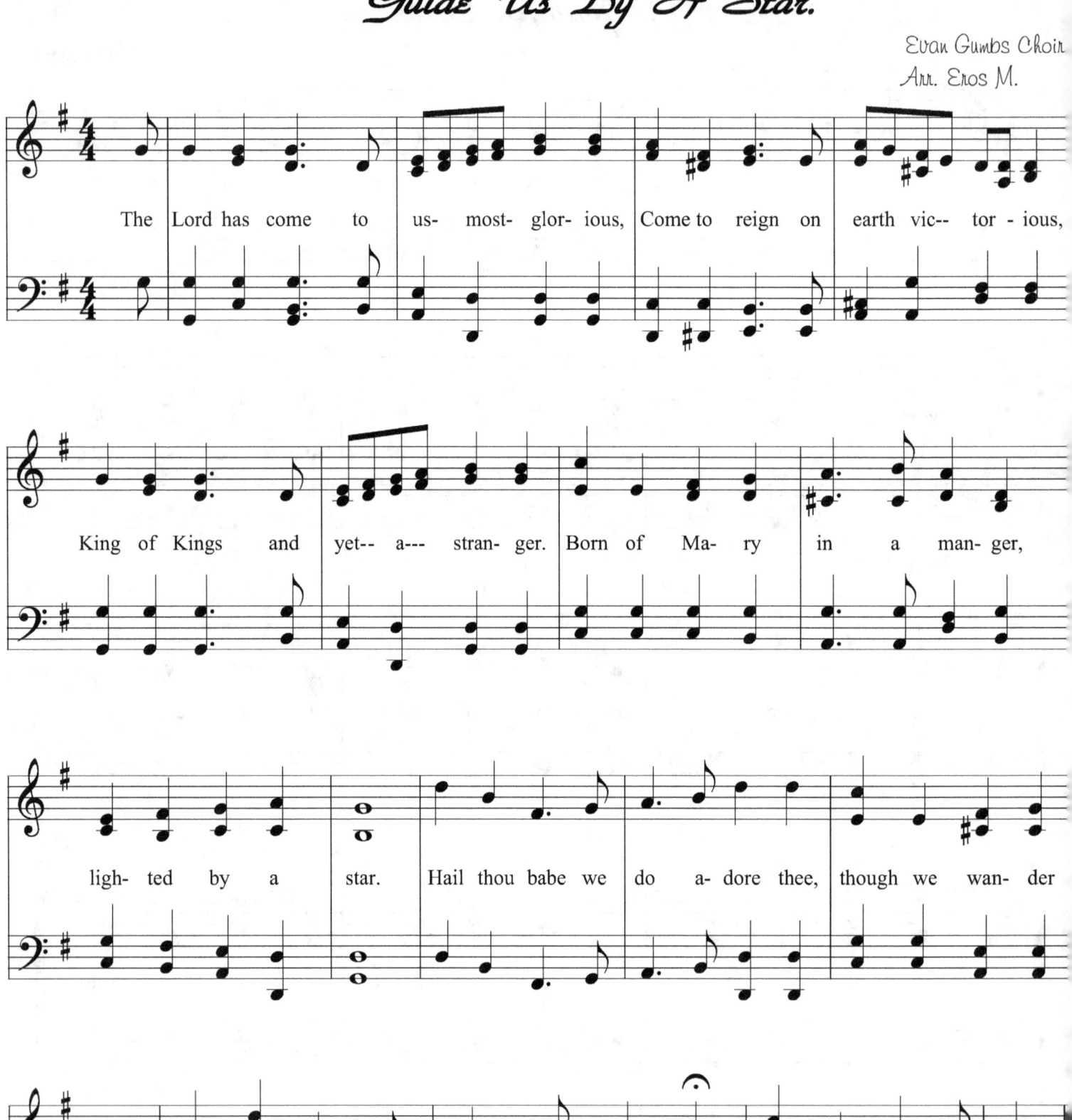

The Lord has come to us- most- glor- ious, Come to reign on earth vic-- tor - ious,

King of Kings and yet-- a--- stran- ger. Born of Ma- ry in a man- ger,

ligh- ted by a star. Hail thou babe we do a- dore thee, though we wan- der

far, Lead us to thy home in glo-- ry, Guide us by a star.

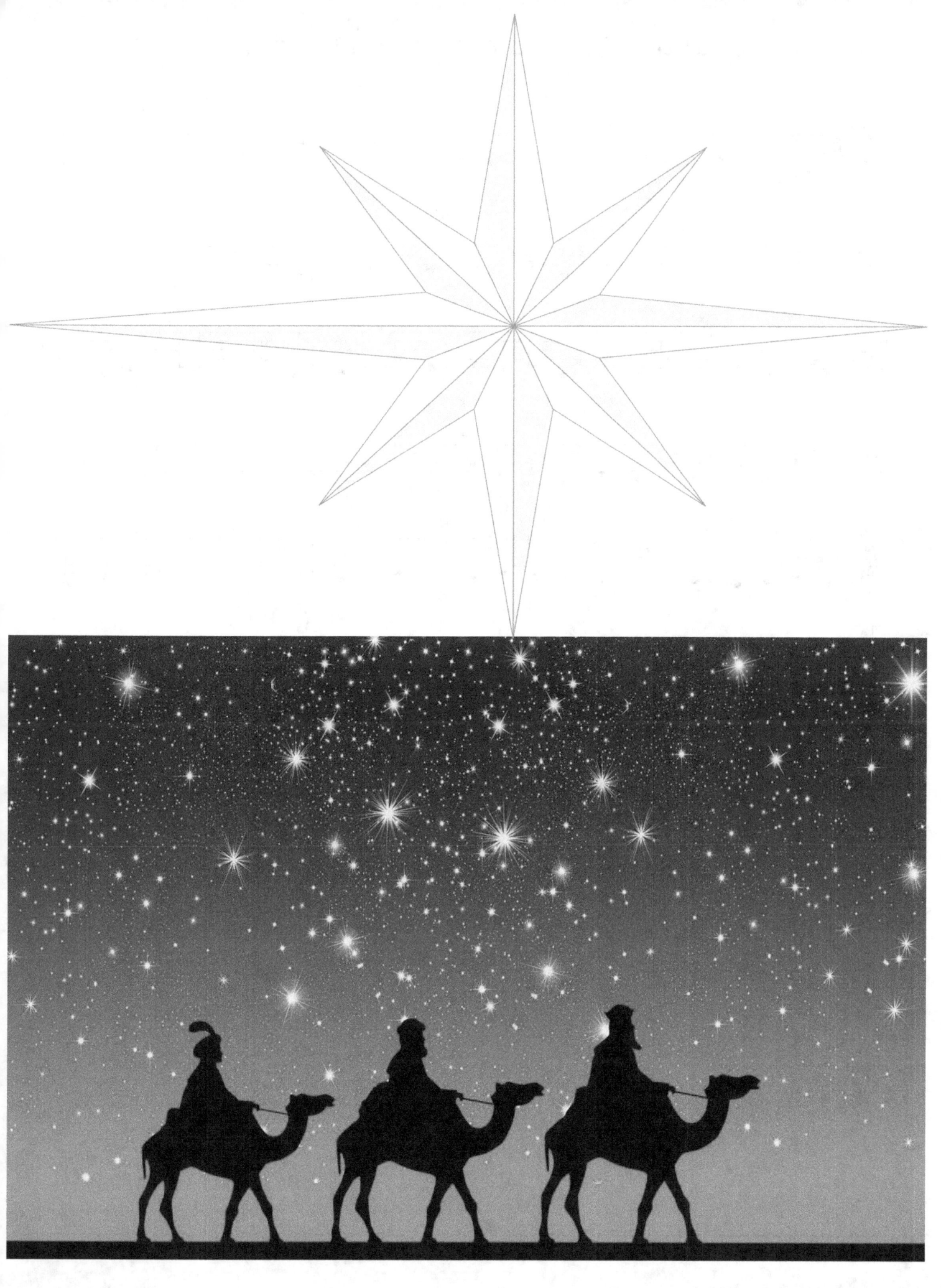

Take 5 in C for Right Hand

Claire

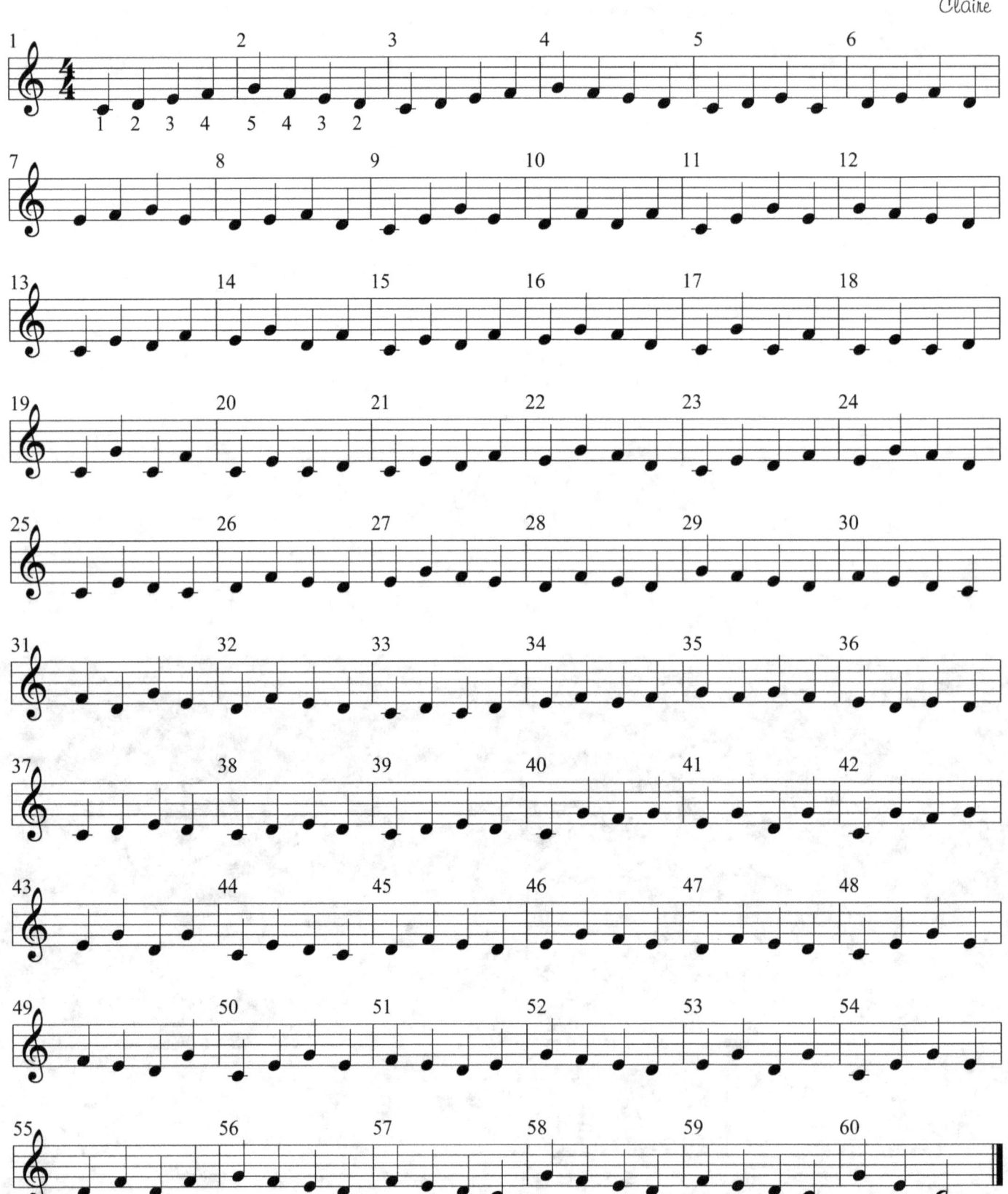

Take 5 in C for Left Hand

Claire

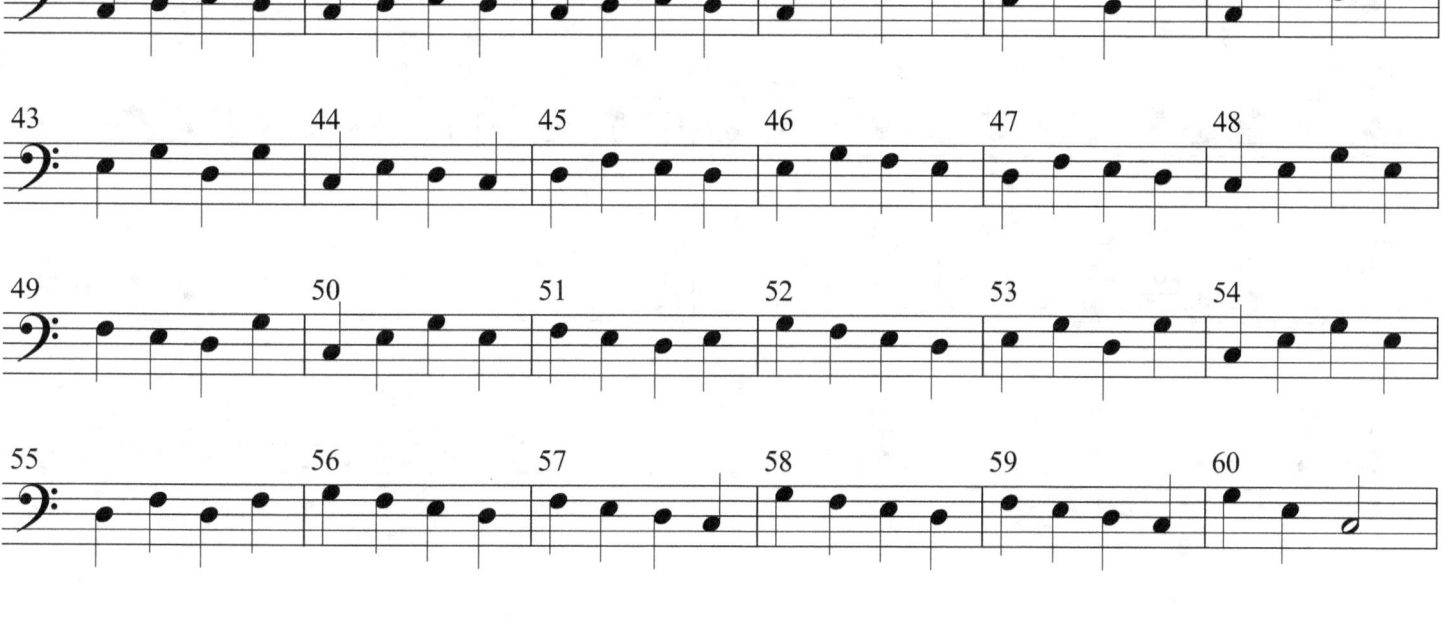

Take 5 in G for Right Hand

Claire

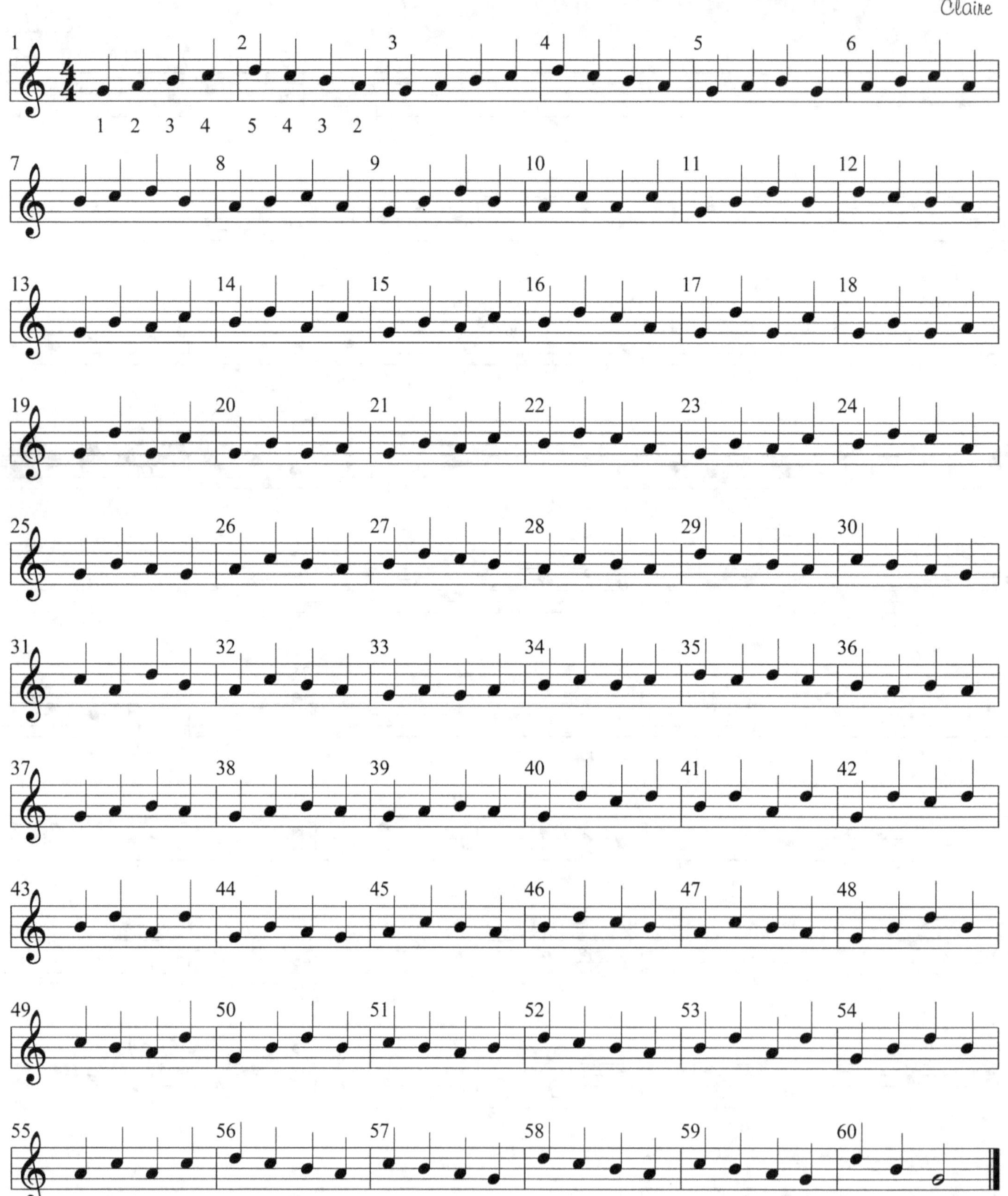

Take 5 in G for Left Hand

Claire

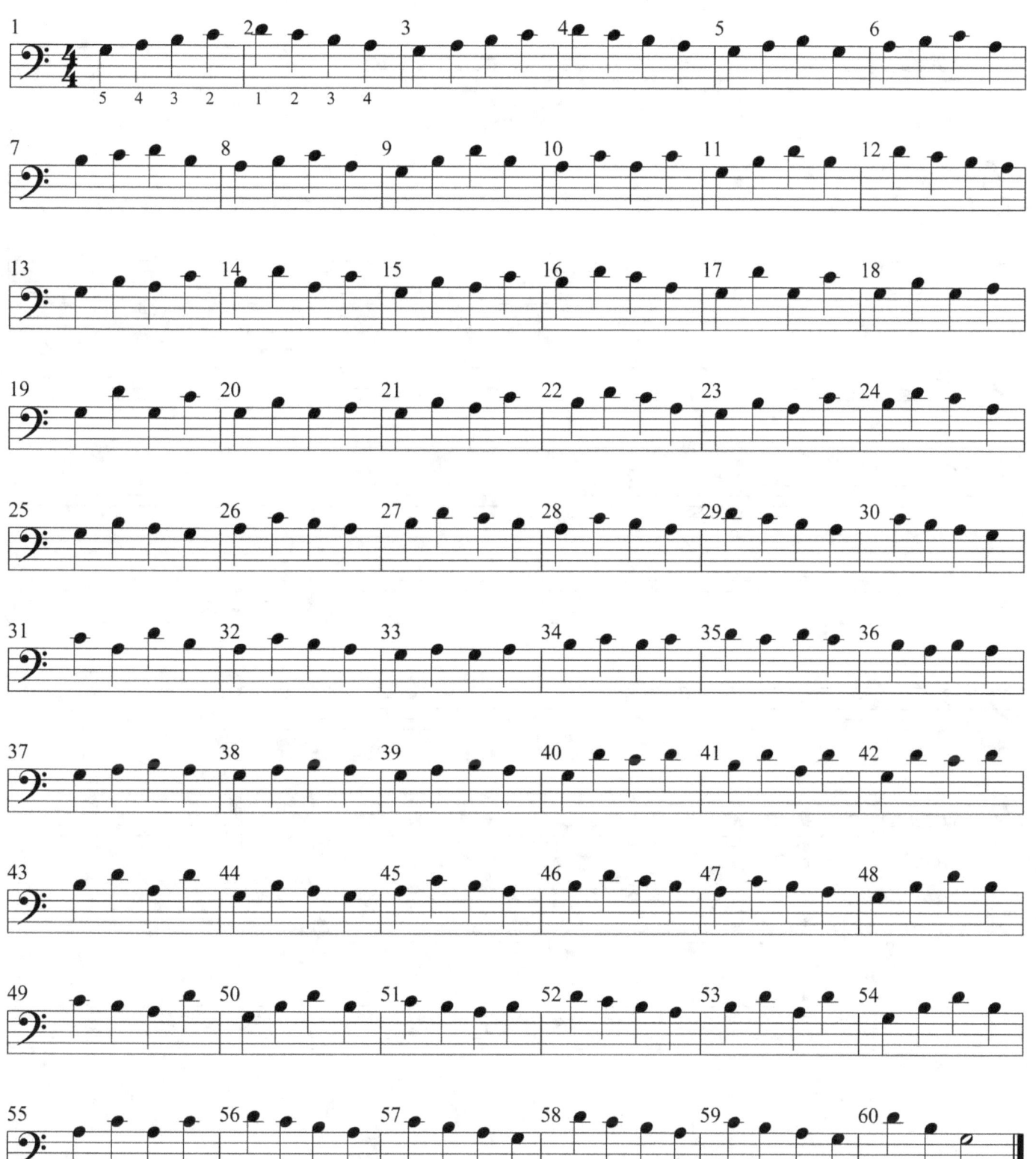

Left Hand Pairs in C.
Claire's Traditional Carolbook Practice Pieces

Chord of C

Left Hand Pairs in G.

Claire's Traditional Carolbook Practice Pieces

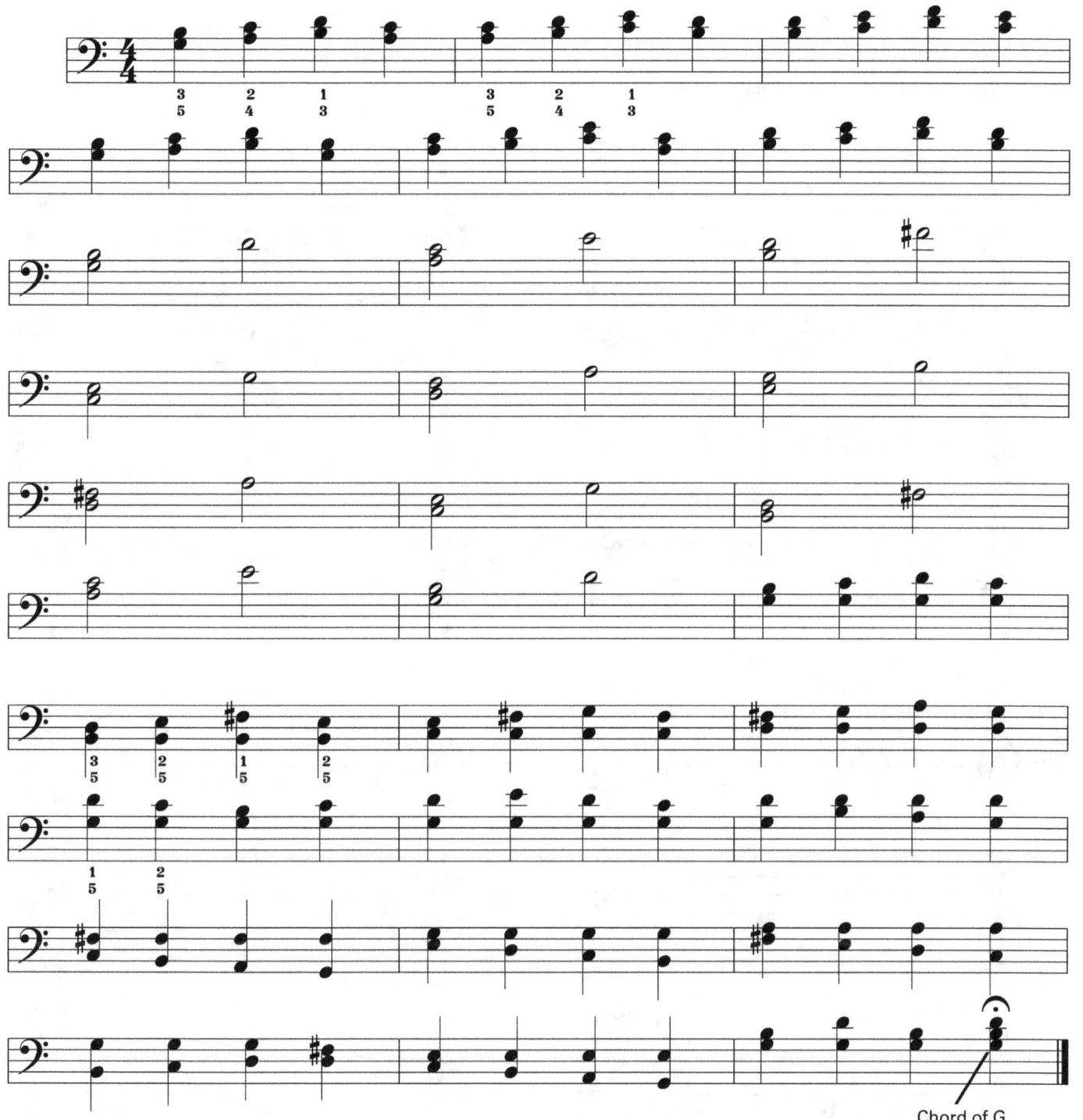

Chord of G

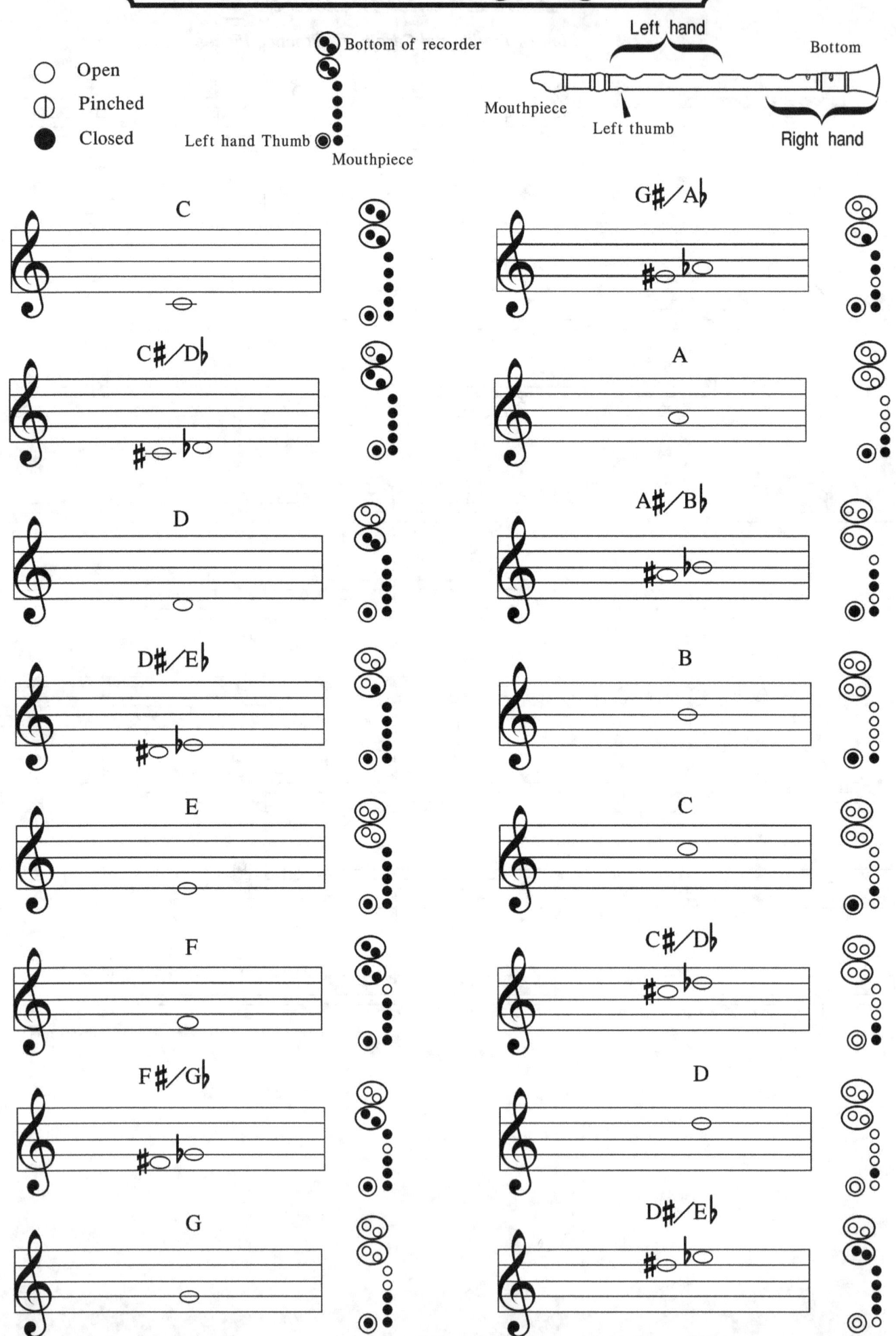

GUITAR CHORDS

C MAJOR   D MAJOR   E MAJOR   F MAJOR

G MAJOR   A MAJOR   B MAJOR   C MINOR

D MINOR   E MINOR   F MINOR   G MINOR

A MINOR   B MINOR   C 7th   D 7th

E 7th   G 7th   A 7th   B 7th

Remember the strings on the guitar are (from the base): E A D G B E.

X muted string.

115

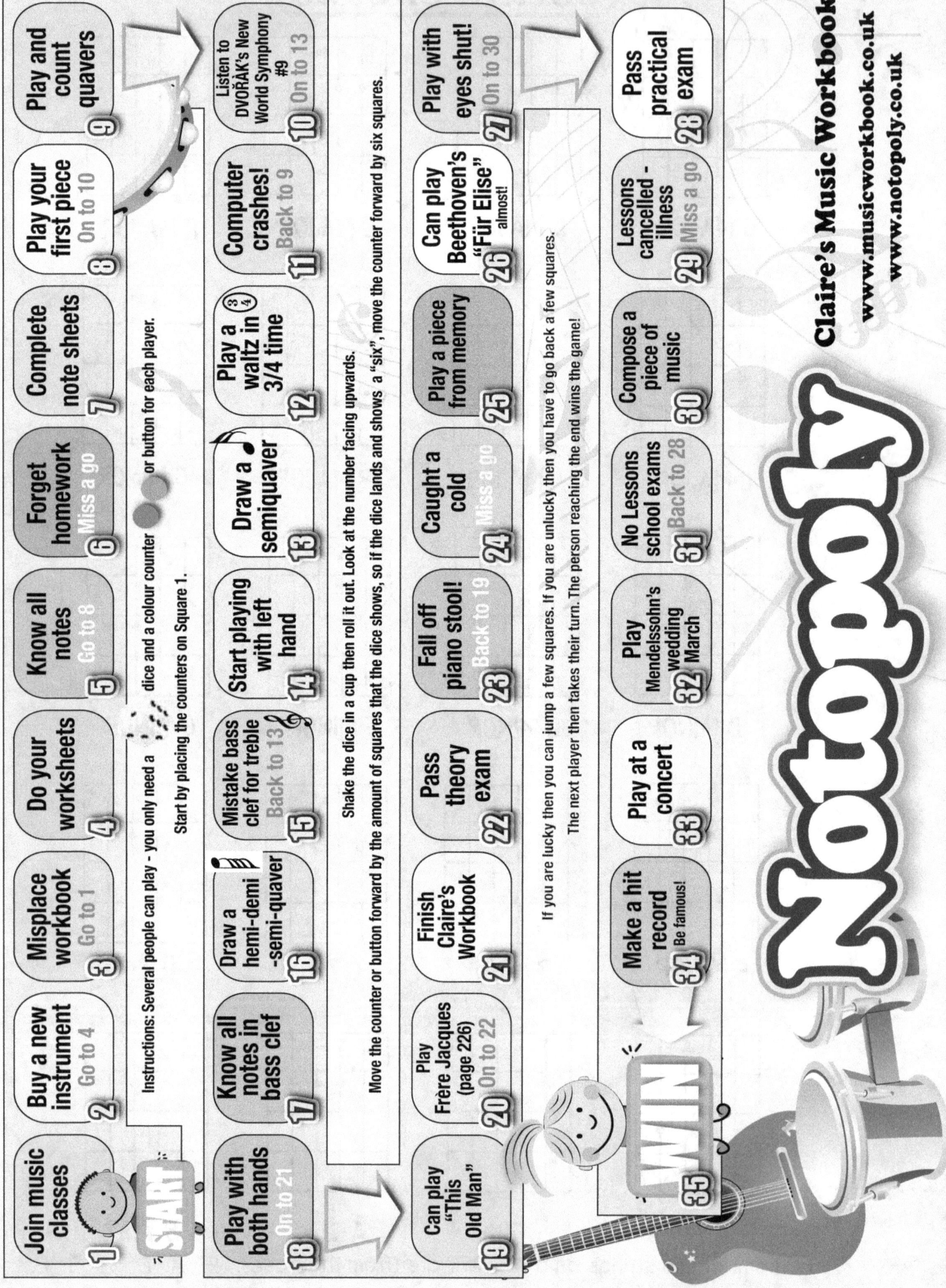

Notopoly

Claire's Music Workbook

www.musicworkbook.co.uk
www.notopoly.co.uk

1 Join music classes — START

2 Buy a new instrument — Go to 4

3 Misplace workbook — Go to 1

4 Do your worksheets

5 Know all notes — Go to 8

6 Forget homework — Miss a go

7 Complete note sheets

8 Play your first piece — On to 10

9 Play and count quavers

10 Listen to DVOŘÁK's New World Symphony #9 — On to 13

11 Computer crashes! — Back to 9

12 Play a waltz in 3/4 time

13 Draw a semiquaver

14 Start playing with left hand

15 Mistake bass clef for treble — Back to 13

16 Draw a hemi-demi-semi-quaver

17 Know all notes in bass clef

18 Play with both hands — On to 21

19 Can play "This Old Man"

20 Play Frère Jacques (page 226) — On to 22

21 Finish Claire's Workbook

22 Pass theory exam

23 Fall off piano stool! — Back to 19

24 Caught a cold — Miss a go

25 Play a piece from memory

26 Can play Beethoven's "Für Elise" — almost!

27 Play with eyes shut! — On to 30

28 Pass practical exam

29 Lessons cancelled - illness — Miss a go

30 Compose a piece of music

31 No Lessons school exams — Back to 28

32 Play Mendelssohn's wedding March

33 Play at a concert

34 Make a hit record — Be famous!

35 WIN

Instructions: Several people can play - you only need a dice and a colour counter or button for each player.

Start by placing the counters on Square 1.

Shake the dice in a cup then roll it out. Look at the number facing upwards.

Move the counter or button forward by the amount of squares that the dice shows, so if the dice lands and shows a "six", move the counter forward by six squares.

If you are lucky then you can jump a few squares. If you are unlucky then you have to go back a few squares. The person reaching the end wins the game!

The next player then takes their turn.

Treble Clef

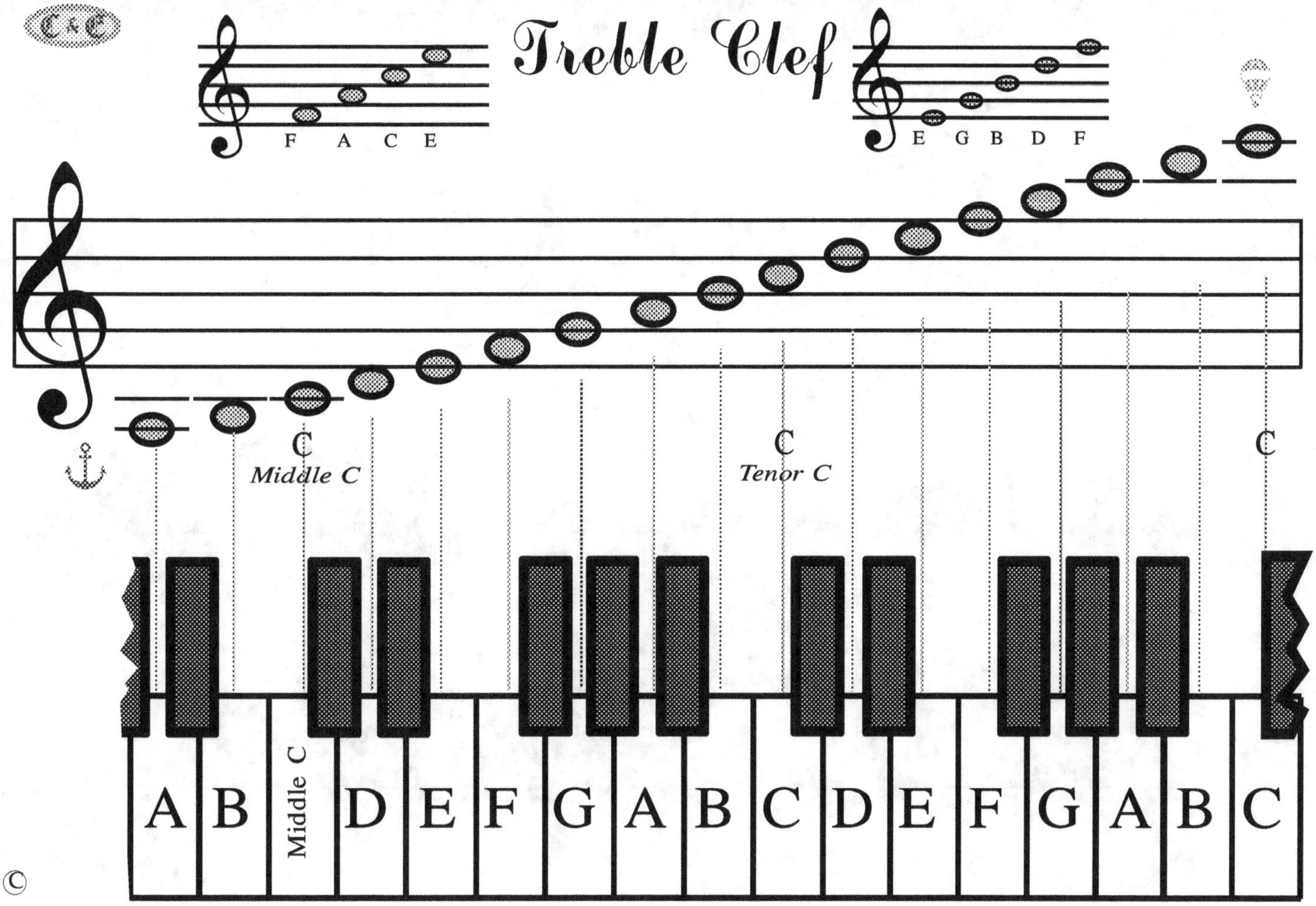

Bass Clef

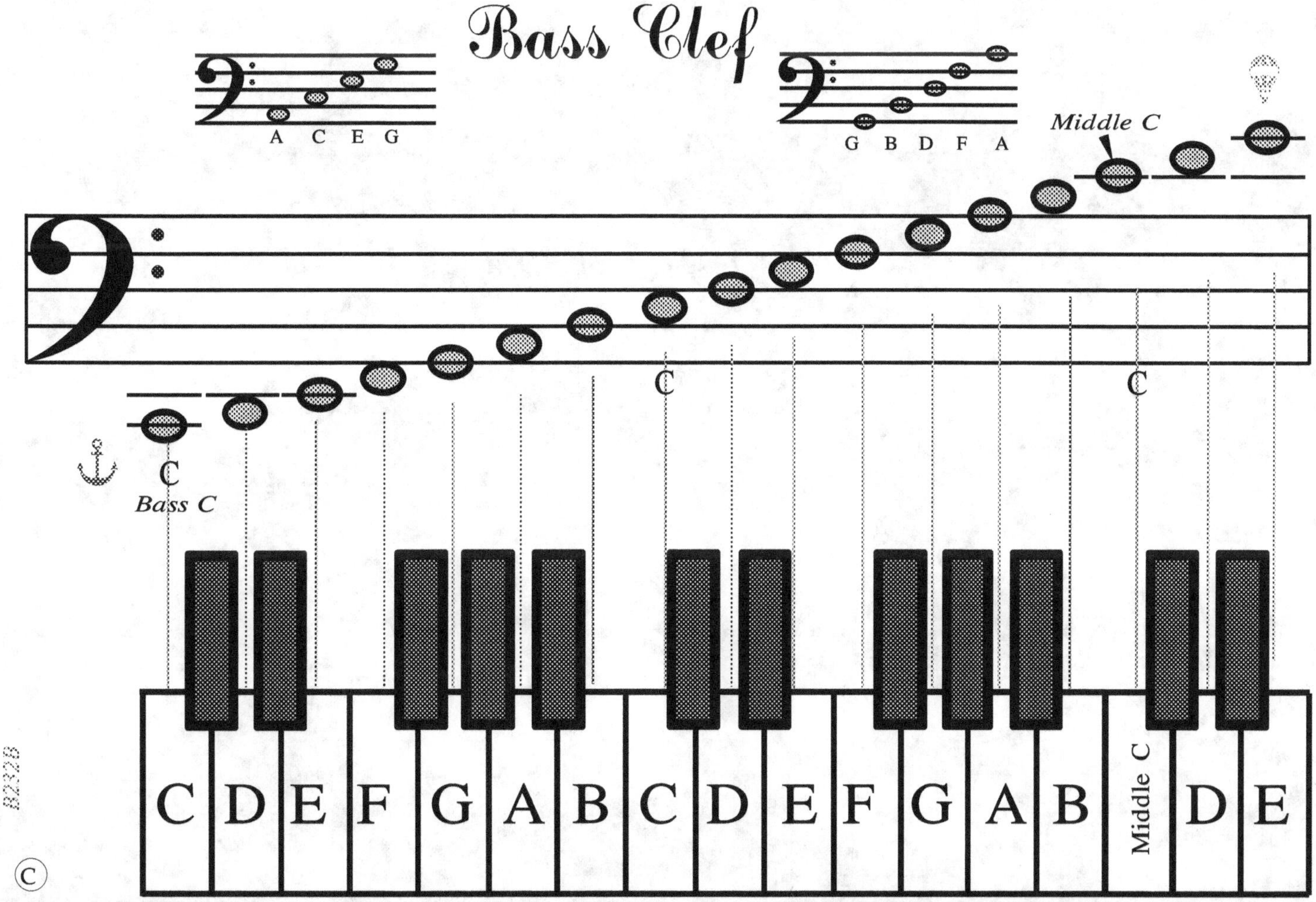

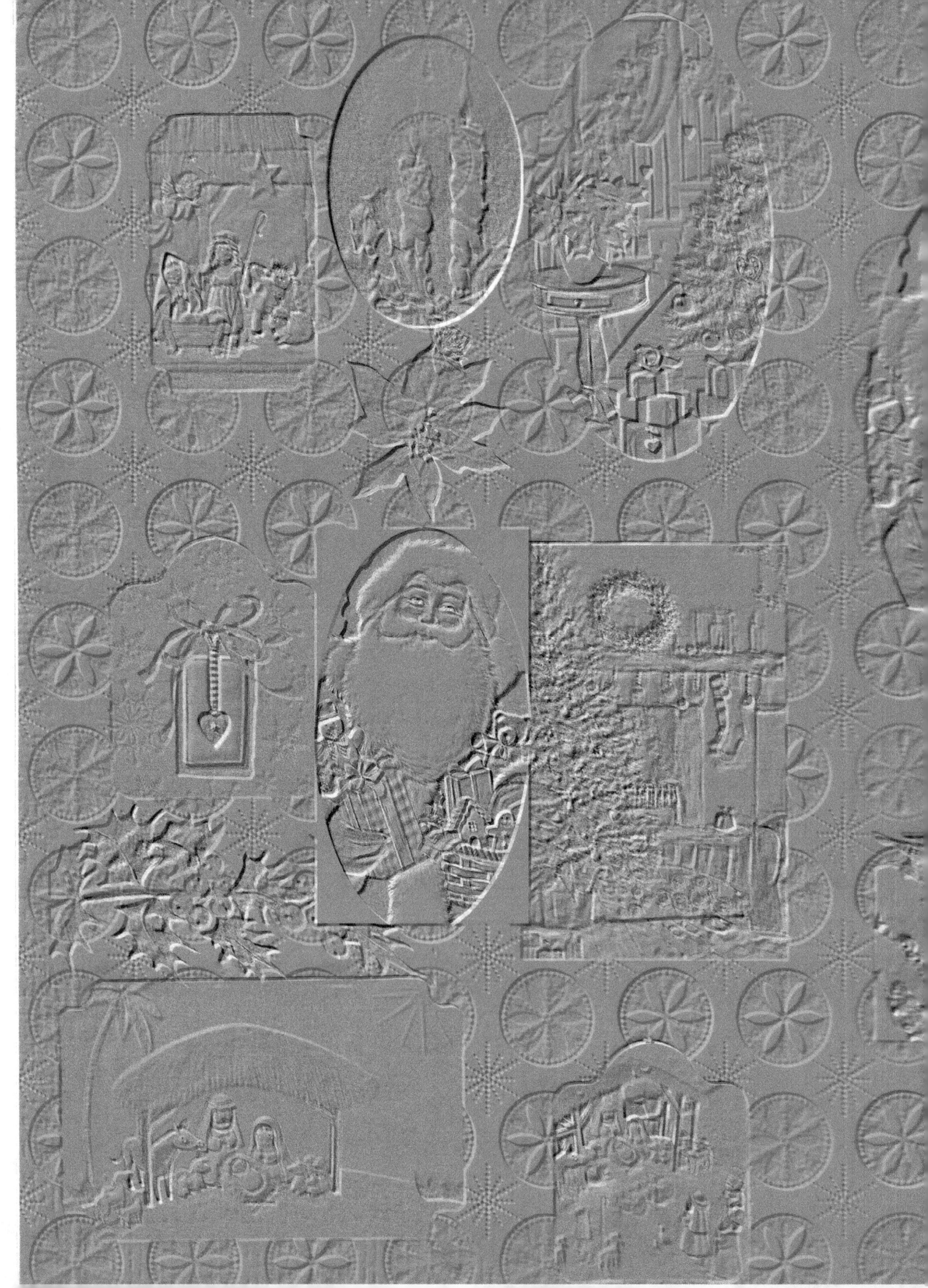

➢ New edition with over 50 traditional tunes, "Guide us by a Star", Christmas Hymn, Auld Lang Syne
➢ Created and inspired by young people - not just old reprints
➢ Modern arrangements to suit the modern piano, keyboard, string and wind instruments
➢ Simple progressions- most are two note bass harmony
➢ No big jumps - octave stretches a rarity!
➢ No long stretches - ideal for small hands
➢ Harmony is retained while maintaining simplicity
➢ Rhythm is maintained
➢ Two easy keys - C major and G major, one sharp
➢ No key signatures used in most pieces
➢ Easy for guitar players who can recognise basic chords
➢ Guide fingering used minimally – not overdone
➢ Practice exercises based on carol arrangements included in appendix
➢ Playable by amateurs and more advanced pianists, wind and string players
➢ Two versions of three popular carols (English and American)
➢ Every carol has the words edition on the facing page in clear type. Words are free to copy for use in schools, churches, hospitals, youth hostels and similar institutions.

And a new carol, "Little Angels"

This little "music-box" type jingle is very popular with children and is easy to play.

Claire's MusicWorkBook- Music Theory and Exercises - for all instruments.

Ever wanted to read and play music and unable to have lessons, or having lessons but want to progress more rapidly? This book was co-written with a young lady with several years' teaching experience - you too can teach yourself to play the keyboard and piano. This book comes with easy DIY exercises and a modern clear layout but without any colour sketches using up valuable space. You can use this book for formal music exams, GCSE, CXE (Caribbean area) or for your own fun - play popular music from sheet music or light classics. Over 50 tunes graded in difficulty are included. The latest edition now has a steelpan supplement with suggested layouts supplied by the TT Bureau of Standards and Pan Trinbago.

"Claire's Workbook" has evolved over 25 years' teaching experience with students from 4 to over 70 years of age, and originally started as single-sheet handouts for use during class. Over the years, these were improved and developed, and then eventually bound together to help students organize their work. Active feedback and suggestions led to continual improvements based upon helping students with widely differing abilities, backgrounds, ages and experience.

This collection now addresses most of the typical theory requirements of the major examining boards of music, covering from introductory to the next successive stages, Grades 1 to 2 or 3 depending on the examining board. The workbook endeavours to introduce theory concepts gradually thus helping the novice to read and understand notation and theory rather than merely satisfying a particular board's requirements exclusively. While teacher guidance is always advisable to obtain the best from the workbook, it has also been designed such that the more ambitious student can progress with the minimum of supervision, whether in a formal class, school or privately, or working at home. Answers to questions will soon be available on the internet – check webpages for information.

The teaching pages are liberally interspersed with exercise pages. More difficult concepts such as time-signatures and tones/semitones are dealt with diagrammatically. The book has a glossary of Italian terms at the back, along with daily practice pieces. A few easy-play carols along with over 50 well-known and traditional pieces have been included in the appendix. Also included is a variety of manuscript paper with differing pitch sizes. Manuscript books are also available separately as "Claire's VaryScript Manuscript Paper", ISBN 0-9544406-6-8.

Available from Internet booksellers or from publisher:
Eros Mungal, 5 Bryant Avenue, Berkshire, England, United Kingdom. SL2 1LF. ©MMXIX
Tel. +44 (0)794 139 2888 Email cmwbook@aol.com   ISBN (US) 1-55395-678-8
Claire's MusicWorkBook ISBN (Caribbean) 0-9544406-4-1.   ISBN (UK) 0-9544406-0-9

ISBN 0-9544406-1-7

9 780954 440619

www.ingramcontent.com/pod-product-compliance
Lightning Source LLC
Chambersburg PA
CBHW081153180526
45170CB00006B/2055